RUBBER

Vidya Rajan is a science aficionado. She has academic credentials in the biological sciences from four different universities on three continents. For the last seven years, she has written a monthly science column called 'Inner Nature'. Her interest in antifeedants arose from research she did for her doctoral dissertation and from her interest in managing pests without pesticides. She currently works as an adjunct associate professor at the University of Delaware and as a technical writer. She loves dogs and kids, enjoys nature walks, cooking, woodworking, reading, thinking, writing and red wine.

RUBBER

The Social and Natural History of an Indispensable Substance

Vidya Rajan

Published by Westland Non-Fiction, an imprint of Westland Books, a division of Nasadiya Technologies Private Limited, in 2025

No. 269/2B, First Floor, 'Irai Arul', Vimalraj Street, Nethaji Nagar, Alapakkam Main Road, Maduravoyal, Chennai 600095

Westland, the Westland logo, Westland Non-Fiction and the Westland Non-Fiction logo are the trademarks of Nasadiya Technologies Private Limited, or its affiliates.

ISBN: 9789360455873

10 9 8 7 6 5 4 3 2 1

The views and opinions expressed in this work are the author's own and the facts are as reported by her, and the publisher is in no way liable for the same.

Typeset by Mukul

Printed at Thomson Press (India) Ltd

To Steve, Ashish and Samir

Contents

III
Appendices

List of Figures and Tables

Figures

Tables

I

Olin

Preface

Rubber was used over 3,500 years ago in the areas of Central America inhabited by the Olmec, Maya and Aztec civilisations, encompassing modern-day Mexico and Guatemala. Milk-like latex[i] obtained from indigenous trees was collected and processed into a bouncy and rubbery substance they called '*olli*'.[ii] The springiness and utility elevated *olli* into a nucleus around which their mythology and rituals were built. In its latex form, it was symbolic of fertility, and represented the characteristics of milk, semen and blood.[1] Its *olin* form called to

---

i The term 'latex' is used for the milky liquid obtained from plants, some of which contain rubber particles. The particles are coagulated and processed into solid raw rubber known as '*olli*'. *Olli* was variously called '*hule*' or '*caoutchouc*' until Joseph Priestley coined the term 'rubber' after he had used it to rub out pencil lines. I retain the use of the term 'rubber' for both the latex and processed forms unless there is a need for further clarity.

ii The term '*olli*' refers to rubber, and the term '*olin*' means 'motion-change'.

mind the elasticity of the human heart. These cultures devised a ceremonial ball game and carried out sacrifices that ritually represented the lifegiving forces of the sun and moon—customs that were encountered by conquering Spaniards as they sought to colonise new lands.

In Central Africa, rubber-containing latex comes from a tropical vine, but it was more a curiosity than a material of utility because of lower population density and the difficulty of transporting materials; that is, until colonising Europeans recognised it as the same substance as the rubber from the Americas with which they had already become familiar. In Southeast Asia, tree latex contained a different substance called 'gutta-percha', which is inelastic but plastic, and remarkably robust. In the Malaysian archipelago, gutta-percha had been used to make walking sticks, knife handles, bowls and other items since time immemorial. Gutta-percha was brought to Europe around the same time as rubber from the Americas, but its utility was not explored systematically until the mid-nineteenth century, when it was discovered to be a durable coating for underwater cables. Chapters 1 and 2 tell the story of rubber in its earliest documented homeland in Central America, and the part that it played in the origins of the rituals of the Olmecs, Maya and Aztecs.

Rubber was a curiosity until vulcanisation[iii]—the method that the Central Americans had also deployed, albeit using natural plant extracts—was developed. This process helped achieve a rubber material that was more resilient and less erratic in quality, and helped propel its inclusion into a variety of products whose properties could be modified, depending

iii Chemical treatment of raw rubber with sulphur and heat to improve its durability and elasticity.

on whether you sought rigidity or flexibility. Its utility further exploded with the invention and subsequent growth of horseless transport: first, the bicycle, then the automobile. Chapters 2 and 3 tell the story of the elevation of rubber from a substance of curiosity to one of necessity, and the patent battles to establish who, on the two sides of the Atlantic, could legally claim to have tamed it.

Chapter 4 tells of the drive in the Amazon and Congo (previously Zaire) river basins to produce rubber to fulfil the enormous demand from the middle of the nineteenth century to the early twentieth century. A corollary development was the subjugation of the large labour force required to harvest wild rubber with pressganging, hostage-taking and suppression of public disclosure of such maltreatment being common themes. The other uncanny parallel was the recruitment of Roger Casement, an investigator who was despatched by the United Kingdom to document the rumoured abuses on two occasions, first in the Belgian Congo and then in the Putumayo region of the Amazon. The unsparing records of abuses committed by the Belgian state and its agents, verified by Casement and others, galvanised a revulsed public to pressure the government to take action against the perpetrators. As a result, the United Kingdom leaned on the owners of plantations in the Congo and the Amazon to desist from abusing their labour. Meanwhile, rubber seeds were transported out of Brazil and planted in the Far East, where the British had colonial interests and direct control. Less underhanded (yet misguided) efforts to set up rubber plantations in the Amazon by Henry Ford are described in this chapter.

Undeterred by the setbacks encountered by the Ford Motor Company, American tyre company Firestone looked to Liberia in West Africa, a country established by freed slaves and freeborn black Americans, which had a suitable climate for growing rubber trees and a large labour force to harvest the latex. In the meantime, two world wars taking place barely thirty years apart increased the demand for rubber—the vast amounts required, for instance, to make tyres for troop-carrying vehicles and aircraft, gaskets for gas masks and hoses and belts for machinery. In World War II, Japan captured existing Asian plantations, making the Far East a grim focal point of the war. The need for rubber also triggered efforts to research synthetic alternatives or obtain rubber from other plant sources. It is said that the advances made for the production of synthetic rubber would have been celebrated as the greatest scientific accomplishment during World War II, until it was overshadowed by the Manhattan Project's atom bomb. After the war, the widespread adoption of automobiles and the difficulty of recycling vulcanised and synthetic rubber tyres caused stockpiles of discarded material to grow—alongside the increase in demand as automobile production exploded in a newly peaceful world.

There are also issues beyond our present-day concerns and opportunities of the promises and pitfalls rubber holds for the future. How will ever-increasing demand be met? How much will the clearing of virgin forests for new plantations impact a warming planet? What part will natural or synthetic avatars of rubber play if humans spread to other planets as transients or permanent settlers? How can we convert the large stockpiles of discarded rubber to benefit us and not further degrade the environment? Chapter 5 looks at these problems and their possible solutions.

The story of rubber encapsulates the imagination, technology and vision of humans but also plumbs our species' destructiveness and depravity. It is a fitting metaphor for the human story.

1

The Mesoamerican Ball Game

The arrival of the strangers was preordained. The almanac says today is 1 Acatl and the tonalpouque, *the revered head priest of our walled Aztec town of Tenochtitlan, had predicted this and some other strange and unsettling events. He is always right. The god of fate, Tezcatlipoca, speaks through him. The predictions cause Moctezuma II some disquiet, but he has decided that perhaps these strangers represent the gods sending a message. The strangers are from unknown parts, are dressed in strange clothes, speak a strange dialect, wield strange weapons made of an unknown material and are obviously warlike. Moctezuma II treats them to Aztec hospitality and has gifted them an Aztec calendar as well as much gold, which seems to please them inordinately. They attended a ball game and are captivated by it, but aghast by the sacrifice at the end.*[iv]

Hernán Cortés and the other Spaniards visiting Moctezuma II in the walled city of Tenochtitlan in 1519 are mesmerised by the spectacle of the Mesoamerican ball game, *tlachtli*. The

---

iv This is an imaginary diary entry based on the events of the time.

atmosphere is electric. Drenched in sweat, limbs trembling from exertion, a player forces a twisting lunge at the bouncing ball ricocheting off the wall towards him, aiming to strike it with his hip. He misses; the ball grazes his thigh, bounces and starts to roll drunkenly down the sloping side of the court. There is a dismayed roar from the spectators. The stakes of *tlachtli* are high; it is more than just a game. If the ball rolls into the flat oblong trough between the sloping boundary walls, the game is over but, possibly, so is the order of the world. Keeping the ball in play and out of the trough until successfully passing it through the stone hoop on the wall represents the daily tussle to free the sun from the clutches of underground forces—releasing it again to patrol the sky. Failure means cosmic, existential consequences.

Heart thudding, chest heaving, with teeth gritted, the player dives again, calculating a strike against his shoulder, and the ball is back in play even as his collarbone beneath the padding snaps with a loud crack. The crowd roars again, this time in elation as the ball bounces up and away. The game goes on. The players strike the bouncing ball with their hips, shoulders and back, trying to send it through the stone hoop set head-high in the boundary wall.

The players cannot not afford to falter or fail to focus: if they do, they lose their heart—in the most literal way possible. At the conclusion of the game, losers are sacrificed by having their beating hearts plucked out of their chest right there on the field. This ritualistic bloodletting was believed to be what lubricates the motion, the *olin*, of the Sun which then continues to give life to the earth.

Variously called *tlachtli*, *ōllamaliztli*, *ulama*, *pitz*, *pelota* and *pok-ta-pok*, the Mesoamerican ball game had a grisly and spectacular finish. Although the visiting Spaniards led by Cortés were overwhelmed by the sumptuousness of the Aztecs (and then dismayed by the ritual sacrifice), they took particular note of the bouncing ball. They had never seen a ball move autonomously and thought it must be alive. Balls in Europe were made from leather or cloth and did not bounce. The Dominican Friar Fray Diego Durán wrote later of the ball: 'They call the material of this ball "*hule*" ... jumping and bouncing are its qualities, upward and downward, to and from. It can exhaust the pursuer running after it before he can catch up with it.'[2] His astonishment is palpable.

By 1521, the Aztecs were defeated by a potent combination of guile and starvation. Moctezuma II was imprisoned in his own palace and stoned to death by his own people when he was sent to intervene in the Spaniards' favour after they had fired on an Aztec ceremony, killing many warriors. Why Moctezuma II, the head of a warrior tribe, was so uncharacteristically compliant with Cortés' requests is open to speculation. Some scholars assume that Moctezuma II intervened because he thought that Cortés was the god Quetzalcoatl, whose return was predicted in scripture.[3] Or perhaps he was curious about these foreigners from across the sea—in particular, their weapons.[4] After all, the Aztecs used wooden and stone weaponry, which were ineffective against blunderbusses and steel blades made of iron;[5] besides, he had witnessed these weapons in action against other tribes and would have naturally wished to acquire them for himself.

After the resounding conquest of the Aztecs, the last of the great Mesoamerican civilisations came to an end,[v] but not

---

v The Aztecs' immune system had never encountered Old World scourges and was ineffective against European germs, such as smallpox, which consequently killed thousands of indigenous people.

before they had set in motion the wheels of commerce some 400 years into the future.

The Olmec, Maya and Aztec civilisations were located in what is Mexico and Central America today (Figure 1). The Olmecs were the first major civilisation in the area, and occupied the areas covered by the Mexican states of Veracruz and Tabasco. The word 'Olmec' is derived from the Nahuatl word *olmecatl*—a fusion of *olli* (rubber) and *mecatl* (people)—or 'rubber people'. The Olmecs learned how to derive rubber from latex as they became ideologically engaged with the practice of ritualistic sacrifice—later, *tlachtli* fused the two into a ceremonial spectacle. Thought to date back to as early as 2500 BCE, their culture emerged in archaeological records about 1600–1500 BCE. The Olmecs were most productive between 1500–400 BCE, and then precipitously declined for reasons unknown. Some scholars think that was probably due to environmental changes following volcanic eruptions in the Tuxtlas region of current-day Veracruz, which may have made the region unsuitable for farming.[6]

The term 'Maya' is used to refer to a decentralised group of city-states that primarily occupied the Yucatan peninsula and spanned areas covered by today's Guatemala, Belize, Honduras and El Salvador. They were more coastally located than the Aztecs, as well as also more ancient, dating back to before 1500 BCE. The height of their civilisation was probably between 300 BCE and 900 CE. They built many city states with elaborate architecture; husbanded and farmed corn, beans, chilli peppers and squashes; and had sophisticated astronomical devices and calendars. The areas of influence of the Mayas extended to northern Mexico, spreading cultural practices that had originated with the Olmecs.

The Aztecs traced their origins to Toltec predecessors (950–1150 CE) in the basin of Mexico around Lake Texcoco, rising to power in the early 1300s, and declining with the arrival of the Spaniards. The Aztecs established Tenochtitlan (today's Mexico City) as their capital city. By 1428, they had forged a coalition called the 'Triple Alliance' with their neighbouring city states of Tetzcoco and Tlacopan. Having established their hegemony, conquered city states were required to pay taxes and offer tribute materials, including rubber, which did not grow in the highlands. Resentment of the ruling Aztecs caused states such as Tlaxcala, Totonac and Tetzcoco to ally with the Spanish conquistador Hernán Cortés to defeat the Aztecs. Subsequently, the Spanish largely controlled the historical lands of the Aztecs and the Mayas, and set about imposing their culture, traditions and religion.

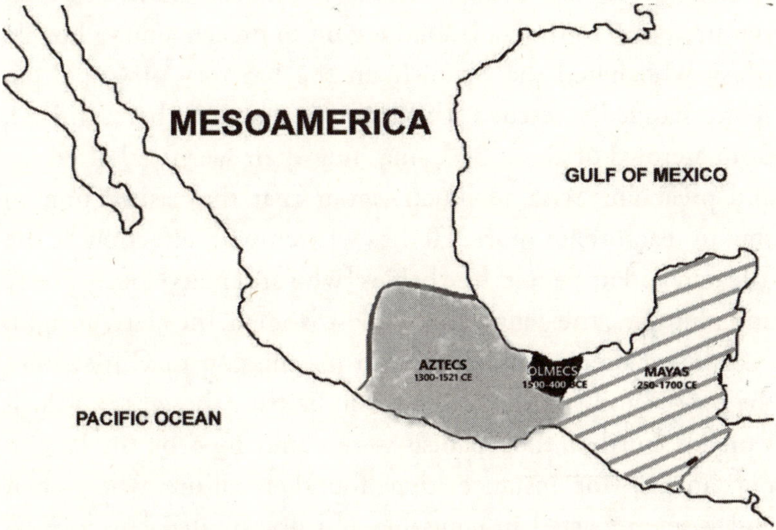

Figure 1: Map showing Mesoamerican empires overlying a map of Central America.[7] *The regions and dates are approximate.*

Very few documents written by indigenous Mesoamericans explaining their philosophy and world view survived the Spanish conquest. Thousands of items, including folding books and deerskin parchments containing holy texts, were burned in 1561 by the overzealous Franciscan monk Diego de Landa for the purpose of eradicating Maya culture in order to instil Christian values. Apparently, de Landa marvelled that 'they [Maya] regretted [this destruction] to an amazing degree … which caused them much affliction'.[8]

Ironically, de Landa's representations to the court when he was summoned back to Spain to explain his actions, as well as his book describing his experiences (*Relación de las cosas de Yucatán*), served to spread knowledge and interest in the very Maya culture that he was trying to suppress. It must be understood that de Landa was not simply a vandal. He had shown extraordinary courage in his commitment to the Franciscan cause and even ventured to into the Valladolid region to preach among hostile Maya who hated the Spanish. In the territory of Cupul, he single-handedly rescued a young boy, about to be sacrificed, from a crowd of about 300, smashing their sacrificial offerings and preaching with so much vigour that they asked him to stay to teach them more. He has written with affection of the Yucatan and its people: 'the babies [who are] marvelously pretty and plump … the gentle and modest women, the alert, upright, disciplined men'.[9] He believed in his mission to Christianise the people and free them from what he truly thought was devil worship. Further, the Spanish were scandalised by the lack of puritanism—for instance, they found a culture where men and women existed in equitable and uninhibited harmony to the point of even sharing baths shameful. But, of course, the imperialist undercurrent of their intentions was undeniably darker. Conquest was not just for redemption. Land, wealth and religion or, in Cortés' words, 'God, gold and glory' were driving aspirations. The priests, de Landa among them, understood that separating the Mayas from their holy texts was a prerequisite to indoctrinating them with Christian values and virtues.

Today, the hieroglyphic writing of the Mayas survives in four authenticated documents, the *Dresden, Paris, Madrid* and *Grolier Codices*[10] and in the carved reliefs of the great pyramids of Mexico and Peru. Ironically, later books disseminating information about the culture were written in Latin script, which the Spanish invaders taught the Mayas. One of the most significant was the *Popol Vuh* (or *Book of the People*), which sets down the religious beliefs and cultural traditions of the Mayas, including the creation and the population of the earth, and those relating to *tlachtli*. The *Popol Vuh* was passed on by oral tradition until it was transcribed into K'iche'[vi] around 1550 CE. Between 1701 and 1703, the Dominican Friar Francisco Ximénez, who was stationed at Santo Tomás Chichicastenango, about 90 miles northwest of Guatemala City, set down the K'iche' and his Spanish translation side by side, making K'iche' accessible to European anthropologists. The book helped to demystify the sacred rites and rituals of the Mayas to the world, thus preserving and promoting them. Fray Diego Durán, he of the 'jumping balls', also described his experiences in his handwritten 1581 book, *The History of the Indies of New Spain*[vii] also known as the *Durán Codex*. Both

---

vi K'iche' is one of several Mayan languages. Also referred to as Quiche. It is still spoken by over one million Maya descendants in parts of Guatemala.

vii However, this book remained uncopied in the library at Madrid, where it was unearthed in the nineteenth century by Jose Fernando Ramirez. Although its seventy-eight chapters contained the Aztec story of creation and many stories gleaned from the Aztecs contemporaneously, this information was not publicised since there was a movement to let the native cultures and observances

the *Popol Vuh* and the *Durán Codex* describe the perceived relationship between *olli*, the lubricating substance, and *olin*, the motion of the sun.

But why the gratuitous bloodletting after a game of *tlachtli*?

In a nutshell: the symbolism harkened back to the philosophy of the divine *teotl*[viii] of the Olmecs,[11] where the bouncing ball represented *yellotl*, the life force of the beating heart. This symbolism linked *olli*—the extraordinarily springy substance from which the balls were made and which the Aztecs identified as the rubber tree's blood—to *olin*, which means 'motion-change'. The symbolism, as described in the *Popol Vuh*, relates the movement of the ball to those of the celestial spheres: the sun and the moon.

The mythology of the Mesoamerican ball game hinges on the exploits of two heroic twins, Hunahpu and Xbalanque. Their father, Hun-Hunahpu,[ix] and uncle, Seven-Hunahpu, were fond of playing the ball game, but were noisy and disturbed the repose of the unsavoury lords of the underworld, the Xibalbans, who invite them to their domain, ostensibly to play the ball game but really to teach them a lesson. Unaware of their intentions,

---

disappear, to be replaced by the religion and cultural practices of the conquering Spaniards.

viii Divinity, but more than just 'god' or even morality. It is the philosophy about how the world exists and operates through *teotl*, described as a 'sacred power, force, or energy' from which the universe, its observed complementary but contradictory dualities, such as life-death; day-night; creation-destruction; male-female, originate. *Teotl* gives rise to itself and the universe, and its motion is a manifestation of *teotl*. The connection of rubber to this philosophy is described later in this chapter.

ix Also spelled *One Hunaphu* in some documents.

the pair accept the invitation and arrive in the underworld, but are murdered—Hun-Hunahpu is decapitated and his head placed in a calabash tree. Xquic, daughter of Cuchumaquic (the head of the Xibalbans), happens to come across the separated head, which spits at her. The spittle impregnates her and causes her to become pregnant with Hunahpu and Xbalanque.

Xquic escapes the underworld to live with Hun-Hunahpu's mother, and gives birth to the twins. At their grandmother's house, the twins find the ball game equipment she had hidden away in the attic after her sons were killed. They learn how to play the ball game on the same court as the one on which their father and his brother had played, and also develop supernatural powers, such as the ability to resurrect dead animals and each other. But the noise they make while they play once again disturbs the Xibalbans, who summon them to take part in a game, just like earlier. The boys enter the underworld, prepared to deal with the Xibalbans' deception. They do so by deliberately losing both the games and their lives, but then, with their abilities, they are able to resurrect themselves. Fascinated, the chiefs of the Xibalbans submit themselves to be killed and revived. The twins oblige them only partially—they do not resurrect them and instead leave the underworld, rising up and up until they are transformed into the sun and moon. *Tlachtli* is thus a re-enactment of this mythological tussle to free the celestial bodies from the clutches of the underworld, and is the oldest recorded team sport in the world. Over time, the balls, the playing courts and the very game itself evolved to reinforce the lived reality of victory and defeat in these martial societies. Today, variations of these games survive, but the civilisations from which they arose and the rituals they represent are largely lost.

It is clear that *tlachtli* was considered an integral part of society: a court from the Chiapas lowlands in Mexico was dated to be over 3,500 years old to 1650 BCE.[12] Dotted around ancient Olmec sites are seventeen colossal 'heads' measuring between 4 and 11 feet tall, around 15 feet in circumference, each weighing several tons, grouped in lines or clusters. Each head has different facial features, but all wear the type of helmet worn in the ball game, the design depending on the status of the wearer (Figure 2). The boulders they were made from were transported from the Veracruz region, about 90 miles away. To transport the boulders and to carve the faces on them was no small feat, so it is assumed that these heads had massive significance. As players whose actions kept the sun and the moon circling the earth, thus preserving life, the veneration would have been well deserved.

The Olmecs were probably the first to discover rubber's elastic properties and utility. Although the details are lost in the mists of time, it is known that they used raw latex as an offering to the gods and as medicine. They increased the durability of the latex using a smoking process, and used the resulting stringy rubber to make balls for the game or as offerings in burial pits. Their mastery of the latex-to-rubber conversion was not their only technological triumph—they were pioneers of many other technologies and creative arts which still amaze.[13] In addition to the construction of colossal heads, they made jade masks fetchingly carved with eye slits for purposes as yet undetermined. Their artistic repertoire included graceful and lifelike animal sculptures—birds, fishes, jaguars—in clay, jade, basalt and greenstone. The Olmecs also developed the first indigenous writing system in the Western hemisphere and invented the compass. That they developed rituals of bloodletting and human sacrifice, the culminating spectacle in *tlachtli* for the propitiation of the forces that maintained life, fits our impression of their fertile imagination.

Figure 2: Colossal Olmec head from San Lorenzo, Veracruz, Mexico.[14]

The Mesoamerican ball game became immensely popular across Central America. Over 1,600 Maya and Aztec ball courts of varying sizes and shapes have been found in sites across Mexico, Guatemala, Belize, Peru and even as far north as Arizona.[15] The format for the game apparently also evolved: the sizes of the courts vary enormously, from 60 feet to over 300 feet in length, although the general 'I' shape was retained (Figure 3). In some game variations, vertical hoops for driving the ball through are present; some variations may even have featured lighter balls with human skulls embedded in them. The heavy padding worn by the players was for the practical reason of protecting them from the ball's impact—a solid rubber ball can weigh several pounds and acquire bone-breaking momentum as it ricochets off bodies and stone walls. It was generally accepted that fragile arms and legs were not used to strike the ball; instead, players hit the ball with their hips and shoulders which were shown to be heavily padded in figurines and murals. Sometimes, paddles were also used (Figure 4). What is not in dispute is that the ball games were important in a social context: the enormous Olmec statuary would have required significant public funds and effort. Evidently, the ceremonial aspects were important enough to permeate every stratum of society, much like football or cricket does in many countries today. Additionally, elaborate murals carved in stone, statues of reclining ball players, interment of ball player figurines and rubber balls in ritual burial pits[16] and the construction of the large numbers of ball courts support the claims of its social and ritualistic value.

Figure 3: Ancient ball court of Monte Alban, in the Oaxaca region of Mexico.[17] Note the sloping sides and a central gully.

Figure 4: A manopla and ball. A solid rubber ball similar to those used in the Mesoamerican ball game from Kaminaljuyu, a Maya site, dated between 300 BCE and 250 CE. The ball is 3 inches in diameter. The manopla or handstone, also from Kaminaljuyu, dated between 900 BCE and 250 CE, is used to strike the ball. A mitten-shaped space has been carved out presumably for the player's hand. The far side of the stone is worn nearly smooth where it struck the ball, putting spin on it. Traces of rubber still adhere to the surface.[18]

After the game, the losing captain was sacrificed on the court by having his chest cut open and the still-beating heart plucked out and held up to provide *olli* to power the *olin* of the sun and the moon. Beheading was also apparently carried out: the sacrifice of a kneeling ball player is seen in some murals (Figure 5), and a decapitated head is held up in another. Balls with superimposed heads are seen on panels at the Great Ball Court in Chichen Itza. That might signify another grisly twist in which the decapitated heads were later inserted into the balls, which would make them lighter too, with hollow skulls replacing some of the heavy rubber material.[19]

Figure 5: Stone carving of the beheading of a ball player from the South Ballcourt at the archaeological site of El Tajin, Veracruz, Mexico.[20]

In August 2022, archaeologist Juan Yaduen Angelo from Mexico's National Institute of Archaeology and History found over 400 vessels in the Pyramid of the Sun in Chiapas containing 'human ashes, coal, rubber and plant material'.[21] He inferred that when important people like rulers died, they were cremated and their ashes were mixed with latex and other materials to form a ball; it is possible the belief was that such a ball would give the deceased a new beginning, perhaps as a celestial object, in the afterlife.

Over time, the ball game morphed from religious ritual to diplomatic ceremony. Elaborate panels depicting deities and royal figures playing the game have been found in various places; it is even conjectured that the game may have sometimes substituted for actual war. But the stakes would have been high. The losers may have endured a triple loss: the game, the war and their lives. The carved colossal heads wearing helmets could indicate that either Olmec rulers played the ball game, or that players became rulers. In 2004, a panel depicting the Maya king Taj Chan Ahk was found at the site of a royal ballcourt in Cancun, Mexico.[22] Altars on either side of the field show images of the king in his full regalia playing against the ruler of a subordinate state. The quality of the panels implies that this was an important event in the social calendar, akin to the pomp and tradition of the Superbowl in the United States, with the added sacrifice of the losers to thrill the crowd and propitiate the deities.

To understand why the bouncing rubber ball was germane to the representations in the ritual, it is necessary to delve into the philosophical mindset of the Olmecs, the earliest people to understand the properties of latex and rubber.

According to University of Maryland historian and philosopher James Maffie,[23] the key concept of this philosophy was the *teotl*, a sacred power that exists both as an entity and as a process that begets itself. *Teotl* is the essence of the cosmos: the material, the action and the motion. It represents the ceaseless cyclical duel for dominance and the nature of the cosmos as two faces of the same expression. Thus, *teotl* as motion-change can represent two polar opposites in three separate dimensions. In its *olin* form, it represents up-down, in-out and back-forth. In its *malinelli* form, it represents twisting, churning, gyrating and such circular motions and, in its *napalanta* form, it represents interweaving, shaking, merging and other incorporative motions. These dimensional motions are inseparable and interacting, not contradictory.[24] The nature of such duality has been appropriately captured in the names for the latex of trees, *olli*, and for motion, *olin;* both characterise rubber. *Teotl* was immanent in the material of rubber; it represented both the *it*-ness and the *of*-ness of motion-change. Thus, *teotl* encompasses the world, and rubber is its spokesperson.

The bouncing balls used in *tlachtli* were probably made of latex derived from the *Castilla elastica* tree, which is indigenous to Central America. The tree did not grow in the highlands of the Aztec homeland, but rubber was received as tribute from the lowlands. The latex that oozes from the tree is a tacky liquid that softens when warmed and hardens when cooled. Not all plant latex contains rubber particles, but when it does, the latex can be coagulated or dried into a sort of 'proto-rubber'. This is not yet rubber as we know it—balls made from proto-rubber lose their shape on impact and do not bounce. However, the Olmecs' rubber balls *were* bouncy and *did* hold their shape. The Olmecs also buried rubber balls, and the ones dug up in El Manatí, in Veracruz, Mexico, have survived from about 1600 BCE—over 3,500 years—in the ground. How might the Olmecs have discovered the method to make actual rubber from latex? This is an especially intriguing question, because making rubber from latex is not straightforward.

Dorothy Hosler, Michael Tarkanian and their team at the Massachusetts Institute of Technology (MIT) examined the process which *huleros*—rubber workers—in Chiapas still use. Raw latex is mixed with juice from the *Ipomoea alba* (morning glory) vine. In their publication, the MIT team writes: '750 mL of latex is mixed with 50 mL of morning glory vine extract and stirred with a stick for about 15 minutes until the latex coagulates into a solid mass of rubber of 9.5 cm in diameter which rebounded into the air to a height of about 2 m.' They also learned that the proportions could be varied to produce different properties in the cured material. A 50:50 ratio of latex to morning glory vine juice produced the bounciest ball; a 75:25 ratio made for the most durable rubber.[25] Testing showed that the strain capacity was the same in untreated and treated latex, but that the elasticity (rebound) of the rubber treated with vine juice was doubled due to increased stringiness and stretchiness.[x] The MIT team also describe the two-part process by which the polymer chains join up to make rubber. The morning glory vine juice removes a coating of protein from rubber particles, facilitating a phase where the soluble components of latex and the insoluble rubber chains separate. In the second part of the process, the sulphur-containing components of the morning glory vine juice, sulfonyl chloride and sulfonic acid, crosslink the rubber chains when heated—a process that causes them to adhere to form rubber.[xi] In the absence of the juice of the morning glory vine, latex dries to a brittle brown substance, but, when mixed with it, it turns black and becomes elastic, resembling the rubber we are familiar with. In their paper, they mention that Fray Toribio de Benavente (alias Motolinía), who recorded the Aztec method of processing latex in the *Historia de los indios de la Nueva España*, described the product as 'black, not brown'.[26]

One presumes that the Olmecs were both excellent observers and experimentalists, and may have understood the effects of varying the relative proportions of latex to morning

---

x Strain measures the amount of deformation a material can take before it loses integrity. Elasticity measures the speed of regaining the original shape after removal of the distorting force.

xi The chemistry here is similar to the process of vulcanisation developed later by Goodyear and Hancock in which rubber strands are cross-linked by sulphur and heat.

glory vine juice. But it is not just balls made of rubber invented by Mesoamericans that have persisted through time; other similarly ingenious uses of latex were dreamed up. Latex was used for painting and sculpting, making squeezable bottles, forming elastic strips to secure arrowheads to arrows, for use as medicine, for burning for light and for coagulating on feet, hands and clothing to leverage its protective and waterproof qualities which were so desirable in tropical jungles with all manner of wet and pointy things everywhere. And, of course, there is the remarkable survival of 3,500-year-old rubber balls at El Manatí, Mexico. How the Olmecs calibrated their formulas is not known, but the fact that their artefacts have survived over three millennia in the ground is proof that they had significant expertise and imagination. Ron O. Cook speculates that those massive head sculptures could have been transported for miles using rubber balls as rollers.[27] Could the Olmecs have been the inventors of vehicular motion? We can only speculate.

Eventually, rubber moved from being a curiosity of a geographically isolated culture to a mainstream product due to its utility and versatility. As rubber products were documented, and as bouncing balls and ball players were taken back to Europe for exhibitions, interest grew in the fascinating properties of latex from oozing trees. These properties were discussed and shared by enthusiastic colonialists who arrived later, including from other European countries, tasked with documenting the flora and fauna of the New World. The helpful indigenous people shared knowledge of these items with the Spanish, showing them how latex was tapped and processed into rubber. Europeans discovered other useful attributes—for example, that rubber would rub out marks made by pencils. But rubber just did not get much attention in the Old World in the early days—there was just so much already to process from the voyages of Columbus and Cortés, and bouncing balls were not as dazzling as gold or exotic animals. About 300 years after the first voyagers brought bouncing balls to Europe, Nathaniel Hayward, Charles Goodyear and Thomas Hancock discovered that vulcanisation—the processing with sulphur and heat treatment—gave rubber desirable properties such as elasticity, thermostability and durability. The unearthing of these and other properties jumpstarted the interest in rubber. Then, the economics of supply and demand took over.

2

Fruits of Discovery

Christopher Columbus returned to Spain from his first transatlantic voyage in the year 1493 with stories of a strange herb (presumably tobacco) which was used in the New World and a plethora of other show-and-tell items: 'In advance marched a group of some half-dozen New World Indians and a squad of sailors from the ship Niña. The Indians wore gold ornaments and carried spears and arrows, while the sailors bore aloft forty parrots of gorgeous plumage, besides other birds, together with rare plants and animals, including a five-foot-long iguana, its back bristling with spines.'[28]

Michele de Cuneo, a Genovese man who accompanied Columbus in 1493, describes a tree the wood of which burns like a torch and yields 'an excellent turpentine'—probably torchwood, *Amyris elemifera*.[29] Another merchant, Giambattista Strozzi, describes 'trees which make wax.'[30] According to botanist Jeremy Purseglove, these trees were most likely *Castilla elastica*, which would grow at that latitude. On this voyage, Columbus is said to have seen young boys playing on the beaches of Hispaniola (now Haiti/Dominican Republic),[31] with a rubber ball that bounced—something that the balls made of leather in Europe were incapable of—and he is said to have acquired it to bring back to Europe.[32]

In 1525, the historian Pietro Maître d'Anghiera, later Count Palatine, noted in his *Decade of the New World* that '*gummi optima*' was made from the white juice of a tree, which was then dried and smoked. In 1528, Hernán Cortés sent back Mesoamerican ball game players to the court of Charles V of Spain where they were drawn by Christoph Weiditz, a visiting German artist (Figure 6). There are two ball players facing away from the viewer in the drawing. The ball is suspended in the air between them, seemingly struck by the hips or buttocks of the player on the right, who is crouched, twisting his neck as if to observe the initial lift of the ball. The stances and musculature of the players show extreme athleticism. The annotation reads: *Auf soliche manier spilen die Indianer mit ainem auf geblassen bal mit dem hinder. On die hend an Zue Rieren auf der Erdt haben auch ain hardt leder for dem hindern dar mit er vom bal den widerstreich Entpfacht haben auch solich ledern hent schuech an.*[33] This roughly translates to: 'The Indians play with an inflated ball with their butts, keeping their hands from touching the ground. They wear leather on their butts and on their hands.'

Figure 6: Mesoamerican ball players in the court of Charles V in 1528. Drawn by Christoph Weiditz.[34]

The Spaniard observed that locals dipped their clothing, objects and even their bare feet in latex and smoked them over a fire to obtain waterproof material, bottles and bespoke shoes.[35] The waterproofing qualities of latex were quickly adopted by European visitors to the Americas, who used them to coat their long stockings, hats and boots before embarking on trips into the jungle.[36] Bags made from fabric impregnated with latex had water-resistant qualities and were useful alternatives to ones made of leather. During this time, there arose a modest interest in waterproofing, and latex-permeated fabric and shoes made in Mexico trickled steadily to North America and Europe, but beyond that, it remained merely an interesting oddity.

In 1736, a package arrived at the French Academy of Sciences in Paris from Quito (then in Spanish-administered Peru,

Ecuador). It contained a sample of *caoutchouc* (unvulcanised rubber) collected by Charles Marie de La Condamine,[37] along with a note describing the *Heve* (sic) tree as its source. He described the process by which, following a cut made in the bark, an oozing milky substance (which he called 'latex', after the French word for milk) was collected and shaped into products such as syringes by natives on the bank of the Amazon: 'They make bottles of it in the shape of a pear, to the neck of which they attach a fluted piece of wood. By pressing them, the liquid they contain is made to flow out through the flutes and, by this means, they become real syringes.' However, the tree de La Condamine described was likely *Castilla elastica*, the Mexican rubber tree, rather than *Hevea brasiliensis*, the para rubber tree which he would encounter on a journey down the Amazon a few years later.

Charles Marie de La Condamine was a mathematician, soldier, geographer and a member of the French Academy of Sciences. The journey de La Condamine had undertaken had a different mission altogether from discovery: it was to measure the distance of a degree of the latitude at the equator in order to settle an argument that had arisen between supporters of René Descartes' suggestion that the earth was 'lemon-shaped'—that is, expanded at the poles and flattened at the Equator—and the followers of Isaac Newton, who had calculated that the earth was oblate or 'mandarin-shaped', meaning it was expanded at the Equator and flattened at the poles. Besides being an academic battle, it was also a political one. The French and the English were both trying to establish accurate maritime navigation, which translated to potential global supremacy given the colonisation and trading opportunities of the time. Starting with Columbus' journey, the Spanish had demonstrated their derring-do in ocean navigation overseen by a branch of the Bourbon family of France—a successful Franco–Spanish alliance. The English were no laggards either. The British Parliament had established a £20,000 prize under the Longitude Act of 1714 for anyone who could build a clock which could accurately help sailors calculate their position on featureless seas.[xii] Whereas latitudes (the distance north or south of the equator) could be calculated by measuring the angular distance of known stars relative to the North Star with sextants, longitudes (the distance east or west of a location) could not.[xiii] When a ship was sailing along a latitudinal line and its longitudinal position changed, the stars held their relative position in the sky, but the sun rose and set earlier or later. So the best way to gauge longitude was to have two clocks set to the same time when departing the port, and adjusting just one of the clocks to the time of sunrise. The difference in time between the clocks could then be translated into the distance from the port of departure. The problem was that the distance between longitudinal lines was not known with accuracy, because the shape of the earth was not known for certain, and lemon-shaped and mandarin-shaped earths would translate to different longitudinal distances at different latitudes.

---

xii A spellbinding description of the work of clockmaker genius John Harrison's pursuit of this prize is given in Sobel, D., 2005. *Longitude: The true story of a lone genius who solved the greatest scientific problem of his time*. Macmillan.

xiii A couple of mnemonics to remember the difference between longitude and latitude: 'Longitudes are like long ladders, but lats are flat' or the rhyme 'Latitude, flatitude, round and round; longitude lines go up and down' (from Jennifer Bazzit of Thrive in Grade Five at https://thriveingradefive.com).

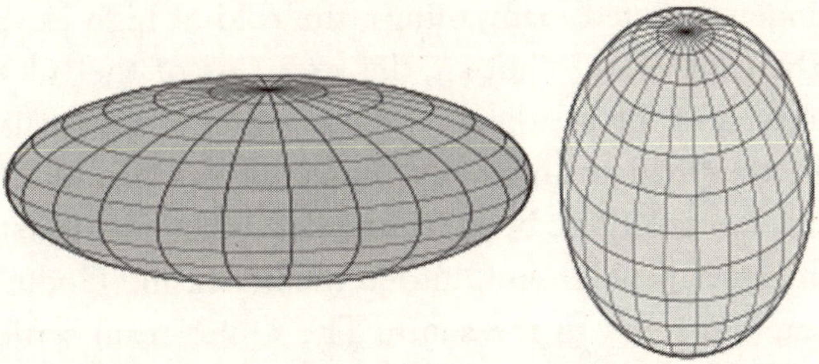

Figure 7: Distinguishing between two possible shapes of the earth; on the left is the 'oblate mandarin shape' suggested by Newton and on the right is Descartes' 'prolate lemon shape'. The shape of the earth could be inferred by measuring a degree of latitude at two locations as far apart as possible. The French equator team chose Lapland near the North Pole and Ecuador near the equator to make the measurements.[38]

In 1735, the French Geodesic Mission, initiated and aided by the offices of Jean-Frédéric Phélypeaux, Count of Maurepas and *Ministre de la Marine* (Minister of the Navy) to Charles XV, set out to conduct measurements to establish which shape was right by measuring the length of a degree of latitude at the equator to compare to the measurements of a team despatched to Lapland near the North Pole. Two widely separated north–south points could be established on land, and the distance between them measured accurately. Their latitudes could be established by the position of the stars and the curvature of the earth in between calculated. By comparing the curvatures at the equator and North Pole, the shape of the earth could be inferred.

The French equator team consisted of three key members: Louis Godin, the team leader, and Pierre Bouguer and de La Condamine. Both Bouguer and de La Condamine chafed under Godin's inept leadership, and things got off to a poor start when de La Condamine decided to travel separately to Quito, which is when he first encountered latex tapping. The team had also underestimated many things: the cold at high elevations near the equator, the thin air, the steepness of the volcanoes, the vagaries of the weather and the hostility of the locals even though they had Spanish government emissaries to smooth the way. In June 1736, Bouguer and de La Condamine started their measurements from Quito in the north, and Godin from Cuenca, 280 miles to the south. The Quito team settled on an initial baseline 7.5 miles long on the flat Yaruquai plateau, which they painstakingly measured out with poles 20 feet long, laid end to end. From each end of the baseline, they measured the angle to a distant elevated 'station'[xiv] (such as a mountain top). They then used basic trigonometry to work out the distance to the station by a process called triangulation.[xv] Then they physically climbed to the mountain top station to make the next measurement. This was tedious work, and they finished their initial measurements in 1739, but disagreements kept them working independently for three more years despite knowing that the Lapland team had already completed their work and established that the earth was oblate, as Newton had theorised.

---

xiv The points that were surveyed were called stations. Once the distance to a station was obtained, the surveyors moved to that station and made measurements to another station. Gradually, the surveyors built up a map of the area by overlaying it with a series of triangular measurements.

xv Triangulation is a survey technique to measure long distances accurately. This process uses one length measurement and two angle measurements to a distant 'station' to get the lengths of all the three sides using trigonometry. The area to be surveyed is covered in a network of triangles calculated from different stations called 'triangulation points'. Using the triangular grid, distance can be calculated accurately between any two points within the surveyed area.

After the measurements were finally completed, each went his own way, with de La Condamine choosing to travel down the Amazon by raft, taking four months for the journey, with pauses to investigate reports of the anti-malarial properties of the cinchona tree and tales of warlike women called the Amazons. He collected about 200 specimens, including several seedlings of the cinchona tree, and seeds of vanilla, sarsaparilla, cacao and guaiacum, which he gave to the naturalist and mathematician Georges-Louis Leclerc, Comte de Buffon and the director of the Jardin du Roi (now called the Jardin des Plantes), the main botanical garden in France. Further, de La Condamine described his Amazon journey in a publication he called *Journal du voyage fait par ordre du roi, a l'Équateur*, and succeeded in convincing the French Academy of Sciences to explore the material properties of the *caoutchouc* he had mailed from Quito, with Francois Fresneau becoming midwife to the project.

Francois Fresneau and Charles-Marie de La Condamine had met in Cayenne, French Guiana. An engineer by profession, Fresneau had been tasked with shoring up the fortifications in Cayenne. The project was considerably more involved than he had anticipated—the fortifications required reconstruction. While he was waiting for funds to be made available, he had indulged his other passion, botany—discovering plants and assessing which could be sent to the Jardin du Roi. He also met de La Condamine, who showed him samples of *caoutchouc*[xvi] that he had collected, exciting in Fresneau a new passion: rubber. Eventually, de La Condamine left for France in 1743, but Fresneau continued to observe and study the methods for making rubber from latex and fashioned items that he sent

xvi To maintain narrative, I will use the term rubber rather than *caoutchouc* subsequently.

home. He also wrote a letter about it in 1746 to the Count of Maurepas, who had been behind the French Geodesic Mission but who apparently disregarded Fresneau's letter. Subsequently, Fresneau moved back to France and wrote a document about rubber, explaining its properties and insisting that this strange substance had immense potential. Eventually, his document landed at the French Academy of the Sciences and made its way to de La Condamine. Since Fresneau was in poor health, de La Condamine presented this as a paper to the Academy in 1751.

Fresneau slowly recovered his health and started working on rubber in his laboratory in his ancestral home, La Gataudière. His efforts were rewarded when Jacques de Vaucanson, an accomplished inventor, sought information on rubber through a government minister, and is credited with having created and used the first flexible rubber tube for his invention of an amusing automated 'Digesting Duck' which could flap its wings, eat grain and defecate a green material (later shown to be breadcrumbs and green dye rather than digested grain).[xvii] Fresneau wrote a report for the government on his experiments, including the use of turpentine to dissolve rubber for use in waterproofing fabric. Again, Fresneau reached out to de La Condamine, who suggested it be rewritten as a scientific paper, which was then presented at the Academy in 1765.

---

xvii In 2006, the Belgian artist Wim Delvoye created a 'Cloaca Machine' which mimics the human digestive system and turns real food into real faeces which looks and smells like human faeces. It can also produce various types of faeces, including diarrhoea. Apparently, the faeces is bagged and sold under the Cloaca brand to art dealers and collectors; so far all the faeces produced has sold out. De Vaucanson would be impressed.

By the 1770s, rubber was mainstream, although expensive. Edward Nairne, an English engineer who invented and patented several electrical machines, is said to have inadvertently picked up a piece of rubber that was lying around and used it to erase pencil marks. Maybe he did not have a piece of bread, which was until then used for that purpose. Nairne started selling these at the exorbitant price of 3 shillings (36 pence; equivalent to a day's wage for a workman at the time). Joseph Priestley, who made the discovery that plants released oxygen and that it was the gas that sustained life, is also often given credit for the discovery of the erasing ability of rubber. But some admirable sleuthing to establish the authenticity of this claim by Laurel Thatcher Ulrich, a history professor at Harvard, revealed that Priestley had documented seeing it in Nairne's store, but not that he had actually bought it or used it.[39] Ulrich found a footnote in *A Short History of Chemistry* by J.R. Partington referencing Priestley's 1770 book, *A Familiar Introduction to the Theory and Practice of Perspective* (which presumably needed a lot of drawing and erasing), as an addendum:

> Since this Work was printed off, I have seen a substance excellently adapted to the purpose of wiping from paper the marks of a black-lead-pencil. It must, therefore, be of singular use to those who practise drawing. It is sold by Mr. Nairne, Mathematical Instrument-Maker, opposite the Royal-Exchange. He sells a cubical piece, of about half an inch, for three shillings; and he says it will last several years.

William Henry Playfair commented on Edinburgh's revival during the years after the Napoleonic Wars that 'nothing good in Architecture can be effected without a monstrous expenditure of patience and Indian Rubber…'[40] Rubber remains the preferred term today and has even expanded its domain as the slang word for condoms, which were made of latex.[xviii]

To the Portuguese who had been in Brazil working with locals to tap for latex, rubber was also not much more than a curiosity. In the early 1700s, the Portuguese had sealed Brazil off from any commercial exchange with the rest of Europe, so that all the gold and diamonds recently discovered there could flow to Lisbon and directly into the coffers of King João V, who ruled from 1706 to 1750. José I, who succeeded him, ruling from 1750 to 1777, also had a narrow perspective of the utility of rubber. He had sent his boots to Para (now Belem) for waterproofing, and a waterproof coat made of fabric treated with rubber had been presented to him in 1759. Only a few items, such as rubber bottles, made it out to countries allied with the Portuguese, including into the British colonies in America, arousing public interest, but the supply was not adequate for rubber to hold anything more than novelty value. Portugal's overseas interests in Brazil meant they had to use seafaring ships, but only at the pleasure of the powerful British Royal Navy which could challenge any comers. This required Portugal to maintain friendly relations with Britain. Another reason the Portuguese had for maintaining this friendship was that Britain was a major slave-trading nation which used the port at Lisbon as a stopover, bringing in the riches of the Atlantic Triangle Trade.

In 1789, the French Revolution had caused upheaval in Europe, especially amongst the aristocracy. But upheavals

xviii Although condoms have been made of other materials for many centuries including silk, leather and animal intestines, latex was probably in use since the 1770s, prior to vulcanisation (John Loadman, personal correspondence).

continued after the revolution and the fall of the *ancien régime*, when Napoleon Bonaparte, a renowned military general and initiator of the French Revolutionary Wars, took over as First Consul of France. In 1793, Portugal allied closely with Spain and Britain due to the horror felt by the ruling classes of Europe following the French Revolution and the execution of Louis XVI. But then, Napoleon invaded Spain and forced the Peace of Basel in 1795 under which Spain broke its treaty with Britain and joined forces with France. Then, in 1799, he mounted a coup to overthrow the Directory that then ruled France, all the while remaining on the warpath against Britain and anyone who sided with it. Under Napoleon's instigation, Spain invaded Portugal in the War of the Oranges in 1801 and, under the Treaty of Badajoz, demanded that Portugal stop British ships from entering its ports. In 1803, Britain broke the short-lived Treaty of Amiens signed in 1802 and declared war on France. Needing money to support the war effort, Napoleon negotiated the Louisiana Purchase Treaty of 1803 with US President Thomas Jefferson, ceding a swath of 828,000 square miles across the middle of the new country of America for a price of 15 million dollars. Through it all, Napoleon entrenched his domestic standing, and crowned himself Emperor of the French in 1804.

Napoleon's bellicosity and his hostility towards Britain dominated Europe for the next decade. In 1805, he gathered together thirty-three ships of the navies of France and Spain—including the largest warship of the time, the Spanish ship *Santisima Trinidad*, equipped with 140 guns—under the command of Admiral Villeneuve, seeking to invade Britain. Arrayed against him was the small but powerful British navy comprising twenty-seven ships under the leadership of the experienced Admiral Lord Nelson aboard his flagship, *HMS*

Victory. It did not help that Admiral Villeneuve had memories of a previous defeat of the French navy by then Rear Admiral Nelson in the Battle of the Nile in 1798, and was probably not eager for a repeat confrontation. It would appear that his apprehensions were founded. The ensuing Battle of Trafalgar was a rout of Napoleon's navy. Admiral Nelson's bold tactics and the relative inexperience of the French naval commanders (since many of their most able officers had been executed or pushed out after the French Revolution) resulted in a British victory.[xix] As the British and captured French ships turned to head back to England, a massive storm broke in the English Channel, battering both the victors and the vanquished for three days. When it ended, all British ships managed to return to port, but with only four captured French vessels. Except for two vessels that had been recaptured by the Spanish, all the others had been sunk by the British or by the storm. With Britain's naval forces victorious, Portugal was again under pressure from both sides: from France to join the Continental Blockade to exclude the British from mainland Europe's ports, and from Britain to do no such thing.

In 1807, frustrated by their refusal to submit willingly, Napoleon ordered Portugal's indisposed Queen Maria I and her son, Prince Regent João of Braganza (later João VI), to stop trading with the British. They did so, at least overtly. But Napoleon also demanded that Portugal declare war on Britain, detain British traders and seize their merchandise, which the Prince Regent refused to do. Napoleon's Grande Armée had meanwhile scored victories over most of mainland Europe, uniting Prussia, Russia and parts of Central Europe

xix Admiral Nelson, though, was mortally shot by a French sniper, and a plaque on *HMS Victory*, now moored off Portsmouth, indicates the spot where he fell.

with the Treaty of Tilsit, 1807. Motivated to pursue further consolidation against the British, Napoleon invaded and occupied Portugal with Spain's assistance in November 1807. But the birds had flown the coop. To sidestep Napoleon's wrath, the Portuguese court had quietly decamped to Brazil earlier that year under the protection of the Royal Navy of Britain, and began governing Portugal from its South American colony. The Prince Regent then decreed that Brazil, which had thus far remained sealed for trade, should open up to friendly nations in the *Decreto de Abertura dos Portos às Nações Amigas* (Decree of Opening the Ports to Friendly Nations), the immediate benefactor being Britain. This series of historical events ultimately made possible the transit of rubber harvested in Brazil to Britain and to America, where it eventually came to the attention of Thomas Hancock and Charles Goodyear, who would go on to mould the rubber story four decades later.

Napoleon turned his wrath on his inconstant Spanish ally and deposed Charles IV as well as his son Ferdinand VII. He then installed his brother Joseph Bonaparte as Joseph I under the Bayonne Statute to the Spanish throne. This touched off the Peninsular Wars, a rejection by Spain and Portugal of Napoleon's governance. In 1812, in an act of hubris, Napoleon invaded Russia in the winter. This was a folly in line with the advice given later by General Douglas MacArthur to JFK about how 'anyone wanting to commit ground troops to Asia should have his head examined'.[41] The Grande Armée suffered a humiliating defeat, puncturing Napoleon's reputation as a general par excellence. Subsequently, this emboldened the Sixth Coalition comprising Austria, Prussia, Russia, Spain, Portugal, Germany, Sweden and Britain to assemble and collectively defeat and depose Napoleon, exiling him to Elba in 1814. Napoleon escaped in 1815, and returned to his throne in

Paris the same year, but was soundly defeated once again at the Battle of Waterloo. This time, the British imprisoned him on the remote island of Saint Helena, where Napoleon appears to have died from stomach cancer, illness arising from poor living conditions or arsenic poisoning—or perhaps a combination of all three—at the age of fifty-one.

Why are the Napoleonic Wars relevant to rubber? The turmoil of the Napoleonic era and his rejection of trade with the British, who, at the time, controlled the oceans with the most powerful navy in the world, affected the French exploration of the Amazon that de La Condamine had begun. France and its superb scientific and military communities had been at the forefront of innovations such as canned food; submarines; steam-powered warships; the development of inland waterways to move their materiel;[xx] rifles (which replaced muskets); semaphore-based communication; battlefield triage using 'flying' ambulances drawn by fast horses to reach the wounded more quickly; and pioneering the examination of soldiers' craniums with elastic rubber catheters to locate embedded bullets and using trepanation to remove them, thereby relieving brain swelling. On the other hand, war made it harder for the French to travel across British-dominated waters, and the loss sustained by France due to the sale of the central swathe of America in the Louisiana Purchase Treaty may never be measured. The standoffs with Portugal, the only country with access to rubber, and with Britain, which had worldwide commercial interests and a powerful navy to protect them, were counterproductive. Although it is counterfactual, perhaps access to rubber would have spurred Napoleon's military to find

xx Materiel is a term referring to equipment and supplies used by an organisation, usually the military. Material is a general term for the type of matter from which an item is constituted.

other innovative uses such as coating wagon tyres to produce even faster 'flying' ambulances. Regardless, France failed to capitalise on the initial impetus on rubber research that de La Condamine and Fresneau had begun.

There was one other, fraught, connection between Napoleon and rubber. In 1864, Napoleon III, the nephew of Napoleon I, sent Archduke Maximilian, brother of Franz Joseph I, the Emperor of Austria and King of Hungary, to Mexico in 1864 to establish a regime that would align with the French. But the venture was mired with diplomatic complexities and political instability, and went poorly. In 1867, the Mexicans under Benito Juárez revolted; and Maximilian and two of his generals were shot by a firing squad.[42] Before he was summarily despatched, he supposedly made a short speech, handed each member of his firing squad a gold coin, pointed at his heart and uttered, 'Aim well, *muchachos*.' Maximilian's wife Charlotte was in Italy at the time of her husband's execution to plead for French military support from Napoleon III, but he refused her request again and again. As a result, she would suffer mental instability until she died in 1927 at the age of eighty-seven. And since Charlotte's oldest brother and heir to the Belgian throne, Louis Philippe, had already died in infancy, it was her younger brother, the Duke of Brabant, who inherited the Belgian throne and subsequently grew up to become none other than the infamous King Leopold, Butcher of the Congo.

3

Patent Battles

Mesoamericans had used latex as a protective substance from time immemorial. It was a substance that was plentiful and readily available to them—if one product wore out, they could make another with little effort; they did not need to innovate for durability beyond their immediate needs. In other places, nomadic, animistic and hunter-gatherer societies believed that living things possessed spiritual power, and treated land as a shared resource for all beings, taking only what they needed and sharing information freely without restraint or expectation of reward. The indigenous people the Spanish encountered freely demonstrated the bounce of rubber balls and showed them how latex could be used for waterproofing. The information was eagerly received even though remuneration of equal value was not exchanged during or after these voyages of 'discovery'.

On the other hand, settled cultures that grew out of valuing land—farming the earth, domesticating animals, establishing dwellings, accumulating materials, building social communities, specialising in trades—placed a greater value on information, and produced legal frameworks for sharing intellectual property that gave the innovator some monetary benefit. The first patent systems were Greek and described in 500 BCE.[43] By the time the great European explorations of discovery got underway in the fourteenth century, patent systems were well established in Europe. In the United States, Thomas Jefferson established the patent system in the year 1790. Applications for patents were carefully scrutinised, but the amount of time it took to thoroughly examine an application and assess its novelty became cumbersome. Therefore, in the early nineteenth century, the US patent office moved to a system where examinations were curtailed and patents were registered rapidly without the need to demonstrate adequate testing, prototype creation or reproducibility. This lowering of barriers allowed patent speculators to take a legitimate invention and register it with barely any changes, putting the onus on the inventors to engage in lawsuits to protect their rights to receive royalties. Subsequently, the Andrew Jackson administration re-established examinations and, in 1836, public access to patents was granted—measures which went some way to restoring the legitimacy of the US patent system.

There remained a difference between European and American patent systems that was not resolved until the America Invents Act of 2011 (implemented in 2013) which included a provision regarding *when* a patent is issued.[44] Before 2013, the US patent office assigned patents to the first person to invent something, and keeping accurately dated records of the process was necessary to resolve the problem of who first came up with an invention. By contrast, the new legislation directed the awarding of patents to the first person to file, in line with the rest of the world. Detractors have argued that this change benefits big businesses whose in-house patent filing systems are quicker than those available to a garage inventor. It was precisely this issue of precedence that Charles Goodyear and Thomas Hancock clashed over in British courts. Charles Goodyear did not patent his sulphur-and-heat-based vulcanisation process until 15 June 1844[45] although he claimed he had invented it in 1839 and tested it for five years. But Thomas Hancock had filed a preliminary patent in 1843, adding more information in a patent filed in 1844.[46] And therein lay the rub, not only because of suspicions of theft of technology, but of incompatible patent systems facing each other in court. When the adherents of one system met the adherents of the other, things could get fairly heated, because a decision could have substantial economic value. The patent battles for ownership of the process of vulcanisation are the subject of this chapter.

By the early nineteenth century, the British and the Americans had realised that rubber-waterproofed items could become highly popular merchandise, particularly in damp and cool Britain and New England. However, the items were not suitable for their weather. The 'thermoplastic' properties of contemporary rubber were such that items made from it were elastic and could flex at moderate temperatures, but tended to get sticky in the summer and rigid in the winter. Innovators worked to understand and improve the durability and utility of rubber, and their goal was a process that resulted in rubber that held its shape, while retaining its desirable elastomer qualities independently of the temperature. Foremost among the innovators were Charles Goodyear from the United States and Thomas Hancock from Great Britain, but there were others[xxi]

xxi For example, François Herrissent and Pierre Macquer discovered that rubber could be dissolved in turpentine and ether and Freidrich

such as Nathaniel Hayward;[47] the brothers Walter, John and Charles Hancock; Charles Macintosh; Edwin Chaffee; William Ely; Horace Day—they flit in and out of the narrative, helping or hindering the primary rivals. Most of the story in the next section is recounted from Richard Korman's biography of Goodyear.[48]

Charles Goodyear was born in 1800 in Connecticut. His father, Amasa, had a hardware business, but Charles was unfortunately lacking in sufficient business sense to turn a profit: a business he started in Philadelphia went bankrupt. In fact, bankruptcies, debt and debtor's prison were regular features of his life, as also was the birth of children and, on occasion (sadly), their death. Charles's obsession with making rubber into a usable product has rightfully become stuff of legend, but less commented on is the fact that Charles was fortunate in his family and the friends who indulged and bankrolled his monomania. His wife Clarissa was as patient as she was penurious, and his well-to-do brother-in-law, William De Forest, frequently stepped up to rescue him financially.

Charles Goodyear's life story excites compassion and admiration, and is truly a triumph of doggedness. The time around his birth was one of great turmoil, with the Napoleonic Wars sputtering in Europe and the War of 1812 raging between Britain and the United States. The ensuing fluxes in trade would affect his livelihood. In contrast to his later life, his early personal life appears to have been quite stable. His Calvinist New England upbringing instructed him at an early

---

Ludersdorf in Germany also discovered the importance of sulphur. They do not enter this story.

age in piety, self-reliance and hard work. He was precocious, bright and full of ideas for inventions, but he was small, thin, physically frail and often sick—issues that lasted throughout his life. His father's hardware store sold clocks, farm tools and also other things Amasa had invented and patented: tempered round-tined table forks, an enclosed oil-burning lantern, a molasses-gate and a spring steel hay fork. The spring steel hay fork was lighter and springier than traditional forks and, more importantly, it was popular, bringing both recognition and substantial remuneration. Amasa also made and supplied the US military with buttons for uniforms during the War of 1812. A Connecticut neighbour of the Goodyears' was Eli Whitney, who had invented the cotton gin.[xxii] Alas, Whitney's patent had been widely infringed and he received no royalties; a lesson to Charles about vigilance over intellectual property.

Although Charles initially went to school locally, at sixteen he was enrolled in a Congregationalist school in Ellsworth, Maine, which was run by a popular and vigorous preacher, Reverend Daniel Parker. Although he was regarded as an excellent teacher, Parker complained about the hard work and poor pay. But he was committed to his congregation. He floated his poorer flock cheap loans, maintained joint business ventures with some townspeople and supported an orphan. When the congregation grew in size, another school opened in the area, making him resentful. His employment and business relationships soured, and he demanded to be dismissed. When he was, albeit for having too much involvement in 'worldly matters', Parker sued for slander. His schooling thus disrupted, Goodyear returned

xxii The cotton gin efficiently separated the fibres of the cotton flower from the seeds. This speeding up of the process made cotton-growing more profitable and increased demand for slaves to plant and pick it.

home. For a time, his tutor was William De Forest, a successful businessman who later married Goodyear's sister Harriet and became a source of moral and financial support.

In 1824, Charles married Clarissa Beecher, whom he had known since childhood. They moved to Philadelphia, where Amasa already had a customer base, and set up their own hardware store which sold only goods 'Made in the USA' by the Goodyears themselves or by others on a commission basis. Due to locals feeling animosity towards Britain following the War of 1812, resulting in protective import tariffs levied on foreign goods by the US government, the store's patriotic stand soon proved visionary. Sales were brisk, and business rapidly expanded to other states. They were prosperous enough to commission a painting around 1830—Charles holding his two-year-old daughter Cynthia in his lap with his older daughter, six-year-old Ellen standing beside him. Clarissa, however, is not in the painting.

Now that his family and his business had successfully stabilised, he started partnering with other inventors and started to speculate in real estate. In an effort to leverage more sales, he extended credit to southern farmers, which all went very well, at least until the Tariff of 1828. Also known as the 'Tariff of Abominations', this law levied a tax of 38 per cent on imported goods and 45 per cent on raw materials. The purpose of the tariff was to incentivise domestic manufacture over the purchase of cheaper goods from England, which was only too willing to unload goods in the American market since they could not trade with the European continent due to Napoleon's blockade. The southern states particularly resented this tariff because theirs was not an industrial economy, whereas the northern states preferred it since their manufacturing base was stronger. This resulted in a standoff within the federal government between President John Quincy Adams, a northerner, and his own

Vice President John C. Calhoun of South Carolina as well as Calhoun's supporters, including Martin Van Buren and Andrew Jackson. The irony was that the bill, written by southerners including Van Buren and Calhoun, was deliberately framed in a way to hurt both imports from manufacturers in Britain as well as in New England. The writers were sure it would fail in the Congress but the plan backfired: the bill passed, and President Adams signed it—much to the southerners' astonishment and chagrin. Unfortunately for businessmen such as Charles Goodyear who had extended credit widely, it caused the southern farmers to renege on paying their debts. Goodyear was ruined. And he still owed $12,000 to his creditors.

That was just the beginning of Goodyear's trials. Like the parable of Job in the Bible, over the period from 1830 to 1834, the blows kept falling. He was sent to debtor's prison; two of his children, Clarissa and Sarah died; he borrowed money repeatedly from De Forest; he lost all his real estate and hardware investments; he surrendered his patents. Then it got worse. To rescue him, his father parted with his fork patent—and then with his house and farm in Connecticut. Worst of all, Charles Goodyear's reputation as a businessman was ruined. With so much misfortune tumbling down on his head, Goodyear decided that invention, rather than ironmongery and storekeeping, was to be his salvation. Visiting New York in 1834, he had walked past Roxbury India Rubber Company's storefront in Manhattan and had seen a life-preserver whose valve he thought he could improve.[xxiii] When Goodyear took his improved valve back to the store, the agent fatefully told him to

---

xxiii India rubber was the common name given to articles made of latex from South America. It may be a hangover from Columbus' mistake in thinking he had found a western route to India.

work on improving rubber rather than the valve. Roxbury India Rubber Company was struggling because rubber's recalcitrance to being worked and the stink it produced in warm weather was causing the many companies that had excitedly adopted the new material to go bust. Goodyear obtained a sample of rubber. It was the summer of 1834, and Charles Goodyear was thirty-four years old.

Between 1834 and 1837, joy and sorrow stalked Goodyear. A child, William Henry, was born in 1834 but died within a year. His family had moved back to New Haven, Connecticut, and Goodyear initially distracted himself with work on boat construction but it did not pan out. He returned to rubber. He found investors, whom he beguiled with his charm and enthusiasm: De Forest again; William Ballard, a knife manufacturer; Thomas Bradshaw and Stephen Moulton who carried rubber samples to England to show Thomas Hancock; Ralph B. Steele, a stove dealer; Abijah Osborn; Milo and P.B. Hine; Jesse Worcester; and William F. Ely, who became his uncomplaining 'silent' partner and source of funds. Goodyear experimented endlessly with both raw latex and rubber in order to be able to fashion products which would retain their shape and consistency. He mixed rubber with a variety of powders, dipped it in a variety of chemicals, heated and cooled it, kneaded and rolled it, glazed and embossed it. All of the methods were unsuccessful. One anecdote is that of a young workman Goodyear had hired, who had dipped his trousers into a drum of latex the previous night and laid them out to dry. The next morning, the trousers were dry, and the young man put them on. Goodyear was stunned—it was as if the only formulation that was actually needed was for the latex to dry. But the day wore on and the young man sat on a chair to stir a pot of latex before a fire. As he and his trousers warmed up, the latex melted and glued him to the chair. He had to be extracted from his trousers, which caused much merriment. Goodyear continued his experiments. And another boy child, named William Henry after his deceased older sibling, was born.

Goodyear also continued to move and borrow money, leaning heavily on family, friends and the cold comfort of debtor's prison. In prison, he carried on his tests, relying on Clarissa to bring him rubber and her rolling pin to dust the rubber with magnesia and talc before rolling it into sheets, hoping their absorptive power would keep the rubber dry. It seemed to work; so, when he got out of prison, he made several hundred rubber overshoes, filling them with magnesia. But warmer weather arrived before customers did, and the overshoes collapsed into sticky globs. He mixed in two other powders—magnesia and quicklime—but to no avail. He painted the shoes, then stripped the paint using nitric acid in order to repaint them and found that the nitric acid had dried out the rubber. He was elated! He sent samples to President Jackson, Vice President Calhoun and Senator Henry Clay. He applied for a patent, funded by William Ely. He rushed over to the Roxbury India Rubber Company store with his sample and met an original shareholder, John Haskins, who invited him to the factory at Roxbury.

At Roxbury, they had not been idle. Edwin M. Chaffee, one of the founders of Roxbury India Rubber Company, had built a $30,000 machine he called 'The Monster' that pummelled, shredded, pounded, heated and rolled the rubber until it submissively formed smooth sheets without having to first dissolve it in turpentine.[xxiv] Since distilling turpentine from pine

---

xxiv Rubber is a hydrocarbon and dissolves in turpentine, which is a volatile solvent first distilled from pine tree resins, and later obtained in larger amounts from petroleum. The solubility of rubber

resin was costly, their savings from not having to use the solvent was the key to their solvency! Goodyear requested several thousand yards of rubber for his tests but Roxbury demanded payment, which Ely was asked to supply. Goodyear still was not done. He asked for experiments with pigments to be conducted. He appropriated the work of two workers, L.S. Maring and John Nash, both of whom had made small improvements to rubber, promising them payments from the vast amounts of money that would flow in eventually. He hatched plans to buy the Roxbury factory. His disquieting presence was such that, eventually, he was asked to leave Roxbury. The manager, Samuel Armstrong, was quoted as having said, 'Goodyear will get tired of building castles in the air after a while.' Not so. Goodyear continued to place orders with Roxbury for rubber sheets. And he was soon to meet Nathaniel Hayward, who would catalyse Goodyear's successful rubber vulcanisation quest.

In 1937, fellow American Nathaniel Hayward was twenty-nine years old and had been with the Eagle India Rubber Company in Woburn, Massachusetts, since 1834. He was the opposite of Goodyear. Where Goodyear was educated, Hayward was illiterate; where Goodyear was humoured as a crank, Hayward was a solid businessman. But both shared the rubber passion. In 1934, Hayward had heard of rubber and resolved to solve its problems. The story goes that he had a dream one night of rubber, sulphur and lampblack being 'all that were necessary to make India Rubber'. It didn't work. So he made a witches' brew of all the chemicals he had collected and threw rubber into it. It worked! The rubber that emerged

---

in turpentine is a property which was discovered by Frenchmen Francois Fresneau, François Herrissent and Pierre Macquer around 1749.

was so promising he was offered an immediate position with the Eagle India Rubber Company.

Nathaniel Hayward had spent the previous three years developing his process using sulphur. He discovered that sulphur and exposure to sun caused rubber to 'set' into a reliable and stable material. His process was not patented—Hayward was not literate enough to negotiate the process of patenting or the litigation that might follow. Although he had bought out the Eagle India Rubber Company, an economic recession had depressed orders. So Nathaniel and Martin, his brother, made and sold machinery to Roxbury India Rubber Company instead, including a machine with heated rollers and a spreading knife to produce perfectly flat sheets of rubber, which may have been the inspiration for Chaffee's 'Monster'. Roxbury India Rubber Company had reached out to Hayward's Eagle India Company to request some of his high-quality sheets of rubber to fulfil Goodyear's orders. Fearful of his sulphur process being discovered—Goodyear's reputation for opportunism had preceded him—Hayward omitted sulphur from the rubber processing. The sheets were not satisfactory. So Hayward again applied his sulphuring process, and the improved sheets made their way to Goodyear, who approved them. He also caught the scent of brimstone.

Intrigued, Goodyear travelled up to Woburn to see the plant, but Hayward would not allow him inside. In frustration, Goodyear confronted him—if he used sulphur, to say so, or he would apply for a patent for the use of sulphur on rubber. Cornered, Hayward confessed his illiteracy and his use of sulphur. Goodyear became charming. He persuaded Hayward to sell him the Eagle India Rubber Company and then employed Hayward for $800 a year, with the understanding that Hayward's employment was contingent on orders coming in. He offered to file a patent in Hayward's name and be named as the assignor, which Hayward gratefully agreed to. The US patent 1,090A was applied for on 23 November 1938 and granted on 24 February 1839: 'Improvement in the mode of preparing *caoutchouc* with sulfur for the manufacture of various articles.'[49] They worked together to optimise Hayward's sulphur-and-solarisation procedure and Goodyear's acid gas treatment, and were awarded a contract for mailbags from the United States Postal Service (USPS). *The Boston Post* trumpeted Goodyear's wonderful product. Hayward was not mentioned,[50] and his name is still absent from historical websites paying homage to rubber manufacturing in Woburn.[51] Goodyear cheerfully promoted the bags they had made for the USPS, colourised with pigments to make them attractive. He took his family on vacation, secure in the feeling that he had turned the corner at last. They returned to find the bags had decomposed; the handles had not even been strong enough to hold up the weight of the bags when empty. Perhaps the problem lay with the colouring agents, which had not been tested in the process. In any case, it was a disaster.

Despite being unable to fulfil the postal order, Goodyear and Hayward continued to manufacture other rubber materials, but Goodyear's obsession slowly became a millstone around his family's neck. His parents and Clarissa demanded he throw in the towel and return to hardware. His silent partner, William Ely, was almost destitute. One day, as Ely sat in a small room heated with a single stove, Samuel Armstrong (the manager of the Roxbury India Rubber Company) approached him to request overdue payment, but Ely told him to come back later. Ely claimed that, at the time, he had been holding a piece of Goodyear's rubber and had tossed it angrily towards the stove. Armstrong left, and returned to find Ely holding the piece of charred rubber. It had been transformed into a blackened leathery material, sturdy but flexible. A Goodyear biographer, Richard Korman, reports Armstrong to have later said 'Ely appeared a good deal excited at the time, and thought it was a new feature in India rubber.' Ely showed the piece to Goodyear a few days later, and Goodyear professed his surprise at this transformation of the rubber. He began searing pieces of treated rubber. But, as Goodyear later told the story, it was he who had made the discovery one night when he had touched a piece of rubber to a hot stove.

Goodyear became obsessive. He experimented endlessly, trying to char the rubber just so. He went to the Woburn factory, but it took him time, effort and money to test the exact method of heating. Heating too quickly at too high a temperature caused the rubber to burn with a ghastly effulgence; to cook it too slow meant it failed to achieve the right temperament. Again, he used every cent he could lay his hands on, including pawning his children's schoolbooks, not paying his creditors and making his family scrounge for food and wood for heating. His elderly parents were in tears. 'Once, we were rich,' Amasa said to a neighbour. Goodyear was hauled off to debtor's prison again and again. He was beset on all sides: Ely was demanding rubber goods to sell in his store as part of their long-time agreement; Hayward was not promptly and efficiently fulfilling orders according to their agreement; Clarissa was pregnant again; Goodyear was destitute again; and his child, three-year-old William Henry—the second little boy they had named William Henry—died. Frustrated by Charles' fantasies, his brother Amasa Jr. and his father Amasa decided to restore their own dissipated fortune by importing pineapples from Florida, and so moved there. But within a short time, they all sickened with yellow fever and died. This prostrated Goodyear for a short time, but he took it as a sign to persevere. Charles's mother moved away to live with her son Robert in Connecticut. Goodyear scrounged a little money from friends and acquaintances, and sold a certain Horace Cutler on his ideas but could not deliver on them, which severed the relationship. Goodyear ended back in debtor's prison. In 1842, he sent a sulphur-treated sample with Stephen Moulton to Britain, where he hoped that he would have better luck than in the US, and better luck than with the acid-cured sample he had sent previously to Britain with his doctor, Thomas Bradshaw. Moulton, who was young and quite unsuited to business intrigue, showed the samples to Charles Macintosh, Thomas Hancock's business partner. Although impressed with the quality, Macintosh told Moulton that Goodyear should patent the process and then come in person to talk about licensing. Moulton acquiesced, but left the samples with Macintosh on the condition that they were not used 'to the prejudice of Mr. Goodyear'. Independently, Goodyear himself finally came to the decision that he must patent his sulphur treatment process if he was to reap any benefit.

On 15 June 1844, Goodyear was awarded US patent 3,633 'Improvement in India-Rubber Fabrics'.

His claims were:

> 1. The combining of the said gum with sulfur and with white lead, so as to form a triple compound, either in the proportions herein named or in any other within such limits as will produce a like result; and I will here remark that although I have obtained the best results from the carbonate of lead, other salts of lead or the oxides of that metal may be substituted therefor, and will produce a good effect. I therefore under this head claim the employment

> of either of the oxides or salts of lead in the place of the white lead in the abovenamed compound.
> 2. The formation of a fabric of the India-rubber by interposing layers of cotton-batting between those of the gum, in the manner and for the purpose above described.
> 3. In combination with the foregoing, the process of exposing the India-rubber fabric to the action of a high degree of heat, such as is herein specified, by means of which my improved compound is effectually changed in its properties so as to protect it from decomposition or deterioration by the action of those agents which have heretofore been found to produce that effect upon India-rubber goods.

Nathaniel Hayward, meanwhile, set up a new rubber manufacturing company and applied for a license to manufacture products using Goodyear's patent. Embittered, he frequently talked of his ill treatment at Goodyear's hands. Although he was in and out of debtor's prison, Goodyear both spoke out against, and took advantage of, an 1841 federal bankruptcy law a few days before it was repealed. He justified his obvious hypocrisy by claiming that the 'provocation' of the benefits of protection from debtors was such that his 'resolution gave way'. He was spared a repayment of $52,629 to his creditors. In 1846, Clarissa bore another little boy, their third child to be called William Henry. Charles Goodyear was forty-six years old.

Englishman Thomas Hancock was born in 1786 into a large family of twelve children, of which four—Thomas, Walter, John, and Charles—had successful livelihoods associated with rubber. Their father, James, had a cabinet-making business, but the effects of Napoleon's trade embargo and the Tambora eruption of 1815 heaped misery on his business and on his family. Of a total of four daughters and eight sons, only six boys made it to maturity.

In 1813, Thomas Hancock began working with his brother John, who made horse carriages from whale baleen and ladies' 'Pilentum' tricycles[xxv] designed to be ridden by women wearing skirts.[52] Then their brother Walter, who was trained as an engineer and designed rubber manufacturing equipment, also joined them. The brothers' interest in rubber came from making waterproof fabrics to help passengers riding in their coaches stay dry. John's factory also used Walter's designs to manufacture rubber hoses, catheters and other medical equipment. Thomas Hancock was inventive, prolific and kind. When John died young, leaving behind a wife and nine children, he took them all into his own home. Hancock was as measured as Goodyear was profligate, but both were equally in thrall to rubber.

Although Thomas Hancock's interest in rubber may have begun with waterproof fabrics, he started to experiment with rubber, making and patenting fasteners, suspenders and some elastic fabrics. He had noted that keeping rubber warm against the skin kept it pliable, and was issued a patent in 1820 for using strips of rubber (which he called *caoutchouc* springs) in clothing, gloves, belts and suspenders. Slices of rubber bottles to make rings for various uses followed. In 1821, he discovered a way to macerate the pieces of rubber left over from previous uses, applying heat to fuse them all together into a uniform

---

xxv No original models have survived, but rubber chemist and author John Loadman and Hancock descendant Francis James tracked down its history for their biography of the Hancock family: *The Hancocks of Marlborough: Rubber, Art, and the Industrial Revolution: A Family of Inventive Genius.*

slug. This process standardised rubber's specifications and made uniformity in products possible. Enthused, he built an enormous shredding device which he called the 'Pickling Machine' and a larger iteration called 'The Masticator' but kept their specifications secret to foil industrial espionage rather than reveal the details in a patent. The workers in his factories were sworn to silence as well.

In 1825, he obtained a license from Glaswegian inventor Charles Macintosh to manufacture a raincoat—the 'Mackintosh'—made from a layer of rubber sandwiched between two layers of fabric. When Thomas Hancock showed that his rubber product was superior to Macintosh's, they made an agreement to use his rubber solution applied by a spreading machine invented by Walter. Hancock formally went into partnership with Macintosh. Macintosh moved to Manchester and built a bigger factory with Walter Hancock's engineering assistance. They installed a steam engine for power as well as larger machinery. In the period between 1820 and 1836, Thomas Hancock received seven patents. In 1832, a worker lured to another firm divulged the secrets of Hancock's rubber technology to his new employer and fresh competition sprung up. In response, Macintosh and Hancock filed a lawsuit for patent infringement against Wynne Ellis, a silk merchant, for infringing Macintosh's 1823 patent for manufacture of 'double-textured cloth'. This was one of the few times that they chose to sue, mostly to set an example. They won. By 1834, forty-eight-year-old Thomas Hancock had already been twenty-one years in business and was recovering from a tragedy: the London rubber factory which had housed his pre-eminent invention, the Masticator, had burned down.

Despite these setbacks, Hancock continued to experiment, and applied for a patent for the Masticator and for the spreading solution of the 'Mackintosh' in 1837. In 1842, Hancock was shown two Goodyear samples which had been brought to England by Stephen Moulton. He examined the material closely and was impressed with its resistance to cold. As he worked, a smell drifted up—the same smell that Goodyear had smelled when handling Hayward's rubber sheets. Sulphur. But he couldn't tell if it had been inserted as a deliberate misdirection or was really part of the process. In fact, he had previously experimented with sulphur himself, and, on 21 November 1843, he applied for a provisional patent which provided protection for an invention for six months before a final patent was filed, a procedure acceptable under English law.[53] In those six months, he methodically tested rubber, sulphur and heat in various combinations. Results in hand, he applied for a patent for his 'vulcanisation' process, the term suggested by his friend William Brockedon, and was issued his patent on 21 May 1844. The patent described in exhaustive detail the various ways for masticating, moulding, spreading and curing rubber, and for reliably obtaining the desired end product. With vulcanisation, rubber became a household item. It was manufactured by the Macintosh Company, with Thomas Hancock as one of the directors, but there were also rubber overshoes arriving from the United States manufactured by Hayward's Eagle India Rubber Company. In 1848, Stephen Moulton also set up a rubber manufacturing factory in Wiltshire using methods that were slightly different from Hancock's. When Moulton's products came to Hancock's notice in 1850, he decided to go to court to challenge their manufacture. But the Great Exhibition of 1851 was going to be opening soon, so he put litigation aside to concentrate on the products for the exhibition, eventually dropping the idea altogether. Stephen Moulton carried on his rubber business until his death in 1880.

In the United States, Goodyear engaged in an orgy of threats of litigation to shut down unlicensed rubber manufacturing using sulphur and heat, a process which he claimed was his invention based on his patent in 1844. To fund the lawsuits, he turned to his patent licensees, drawing them in with his insistence that, by aiding him, their competition would also disappear. He also sold a share of his patent to his lawyer, William Judson, who set up a 'licensed' rubber manufacturing business. In 1849, Goodyear tested a steam-heating process which had been successfully employed and published by Hancock, and filed his own modified version of the patent which simply described any 'artificial heat' as being adequate to the process of vulcanising rubber. The modified patent was granted. He and his associates then went vigorously after Horace Day. Horace Day did have a Goodyear license, but only for shirred rubber materials, which were now out of style. Seeing sales drop, but seeing potential in the manufacture of rubber overshoes for the California Gold Rush, Day took the plunge, but without a license. Judson's legal sharks were circling. Day first tried conciliation, but was rebuffed. Taking umbrage, Day petitioned the United States Congress to disallow the 1849 extension of Goodyear's patent on the basis of '... SHOWING FRAUD and the Necessity of a Law for the Repeal of Fraudulently Obtained Patents', but to no avail. He then took the fight to the public, sarcastically advertising that 'if other people make discoveries which renders your patent obsolete, useless, throw it up – take out another covering everybody's discovery ...' and that '... Truth is not necessary under this new system …' Day and Judson were at each other's throats, although Goodyear was distracted—he was eagerly preparing for the Great Exhibition of 1851 in London. A date was set for the great trial between Day and Judson, supposedly 'at law' by a seated jury, although Judson's team would rather have had an 'at equity' case which would be adjudicated by judges.

Day hired as his trial lawyer the voluble Senator Rufus Choate from Massachusetts, whose presence was as arresting as his oratory. His reputation as the 'Wizard of the Law' was legendary and his successes in rousing a jury to his view were resounding. Choate was notorious for supposedly having spoken the longest sentence known to man at 1,219 words.[54] He had represented Albert Tirrell in the gruesome murder of his lover, Mary Ann Bickford, by first impugning her character and then presenting his client as a sleepwalker who could not be held responsible for what he had done (and Albert Tirrell was subsequently exonerated by the jury). But Judson was no laggard either. Knowing that US Secretary of State Daniel Webster—mentor to Choate and a gifted orator himself—was in debt, Judson dangled vast amounts of money if only the great statesman would take a break from serving the country and represent Goodyear's interests instead. Webster took the bait. All was in place for the 'Trial of the Century' which would be held in Trenton after Goodyear returned from the Great Exhibition of 1851.

Both Charles Goodyear and Thomas Hancock exhibited their rubber products in the Great Exhibition in London's Crystal Palace in 1851. Goodyear's pavilion, called the 'Vulcanite Court', won a prestigious Council Medal, and was seen by millions of visitors. Despite being in the same place at the same time, Hancock and Goodyear appear to have studiously avoided each other. There is no record of their meeting or of even visiting the other's exhibits though this was the crowning achievement of their lives: both their names were to become synonymous with vulcanisation and rubber. But public acclaim alone was not adequate to either; they each wanted to be recognised as the sole genius who had brought rubber to heel.

Goodyear returned to the United States all set to do legal battle with Day. Unexpectedly, the trial that was called was at equity'. This was a shocking and unpleasant turnaround for Day, who had prepared for an 'at law' jury trial. The swashbuckling, high-powered, high-stakes trial closed schools in Trenton and moved the hearing to a larger auditorium. It started with Goodyear's team, the plaintiffs, resonantly begging the question (relying on Goodyear's name recognition) 'If Charles Goodyear is not the inventor of vulcanised rubber, who is?', to surprised silence from the defendants. In time, Day's team trotted out a number of claimants to the title of 'inventor of vulcanisation using sulphur' including Hayward, but the damage was done. Judson had also cleverly sequestered the Eagle India Rubber Company's books and prevented Day's team from supporting their claims with documentation. Choate's and Webster's orations presented dueling versions of the matter, but when the judges retired to consider the verdict, Goodyear's team was already cracking the champagne.[xxvi] They would have to wait

xxvi The Goodyear name was often successful in court, but less so in the court of public opinion. In 2007, Lilly Ledbetter sued Goodyear Tire and Rubber Company for 'intentionally discriminatory pay decisions' in the Supreme Court of the United States, but a hearing was rejected. Justice Samuel Alito wrote the 5-4 majority ruling that 'she could have, and should have, sued' within the 180-day statutory charging period. In response, the United States Congress passed the Lilly Ledbetter Fair Pay Act in 2009, with President Obama signing it into law.

until September 1852 for the verdict to come down, denying Day a jury trial and elevating both Goodyear's claims and stature. Judge Robert Cooper Grier, who was a part of the court making the monumental decision, confessed afterwards that he had not even read the 1,300-page deposition testimony. His judgement was seconded by Judge Philemon Dickerson, whose son was a lawyer for the Judson–Goodyear team, which presented a clear conflict of interest. The case was closed, and Day had lost.

Shortly after the judgement came down, Daniel Webster died, and was eulogised by Rufus Choate. Charles Goodyear's younger brother Nelson died, leaving behind a wife and children and a patent for ebonite, a form of hardened rubber that Goodyear had used for his 'Vulcanite Court' at the Great Exhibition of 1851. A number of Goodyears and others came out of the woodwork to claim the patent (Charles not among them). Charles' other brother, Henry Bateman Goodyear, became custodian of the patent and also provided for Nelson's family. In 1853, Charles's wife, Clarissa, died suddenly from a stroke. Although he mourned her passing and missed her efficient household management, Charles soon met twenty-year-old Fanny in church. They married in 1854. Then they set off for Europe. But Goodyear and his team were not done with litigation. In 1854, in England, Goodyear took Thomas Hancock to court.

Hancock was not intimidated. He retained Frederic Thesiger, First Baron Chelmsford, a former solicitor, Attorney General, and later the Lord High Chancellor. Goodyear teamed up with the French shoe manufacturing firm of Hutchinson, Henderson & Company to claim that Hancock's 'discovery' consisted of simply copying the sample Goodyear had sent via Stephen Moulton in the fall of 1842. Hancock was somewhat flustered under cross-examination by Goodyear's attorney, Queen's Prosecutor Mr Hill, and agreed that he had smelled sulphur on the rubber. But he did have documentation dug out from a drawer of an experiment he had conducted in June 1842 before he even saw the sample. Together with Stephen Moulton's affirmation that the sample had been left 'without prejudice' to be tested, the jury found in favour of Hancock.

In 1855, the great Exposition Universelle was held in Paris, France. Napoleon III, who had seized power just a few years before (and crowned himself emperor just as his uncle Napoleon I had half a decade ago), saw Goodyear's rubber footballs stacked up and mistook them for cannon balls. He invited Goodyear to ride in the carriage with him and Empress Eugenie and apparently asked for the rubber necklace with embedded jewels that Goodyear had in his possession. Goodyear demurred that it was for Fanny, and offered to make another for the Empress. Shortly after, unable to pay his debt for the costs he had incurred for the fair, Goodyear and his French-speaking American partner, Charles Morey, were packed off to jail. They were sent to a prison in the Clichy section of Paris, where a guard watching over Morey shot him dead as he stood looking out of the jail window, thinking that he was trying to escape. Ironically, the court had decided that very day that Morey's arrest had been illegal and that he was to be freed.[55] Goodyear was awarded the Cross of the French Legion of Honor medal by Napoleon III for his 'excellent exhibit and products'. Goodyear's son, Charles Jr., delivered it to him in jail.

Goodyear used the time to ponder his successes and failures. He wrote:

> These trials were not wholly without their advantage; lessons of life were learned from them. If any one is

> desirous to learn more of human nature than he can learn in any other way, or wishes for a moment to look upon the darkest side of life's fleeting shade, let him, for such a cause as debt and misfortune, be placed within the bars of a prison door, without a dollar in his pocket, and in conscious innocence look out upon the world, and reflect upon the wide contrast in his condition with that of those who are enjoying liberty without; while within he finds his fellow sufferers all upon the same level, whether incarcerated for the sum of one hundred pence, or of one hundred thousand pounds. Then, notwithstanding the mortification attending such a trial, if he has (as every human being should have) a good purpose in life for which to live and 'hope on', he may add firmness to hope, and derive lasting advantage by having proved to himself, that, with a clear conscience and a high purpose, a man may be happy within prison walls, as well as in any other (even the most fortunate) circumstances in life.[56]

Goodyear returned to the United States, still in debt, and passed away on 1 July 1860, within a few days of the death of his oldest daughter. He was fifty-nine.

After the 1854 trial, Hancock, too, was engaged with growing his business. He also exhibited in Paris, but history does not record whether Napoleon III stopped at his exhibit. In 1857, he set upon writing an encyclopedic volume titled *Personal Narrative of the Origin and Progress of the Caoutchouc or India-Rubber Manufacture in England*. He sent copies with personal notes to Nathaniel Hayward and Howard Day, and the notes are reproduced in John Loadman's *Tears of the Tree*. No copy or note to Charles Goodyear has been discovered. He leveraged his influence, prevailing on planters to grow more *Hevea brasiliensis*, the Para rubber tree, and increase the production and quality of latex. He recommended to Sir Joseph Dalton Hooker, the director of Kew Gardens to establish plantations in the East or West Indies to grow more rubber trees, to which Sir Hooker wrote back that he was engaged in doing just that. Hancock died in 1865. One of the most significant consequences of his efforts was the increase in production of rubber. In 1842, the total amount of rubber into the UK from all sources was 317,184 pounds. By 1855, it grew to 5,006,736 pounds. The hunger for rubber would increase hugely in the coming decades with the development of the bicycle, the automobile and the pneumatic rubber tyre.[57]

4

Dying for Rubber

Tambora erupted on 10 April 1815. The volcano, on the Indonesian island of Sumbawa, produced the most powerful explosion in recorded human history, spewing forth a volume of 100 cubic kilometres of material.[58] Volcanic explosions are classified by two metrics: the Volcano Explosivity Index (VEI) rankings and their associated descriptions: 8: mega-colossal, 7: super-colossal, 6: colossal, 5: paroxysmal, 4: cataclysmic, 3: severe, 2: explosive, 1: gentle and 0: effusive. The Hawaiian volcano Kilauea which weeps lava persistently is 'effusive'. There have ever been only sixty 'mega-colossal' eruptions with VEIs of 8 spewing over 1,000 cubic kilometres of ejecta, and all are prehistoric. A famous example is the Yellowstone supervolcano, which erupted 600,000 years ago. The most recent (but still in the pre-historic era) was Toba, which erupted near the Indonesian island of Sumatra around 71,000 years ago. Toba's eruption touched off a thousand-year global cooling-off period and caused a genetic bottleneck in human evolution.[59] Next in severity, Tambora's 1815 eruption was super-colossal with a VEI of 7, and ash clouds measuring more than 100 cubic kilometres. Although the volume erupted was a thousand times smaller than Toba's, Tambora's eruption spread dust around the globe, leading to the 'year without a summer' in 1816. Harvests failed. People and animals starved. Horses, which had been the mainstay of muscle power,[xxvii] died in huge numbers, making transportation a problem. Necessity being reputed as the mother of invention, that same year, Baron Karl von Drais de Sauerbrun of Germany invented the *Laufmaschine* (which means the 'running machine' or, as it is more commonly known, the 'dandy horse'), a foot-propelled, two-wheeled velocipede—and the precursor to the bicycle.

Drais was nominally a forest official but, on his own time, he was an enthusiastic and prolific inventor. In addition to the velocipede, he invented the typewriter, a meat grinder, a fuel-efficient cooking stove and draisines—the little open handcarts that are used by service personnel to maintain railway lines. The concept of horseless transport took off after Drais personally demonstrated on 12 June 1817 that he could ride the velocipede at a speed of about 7 kilometres per hour. Road-based innovation stalled for a while between 1820 and 1840, although brisk advances were being made in steam-based transport by rail and by boat. By the 1840s, vulcanisation processes developed by Charles Goodyear in the US and Thomas Hancock in Britain had made rubber a versatile material that was widely available. Of course, while the naissance of horseless vehicles and automation that followed would spur an enormous demand for rubber for tyres, it took a while. In 1845, Robert W. Thompson

---

xxvii The word 'horsepower' represents approximately 740 watts, or the ability of a dray horse to move 33,000 pounds over a foot's distance in a minute, or a pound over 33,000 feet in a minute.

of Britain patented a pneumatic tyre for the 'aerial wheel' and followed it up with patents in France in 1846 and the US in 1847. The tyres were costly and hard to mount, and the steam-powered vehicles they were mounted on were slow. Demand for both automobiles and tyres deflated. By the 1860s, velocipedes and draisines became popular modes of horseless transport.

In 1868, Clement Ader patented rubber coverings on the tyres to make the ride a little more comfortable. Ader was a French engineer, inventor and aviation pioneer. Credited with improving Alexander Graham Bell's telephone, he also established a telephone network in Paris in 1880 and developed the concept for an aircraft carrier. And he applied for the first patent for '*roues caoutchouees*' or rubberised wheels on a bicycle.[xxviii] The story goes that Ader had bought a velocipede for his son, but his son got a headache riding on the bone-jarring, iron-rimmed tyres. So Ader covered the tyres with rubber, which made the ride smoother. The first working automobile, the 1885 Benz Patent-Motorwagen, had three wooden tyres. The 1888 version, No. 3, had solid rubber tyres. It was made famous by Bertha Benz, wife of the inventor Karl Benz, who drove their two teenaged sons, Eugen and Richard to visit her mother in Pforzheim, a distance of 65 miles from Mannheim.[60] It was the first long-distance drive of any automobile. Bertha and her sons returned three days later, comfortably riding in the automobile. The publicity that this trip produced helped the sales of the car, and demonstrated that women were as competent to drive as were men. Also, in 1888, John Dunlop made a pneumatic tyre for his son's tricycle and patented it. Thomson's invention having

xxviii French Patent Number 83,112 in 1868. From *Bicycle Design: An Illustrated History* (2014) Tony Hadland, and Hans-Erhard Lessing, p.59. This was followed by additional patents for rubberised wheels and, by 1869, solid rubber tyres were fairly common.

been forgotten, the Dunlop tyre quickly made its way onto cars as well as bicycles since it absorbed shocks more efficiently than solid tyres, making the ride even smoother.[61] In 1895, the Michelin brothers, Édouard and André, equipped their car with pneumatic Dunlop tyres on a race from Paris to Bordeaux and back. They came last in a race comprising nine other cars because their tyres got punctured so often. However, they were still so enthused by the tyres (perhaps they sensed a business opportunity—they had had to use twenty-four pneumatic tubes on the race) that they started a business selling tyres for vehicles.[62] Rubber demand began skyrocketing, and suppliers from the Amazon and the Congo were quickly gearing up to fulfil demand, all the while inflicting unspeakable cruelty on the indigenous tappers. This domination would end in a few decades, partly because of public outrage at the exploitation, but also because vast quantities of rubber were by then being produced in the Far East from trees grown from rubber seeds purloined from the Amazon basin by British subjects.

On 27 August 1883, the earth shook again.

This time the volcano Krakatoa, in the Sunda Strait between Java and Sumatra, erupted. News of the colossal eruption was quickly carried on gutta-percha-coated underwater cables between Java and Singapore eventually to London, and thence to Europe and the United States, all within twenty-four hours of the eruption. Gutta-percha[xxix] is a tree exudate and relative of rubber from Southeast Asia with waterproofing properties shared with rubber, but with resilience to saltwater that

xxix Gutta-percha is a natural form of thermoset rubber extracted from *Palaquium* trees in the genus Sapotaceae.

outstripped it. Gutta-percha was not the only latex material to be associated with Krakatoa's eruption. Some 15 miles from Krakatoa, sheltering in the lee of a nearby island was the German ship *Berbice,* under the command of Captain William Logan. It was carrying thousands of gallons of combustible paraffin under wooden decks, but miraculously escaped annihilation from the pyroclastic eruption that had fiery sparks falling from the sky onto the ship's masts and sails. Sheltered in Captain Logan's personal chambers was a handwritten note addressed to the curator of the Botanical Gardens in Buitenzorg (present-day Bogor) in Java. In the accompanying package were five seedlings of *Hevea brasiliensis*,[63] a portion of the living confetti scattered around various British colonies in the Far East with the directive to establish rubber plantations, and thereby free the British from Brazilian and Belgian rubber hegemony. The *Berbice*, Logan and the seedlings all survived. These and other plants brought by stealth from the Amazon, specimens that were mercifully resistant to the South American Leaf Blight (SALB) caused by the *Ascomycete* fungus *Pseudocercospora ulei*, allowed the establishment of large rubber-producing plantations to supply the burgeoning demand. More importantly, this new supply of rubber accelerated the demise of the Congo and Amazon as primary sources of rubber, and the associated slavery and abuse of indigenous communities. The drudgery of these indigenous tappers was photographically documented by travellers to the area, among them Walter Hardenburg in Putumayo in the Amazon and Lady Alice Seeley Harris in the Belgian Congo. The ensuing investigation by British Consul Roger Casement would expose the abuses to the world.

With maritime sayings such as 'at 40 degrees latitude there is no law; at 50 degrees latitude there is no God', and with winds named 'the Roaring Forties', 'the Furious Fifties' and 'the Screaming Sixties', sailors were merely expressing their experiences. Before GPS and satnav, sailors on featureless ocean voyages took bearings from the sun's risings and settings, star declinations, chronometers recording time differences,[64] sextants, compasses, the behaviour of animals and how their vessels reacted to wind and water currents. There is no historical record of the ocean crossings of the earliest Australians[xxx] or Polynesians[xxxi]; yet their achievements still evoke awe[65] and disbelief.[66] The earliest recorded circumnavigators, Ferdinand Magellan, Francis Drake and Thomas Cavendish, had to contend with previously unmapped currents and winds. With the advent of sailing ships and navigational aids, trans-oceanic voyages became longer and more frequent.

Navigating the treacherous waters off the southern tips of Africa and South America presented enormous challenges. Cape Agulhas near Africa's Cape of Good Hope means 'cape of needles' in Portuguese. The word 'needles' cleverly referenced both the needle-like rocks that could wreck a ship and a curious observation of the time that north and magnetic north were mysteriously aligned at this place.[xxxii] The stormy

---

xxx Estimated >100-kilometre ocean crossing from Wallacea to Sahul >50,000 years ago.

xxxi Estimated distance across the Pacific from South America to the South Marquesas islands of >4,300 miles around AD 1200. Curiously, both the pre-Columbian Olmecs and inhabitants of Rapa Nui (Easter Island) made gigantic stone sculptures.

xxxii Compass needles pointed to the north at this location because magnetic north and true north were oddly aligned at this point back in the sixteenth century when this point was named. In September 2019, this type of alignment occurred at the Prime

weather and underwater tows caused by the merging of the Indian and Atlantic Ocean currents made disaster a very real possibility.[67] A similar situation exists at Cape Horn, at the tip of South America. These waters were considered so treacherous that even famous sailor-navigators such as Ferdinand Magellan in 1519 and Thomas Cavendish in 1586 negotiated passages in the archipelago near Tierra del Fuego rather than rounding Cape Horn. Such voyagers filled in blank ocean maps with potential ports of call and trading posts to re-provision, repair and otherwise break up long journeys. Thus, trans-oceanic trading routes became established, and the easterly winds near the equator that helped drive the ships from east to west were called trade winds. North of the equator, westerly winds pushed ships towards Europe and Africa. This set up a clockwise route where ships leaving European ports could hug the coastline down to Africa, take on board slaves, travel westwards with the easterly trade winds to the West Indies, South, Central and North America where they would unload the slaves, and load up rubber, cotton, tobacco, sugar and other merchandise produced using slave labour. Then they would use the westerly trade winds to blow them back to European ports. This three-step journey came to be called the Atlantic Triangle.

Other seafaring routes also opened up to the Far East: the overland journey from Europe to Asia along the Silk Road was replaced by the maritime spice route to the Moluccas (part of the Indonesian archipelago). But the maritime journey was difficult because of the enormous distances and the navigation

---

Meridian at Greenwich, UK. Magnetic north drifts over time, and there is a usually a variation which is called 'magnetic declination' which varies by location. Interestingly, the earth's crust is thinner at Cape Agulhas, and the layer below pushed up and drove the breakup of Gondwanaland 180 million years ago.

challenges around the Cape of Good Hope and Cape Horn. Two canals changed all this: the Suez Canal, which opened in 1869 between the Mediterranean Sea and the Red Sea, rendering travel around the Cape of Good Hope null, and the Panama Canal, which opened in 1914, connecting the Atlantic and Pacific Oceans, making it unnecessary to navigate Cape Horn. Trading grew enormously in response, and the whole world was linked by commerce. The main cash crops for trade were spices, grain, sugar, tobacco, tea, coffee, silk, cotton and, of course, rubber. All of these crops were labour-intensive, and the use of forced human labour soon followed.

The use of forced human labour did not suddenly begin in the last millennium. Exploitation of fellow humans has been documented from over 5,000 years ago during the building of the pyramids of Egypt. Vanquished enemies and prisoners of war were typically pressed into servitude, as described in Homer's Iliad. In ancient and medieval times, slave- and serf-labour was openly and unquestioningly used by many societies. The Greeks and the Romans had societies built on slave labour; the Middle East, including the Ottoman Empire, did too. The word 'slave' originates from the term 'Slavs', for the inhabitants of a wide swath of land across Eastern Europe:[68]

> The oldest written history of the Slavs can be shortly summarized—myriads of slave hunts and the enthrallment of entire peoples. The Slav was the most prized of human goods. With increased strength outside his marshy land of origin, hardened to the utmost against all privation, industrious, content with little, good-humored, and cheerful, he filled the slave markets of Europe, Asia, and

> Africa. It must be remembered that for every Slavonic slave who reached his destination, at least ten succumbed to inhuman treatment during transport and to the heat of the climate.[69]

Both Aristotle and St. Thomas Aquinas thought slavery was a natural state and beneficial to both the slaveholder and slave. It is safe to assume that neither of them, in their positions of relative affluence and influence, had the personal experience of being enslaved. On the other hand, St. Patrick, the patron saint of Ireland, and Queen Balthild[xxxiii] of France were both born in England and enslaved as children. In his own authenticated writings dated to the fifth century, St. Patrick describes being captured by Irish pirates around the age of sixteen, and brought to Ireland where he tended sheep in slavery. After escaping back to England, for which he thanked God, he returned to Ireland as a Christian missionary, and was posthumously beatified. He pleaded in his *Letter to the Soldiers of Coroticus*,[70] a British king, to free the Christians he had taken as slaves—his letter reviles the evils of the slave's condition, which he knew about first-hand. In the seventh century, Queen Balthild, consort of Clovis II of Neustria and Burgundy, also expressed her reservations but only of the enslavement of Christians. Born in Britain, she had been sold into slavery as a child, ending up in France. As queen and later regent for her son, she worked to end the enslavement of Christians and of children sold into slavery, a clear indication that she strongly believed that slavery is neither 'natural' nor 'beneficial'. In the *Domesday Book* of 1086, 10 per cent of the population of England is recorded as being enslaved. As

---

xxxiii 626-680 ACE, thought to have been born a noblewoman in England. She was sold into slavery as a child and ended up in Neustria, as a slave to King Clovis's palace manager, Erchinoald.

Christianity spread across the continent, and since the Church had forbidden the enslavement of Christians, the sourcing of slaves moved from England and Western Europe to the Slavs in northern and eastern Europe. Slave traders drove slave caravans to the Arabs and Moors well into the 1900s. Muslim Arabs had a ban on Muslims as slaves, so raiders pillaged non-Muslim North African communities instead for 1,300 years, right into the twentieth century. Eunuchs were particularly valuable in the harems of the Middle East since they could not seduce women, and were 'produced' by forcibly castrating slaves. Once ocean voyages became possible, slaves were acquired from West Africa, which was easier to reach. The first African-born slaves were brought to Portugal in 1441, but African slaves had been traded internally and to the Middle East for centuries.[71]

Slaves were used for dangerous or hard manual labour and for domestic chores across cultures. But slavery across continents really took off when maritime travel opened up the world to widespread commerce. The prevailing winds and currents facilitated the movement of goods, including people. As new lands were colonised, 'guns, germs and steel'[72] facilitated the subjugation of some societies by others. Typically, societies that were adept in ocean travel brought their navigational smarts, technological prowess and evangelical religions to make new conquests of land and labour. Records of navigation and conquest are recent. When merchant vessels started to ply the oceans, trading for commodities that were laborious to produce, slave trade surged. Sugar in the West Indies and Bahamas, cotton and tobacco in antebellum United States, rubber in the Amazon and the Congo river watersheds all required immense effort; effort that was extracted from enslaved human beings. It is undeniable that these slaves did not regard their situation as 'a natural state' and 'beneficial'—many tried to escape; if they were caught, they were viciously punished or murdered.

Others died attempting to escape. Children born to enslaved parents were themselves enslaved from birth, ensuring a steady supply of labour when laws began to catch up with the practice of bringing in slaves from other countries. In December 1806, Thomas Jefferson, himself a slaveholder, in his address to the US Congress in December 1806 said: 'I congratulate you, fellow citizens, on the approach of the period at which you may interpose your authority constitutionally to withdraw the citizens of the United States from all further participation in those violations of human rights which have been so long continued on the unoffending inhabitants of Africa, and which the morality, the reputation, and the best interests of our country have long been eager to proscribe.'[73] The Congress passed a statute forbidding the importing of slaves, which came into force in 1808. But people already enslaved were not set free. That would only happen with Abraham Lincoln's Emancipation Proclamation in 1863, during the American Civil War.

In Britain, Elizabeth I had freed the last-remaining serfs within the island in 1574, but slavery in Britain's overseas colonies was thriving. Slaves imported from Africa before 1807 were used by British landowners on Caribbean island plantations until slavery *per se* was finally abolished after the Slavery Abolition Law received Royal Assent on 28 August 1833. There were many bilateral, trilateral and multilateral agreements the British made to abolish slavery and the transport of slaves. I could not find any unilateral agreements made before 2015 by Britain.[74] The 1926 League of Nations' anti-slavery conventions are still being ratified in member states, most recently by Kazakhstan in 2008. It was not until 2020 that the US states Utah and Nebraska abolished the prison exception, which allowed incarcerated people to be coerced to provide labour, despite constitutional bans on slavery. Colorado, North Carolina, Tennessee and Wisconsin still legally permit it. In California, as of 2018, prisoners who served on firefighting teams earned $1 per hour in the field although the minimum legal hourly wage in California for un-incarcerated labour in 2018 was $11 per hour. In November 2024, Californian voters rejected Proposition 6, which would have terminated forced labour in prisons. There are still places where human beings are held in bondage, such as on 'slave ships' to shell shrimp and process fish, their work extracted without adequate remuneration. Kailash Satyarthi from India was jointly awarded the 2014 Nobel Peace Prize[xxxiv] for his work to eradicate child labour but, according to the Global Slavery Index, about 8 million people in India were being held in modern slavery as of 2018.[75]

Returning to the main narrative, slavery and forced labour were inevitably rampant in the production of rubber, and, consequently, untold numbers of people died miserable deaths in South America, Africa and Asia. About 300 years after the first voyagers brought bouncing balls to Europe in the 1500s, Goodyear, Hancock and others developed vulcanisation and gave rubber desirable properties. Its use in goods—there is a fourteen-page list in Thomas Hancock's *Personal Narrative of the Origin and Progress of the Caoutchouc or India-Rubber Manufacture in England* that spanned a spectrum of its uses from personal to household to industrial which created an enormous demand for raw rubber. The economics of supply and demand took over, starting in the mid-nineteenth century. In his book, Hancock also compiled supplementary tables of the quantity of *Para* (the name for Brazilian rubber) that was

xxxiv Kailash Satyarthi won the 2014 Nobel Peace Prize jointly with Malala Yousafzai.

sent around the world. The quantities of rubber imported into the United Kingdom increased by an order of magnitude in a little over a decade from 222,432 pounds in 1842 to 2,395,344 pounds in 1855. In total, between 1842 and 1855, 18 million pounds of rubber had entered the United Kingdom, 12 million pounds of it from Brazil alone.[76] Brazil's total production in 1855 was 2 million pounds, but in 1879, it was exporting 20 million pounds. In truth, the rubber boom was just getting started. With the industrial revolution and the automobile leveraging its properties, rubber transformed the world and literally set it in motion. The need—and greed—for rubber became monstrous.

There is much poetry in the story of rubber. It has sketched a dramatic journey, heartrending and uplifting by turns; a roller coaster through history showcasing humanity's best and worst, stretching from the malevolence that accompanied its extraction to the ingenuity that moulded its present form. It has inspired politics, art, literature and the poetry of motion. Rubber has built robber barons' kingdoms and brought empires to their knees. Countries have fought over it, conducted espionage and machinated for it. Repugnant crimes carried out by malign actors have revolved around rubber, countered by heroic feats of resilience and resistance. This cut and thrust of realpolitik provides a fascinating retrospective on how the world works; of how rubber lubricates the wheels of commerce by literally making the world go round.

Rubber, silk and cotton are natural biopolymers, but have different chemical compositions. Rubber is a water-repelling megapolymer made from tens of thousands of hydrocarbon isoprene monomers, silk is a protein composed of amino acids and cotton is a carbohydrate with glucose monomers. Since synthetic polymers became widely available only in the twentieth century, natural polymers with their various properties found utility in a host of unrelated fields—rubber for a variety of automotive, waterproofing and tubing uses; silk for fine clothing; cotton in every manner of fabrics, fishing nets, bookbinding, even in shampoo. With the onset of the industrial revolution, demand for these raw materials became so overwhelming that supply—dependent, as we shall see, on the enormous amounts of effort extracted from humans, insects and plants—could barely keep up.

None of these raw materials is amenable to mechanised harvesting; rather, their collection is tedious and slow. Slavery became rooted in extensive polymer-producing operations. Along the southern Atlantic coastline of the United States in the seventeenth century, cotton was not yet being produced in large quantities. Indigo, rice and tobacco plantations had been established, and all of them needed labour for planting, tending and harvesting. Indentured labour was first imported from the poorer areas of Britain. According to David W. Galenson,[77] the use of indentured servants paved the slippery slope to slavery. The numbers of Europeans bound to indenture between 1580 and 1775 in the US is head-turning: about one-half to two-thirds [500,000 of a total of 750,000; largely English] immigrants who were unable to pay for passage entered into a contract of servitude to pay off the transportation debt.[78] Slavery came to the colonies in 1619 with the seizure by two privateer ships, the *Treasurer* and the *White Lion*, of the Portuguese slave ship *São João Bautista* and the subsequent sale in Jamestown, Virginia, of the twenty African slaves onboard.[79] African slaves were expensive so, for a time—into the nineteenth century—smaller landowners paid passage for European labour largely of British and Irish origins. But this set up an interesting biological experiment that led to a north-south divide of the race of workers demanded for indentured and slave labour. It was observed that West Africans were more resistant to the malaria and heat in the south, whereas people of European backgrounds less so. Coehlo and McGuire make a convincing case that, as with the plants they tended, the geographical distribution of bonded African versus European labour were differential responses to disease ecology. Thus, slaves of African origin were put to work in agriculture, and the shift to growing cotton followed in the wake of technical advances in cotton processing such as the use of the cotton gin.[80]

Silk is produced as a single thread extrusion which is spooled around the bodies of pupating caterpillars of the silk moth, *Bombyx mori*. To obtain the silk thread, the cocoon must be dropped into hot water (which kills the caterpillar) and the cocoon agitated to isolate one of the ends of the thread. The thread is then drawn out in a single fibre, to almost a mile long, and spooled. A variety of silks called 'ahimsa silks'[81] where the silkworm is not killed exist, examples being eri, mulberry, tussore and muga; but the collecting and processing of the cocoons has to be done after the moths have exited. The process is time- and effort-intensive, and bonded labour has been reported repeatedly in India despite being outlawed since 1976, although non-exploitative family and cottage productions exist.[82]

Cotton is formed in the flower of the cotton plant. As the plants mature, the flowers open, turning from white to pink after pollination. The pollinated flower develops a 'boll' formed of cotton fibres. When the bolls mature, they crack open for seed dispersal and the function of the cotton fibres is to form a parachute to float the seed to new pastures. Cotton husbandry over millennia has resulted in boll- and fibre-retention, allowing easier collection. But with the fibre being retained, so were the seeds; picking them out was tedious and difficult. Growing, harvesting and especially cleaning cotton were all labour-intensive and, in the seventeenth century, it was not economical, even with slaves. But things changed with the invention of the mechanised cotton gin by Goodyear's Connecticut neighbour Eli Whitney, which allowed enormous quantities of cotton to be processed. Plantations pivoted to cotton, and production, boosted by slavery, increased from 750,000 bales in 1830 to 2.5 million bales in 1850.[83] Slavery in the United States was finally abolished only in 1863 with Abraham Lincoln's Emancipation Proclamation in the third year of the American Civil War.

The third great polymer, rubber, is commercially made from the latex that oozes from damage to the bark of a handful of trees, shrubs and vines.[xxxv] Careless extraction can cause irreversible damage to the plants. In the wild, both the rubber trees in the Amazon and the vines in the Congo were dispersed across the tropical rainforest, and collectors had to spread out into an area, identifying and tapping *Hevea* rubber trees, or slicing and draining the climbing vines of the *Landolphia* genus. In the process, in both regions, trees and vines were more often damaged than not, and, even if they survived, it took years for them to recover. People labouring under oppressive quota

---

xxxv Americas: Guayule shrub (*Parthenium argentatum),* chicle tree (*Manilkara zapota*), Ceara rubber tree (*Manihot glazivovii*) Mexican rubber tree (*Castilla elastica*), Para rubber tree (*Hevea brasiliensis*). *Forsteronia* genus vines; Asia: *Urceola elastica* vine, the rubber tree (*Ficus elastica*); Africa: West African rubber tree (*Funtumia elastica*), lianas or vines in the *Landolphia*, *Clitandra* and *Carpodinus* genus. This information was obtained from the 1914 publication of the Imperial Institute Handbook: Rubber, Its Sources, Cultivation and Preparation by Harold Brown, available on Google Books.

systems were typically not careful and deeper forays into the forest for new plants to tap were needed, costing more time and causing more desperation and damage.

Following the development of the vulcanisation process in the 1830s and motorised vehicles in the 1870s, the thirst for rubber only grew. But European politics was stabilising. Rather than fight each other for minuscule territorial gains as exemplified by the Napoleonic Wars, European nations turned to the enriching strategy of colonising countries in Asia, Africa, Australia and New Zealand. From 1879 to 1912, rubber was predominantly obtained from the Congo and the Amazon. In Brazil, a brutalised indigenous labour force was overseen by an armed militia of British West Africans who did not share common ground with the native workers, and were as lacking in empathy as the largely European overseers. Forced labour was also used in the Congo where vicious punishment and horrifying conditions were documented in the book *Red Rubber* by E.D. Morel.[84] Labour in the Far East, where *Hevea brasiliensis* eventually made its way, was again performed by indigenous labourers with expatriate overseers, often in forced conditions collectively called *corvée*.

Henry Ford dared to differ. A visionary businessman, Henry Ford had established the Ford Motor Company which had built the Model T Ford, an affordable and widely available vehicle that broadened American car ownership to the middle classes, many of whom were workers at his companies earning a fair wage. He envisioned a plantation where native workers were treated fairly and high productivity ensued, just as it had in his factories in the United States. Seeking to sidestep the British monopoly on Brazilian rubber, in 1928, Henry Ford negotiated a 2.5-million-acre site near the Tapajos River near Santarem in Para, Brazil, where his company could establish a rubber plantation called Fordlandia. But it was doomed from the start. The plantation was only accessible by river and its American managers were untutored in tropical agriculture and management, imposing unsuitable conditions on both the trees and the workers. The trees were planted too close together, which made them susceptible to disease, and the native workers crowded together in bunks similarly fell prey to yellow fever and malaria. There was also grumbling about the unwelcome imposition of American puritanism which banned all music, dancing and women from the town. The American-style food served in the cafeteria was also revolting: in the Breaking Pans Revolt of 1930, workers chased the company's managers and cook into the jungle. The Brazilian army showed up and the revolt ended, but it was downhill from there and the project failed by degrees. Fordlandia was abandoned in 1934, with the land eventually sold back to the Brazilian government by a Ford descendant. Meanwhile, the founding of rubber plantations in Asia and the production of synthetic rubber had a seismic effect on natural latex production and costs.

The Congo basin, as perceived in the early 1870s in Europe, was little more than a white patch on a map on the Atlantic coast of equatorial Africa; the area's natural features had not yet been documented. When he was a child of twelve, author Joseph Conrad, born Jozef Konrad Korzeniowski, reportedly put his finger on this area as a place he would like to explore, and fulfilled his early ambitions when he arrived at the riverhead as a steamboat captain. His observations of the maltreatment of the indigenous population and the stories of the human heads used as lawn ornaments feature in his novel *Heart of Darkness*.[xxxvi] The narrator of the book, Charles Marlow, recounts his trip up the Congo River and his hope of encountering the disquieting Kurtz, a notorious but mysterious ivory trader. Ivory was sought after by both Middle Easterners and Europeans, and both groups used African slave labour to obtain and transport it. The ivory was from a species of forest elephant, *Loxodonta cyclotis*, which is distinct from the savannah species, *Loxodonta africana*. Between 1905 and 1912, 30,000 forest elephants were slaughtered each year.[85] Many more humans were slaughtered in the process.

Around the same time as the young Jozef located as an expeditionary goal the white patch on the west coast of Africa comprising the Congo basin, another man in faraway Belgium was actively trying to acquire this land. King Leopold II wanted money, lots of it. He despaired that the longer-established nations had colonised most of the globe, shunting untold wealth into their coffers. Being a young country—Belgium came into being as an independent state only in 1831—it was too late to compete with the established nations over already-occupied lands. When his father died in 1865, Leopold started to put his plan into operation, his eye focused on that white patch. He developed an audacious plan to annex the Congo basin and assume its resources as his personal property.

Leopold knew little about Congo, except that it was ripe for his schemes. He knew there was ivory there. He knew there was a big river down which the ivory could be floated to the Atlantic Ocean, and thence to Europe. As a prince, he had travelled east to the island of Java, at the time a Dutch colony, and wrote that

---

xxxvi Human heads were reportedly used by a real overseer called Van Kerckhoven. In Joseph Conrad's book, *Heart of Darkness*, 'balls' on posts along the fence line to Kurtz's house are native people's heads.

the forced labour practiced there was 'the only way to civilise and moralise these idle and corrupt populations'.[86] Hiding his true intentions by disguising them as altruistic ideals, he proposed to the Brussels Conference in 1876 that the Congo basin would be an ideal region to establish an outpost with the express purposes of fair trade with the indigenous population, who were being enslaved by Arab traders. He, of course, proposed himself as the benign leader under whom such an initiative would thrive. To further promote his value in the region, he established the Association Internationale Africane (AIA) in 1876. Naturally, Leopold was the sole shareholder and funder of the AIA. In the interim he had, with the help of Dutch traders and a consortium of backers, also established the Comité d'études du Haut-Congo (Committee for Studies of the Upper Congo), an organisation with superficial scientific credentials that, in reality, paved the way for the establishment of the infrastructure that would be needed to transport ivory to the coast. Needless to say, after fulfilling its purpose, the committee was quickly done away with, and the financiers were offered full recompense in return for its dissolution. In its place, Leopold quickly established the Association Internationale du Congo (AIC). The initials AIC were quite similar to AIA, and no one appeared to notice. Leopold dissolved the AIA in 1890. In doing so, he had ensured that his activities would not be scrutinised and that there would not be resistance to his schemes from overseers. At last, Leopold was ready to proceed with his actual plan to be in sole control of the Congo. He needed an agent who would travel to the Congo to set up the administrative framework, including securing land,[xxxvii] and

xxxvii Through his partner, Sir William McKinnon, a Scottish shipowner, Leopold II reached out several times to General Charles George Gordon, a decorated and highly regarded

recruited the famed Henry Morton Stanley[xxxviii] following his finding of David Livingstone, the physician, missionary and anti-slavery campaigner who had gone 'missing' in Africa.

Stanley was born in 1842 in Denbigh, Wales, to Betsy Parry, who named him John Rowlands after his father. She was unmarried at the time, although Stanley recounts in his autobiography, bombastically titled *The Autobiography of Sir Henry Morton Stanley, G.C.B.*, that his father had died 'within a few weeks after my birth'. Betsy left Stanley with his maternal grandfather Moses Parry but, when the grandfather died, Stanley was consigned by his foster father Dick Price to a workhouse at the age of six. It was obviously traumatic and left a lasting impression of betrayal as he recounts '… but I then learned for the first time that one's professed friend can smile while preparing to deal a mortal blow, and that a man can mask evil with a show of goodness'. He writes of the workhouse school: 'No Greek helot[xxxix] or dark slave ever underwent such discipline as the

British soldier who was held in high esteem by the British and Foreign Anti-Slavery Society. Gordon was interested due to his affection for the African people, and his objection to slavery. But the British government appointed him Governor-General of Sudan with the mission of evacuating Khartoum which was being besieged by the Mahdists, and he died there in 1885.

xxxviii Stanley was born 'John Rowlands – Bastard' to Betsy Perry in Wales in 1841. After an unhappy childhood, he changed his name, travelled to America, fought for the Confederates and the Union in the Civil War, and then decamped to Africa. As successful as he and his books were, he was not satisfied with the recognition he received in Britain. Thus, he was ripe for Leopold II's advances.

xxxix Serfs in ancient Sparta who worked the land of their masters. Serfs were a class in between slaves and citizens.

boys of St. Asaph under the heavy masterful hand of James Francis', an experience which possibly blunted his emotions to others' traumas and the brutality he would see and inflict as he grew older. After tolerating a particularly violent outburst from Francis, Stanley turned on the older man, beating him until he was unconscious, and fled the workhouse. The boy sought out John Rowlands, his supposed paternal grandfather, who turned him away. Bitter now, he found brief employment in a national school in Brynford as a pupil-teacher; later, he was invited by an aunt to travel to Liverpool where he was promised good employment with his uncle's friend. That promise fell through, and his distrust of people grew. He found work as a butchers' boy and happened to deliver a parcel to the cabin of Captain David Hardinge of the packet ship *Windermere*. The Captain noticed his admiration of the ship, and invited him to sail as a cabin boy to America. And so Stanley did, with nary a backward glance, arriving in New Orleans in February 1859.

In New Orleans, he claimed to have met and been adopted by Henry Hope Stanley, a wealthy cotton broker whose name he would assume. Researcher and biographer Tim Jeal contends that the descriptions matched not Henry Hope Stanley, but James Speake, a grocer who appears to have been his real benefactor.[87] This flexibility with facts was characteristic of Stanley and his autobiography is peppered with inconsistencies which show him in a favourable light. But his catalogued life was remarkable even without embellishment. When the American Civil War broke out, he joined the Confederates but was taken captive in the Battle of Shiloh. He then quickly enlisted in the Union Army but fell sick and was discharged. In 1864, he joined the Union Navy and served on the *USS Minnesota*. He then deserted the navy to become a reporter of the westward expansion, dabbling in overseas reporting. As his profile grew, he was hired by the *New York Herald* to accompany a British military force seeking to free hostages taken by Ethiopia's Emperor Tewodros II—he then broke the story of the British expeditionary force's success. He subsequently reported from several regions across the Middle East, Central Asia and the Indian subcontinent. But his most famous journeys were in Africa, where he tracked down Dr Livingstone[xl] in Ujiji, near Lake Tanganyika. Stanley's description of this encounter in his book *How I Found Livingstone* made him famous, and his book describing his travels earned him further funding from the *New York Herald* and London's *Daily Telegraph* for a trans-African crossing in 1874.

In this journey, Stanley led a group of 356 people, blazing his way across the continent, destroying any perceived threats with force: 'We have attacked and destroyed 28 large towns and three or four score villages.' Nor was he any more considerate to the Africans in his own train: 'The virtue of a good whip was well tested by me ... and I was compelled to observe that when mud and wet sapped the physical energy of the lazily-inclined, a dog-whip became their backs, restoring them to a sound—and sometimes to an extravagant activity.' Towards the conclusion of his expedition, he and what remained of his team were starving. He sent four scouts who arrived in Boma carrying a letter addressed 'To any Gentleman who speaks English at Embomma' which read:[88]

---

xl David Livingstone was a Scottish doctor, Christian missionary, explorer and anti-slavery campaigner. He gained fame as the first European to cross the African continent from west to east. He had 'disappeared' in Africa, and Stanley was sent to 'find' him by the editor of the *New York Herald*. Stanley wrote a self-regarding account including the phrase 'Dr. Livingstone, I presume?' The book and the phrase made him famous, but the pages of the journal on the day of the meeting have been torn out, giving rise to suspicion that Stanley fabricated the story later.

> Dear Sir,
>
> I have arrived at this place from Zanzibar with 115 souls, men, women, and children. We are now in a state of imminent starvation ... but if your supplies arrive in time, I may be able to reach Embomma within four days ... better than all would [be] ten or fifteen man-loads of rice or grain ... The supplies must arrive within two days, or I may have a fearful time of it among the dying ...
>
> Yours sincerely,
> H.M. Stanley,
> Commanding Anglo-American Expedition for
> Exploration of Africa

The following morning, food was sent to the party and they emerged at the mouth of the Congo, sore but alive, with 7,000 miles of continent behind them. Stanley had achieved something tremendous—he had become the first European to travel across the continent from coast to coast, establishing geographical facts: affirming British explorer John Speke's description of Lake Victoria (Lake Nyanza), that Lake Tanganyika was not the source of the Nile, and that the river Lualaba met and became the river Congo, emptying into the Atlantic Ocean.

Even as his fame spread, the sort of social acceptance and veneration he craved remained elusive. The British were not interested in the Congo, as Leopold had established. Stanley therefore agreed to head Leopold's 'scientific exploration' and land acquisition project. In accordance with Leopold's instructions, Stanley left for the Congo in 1878, acquiring up to 1,000,000 square miles of land for the king through gifts of cloth, bribes, intimidation or trickery. Of one treaty, signed on

1 April 1884 by the chiefs of Ngombi and Mafela, Hochschild writes in *King Leopold's Ghost*: 'In return for "one piece of cloth per month to each of the undersigned chiefs, besides present of cloth in hand", they promised to "freely of their own accord, for themselves and their heirs and successors forever ... give up to the said Association the sovereignty and all sovereign and governing rights to all their territories ... and to assist by labour or otherwise, any works, improvements or expeditions which the said Association shall cause at any time to be carried out in any part of these territories ... All roads and waterways running through this country, the right of collecting tolls on the same, and all game, fishing, mining and forest rights, are to be the absolute property of the said Association."' However, it is debatable whether the chiefs knew what they were signing away since the documents were written in French. Stanley stayed on for five more years to make Leopold's new acquisition accessible for transport. He was reputedly a harsh taskmaster, ill-treating those under him with no discrimination. Hochschild tells of the engineer Paul Neve who fell sick and wrote a letter back home: 'Mr. Stanley has taken great care of me during these bad days ... the sort of care a blacksmith applies to repair an implement that is most essential and that has broken down through too rough usage ... teeth clenched in anger, he smites it again and again on the anvil, wondering whether he will have to scrap it or whether he will yet be able to use it as before.'[89] Bitter humour notwithstanding, Paul Neve died. It is unlikely that Stanley was unaware of the abuses that Leopold was committing in the Congo, but there is no evidence that he took any accountability for the innumerable brutalities he had made possible. Stanley was elected a member of the British Parliament between 1895 and 1900. He died in 1904.

Between 1879 and 1882, as Stanley was acquiring land on the south bank of the Congo, the French government authorised the explorer Comte Pierre Savorgnan de Brazza to offer the French government's protection to the lands of King Makoko on the north bank of the Congo. Aware of Stanley's efforts, King Makoko agreed. Leopold used the fact that the French had a foothold in the Congo to pressure Britain and Germany, both of whom distrusted the French, to support his AIA by falsely claiming that he had assured the French that should he, Leopold, wish to sell his holdings in the Congo, Britain and Germany would be the first in line to be given the opportunity to acquire it, rather than the French. Britain and Germany were loath to allow the French more foothold in such a potentially valuable region, preferring that Leopold continue to administer it. The United States was also easy to dupe: they confused the AIA with the AIC, and gave the defunct committee the green light to proceed with their work. Leopold set about with suppressing dissent in the Congo and shipping out ivory. By now it was 1889, and Leopold became aware that there was a burgeoning demand for rubber, obviously available in the Congo, and he was determined to get his hands on it.

But before he could acquire this new commodity, infrastructure to transport products from the interior was required. Land journeys were interminable, but navigating the Congo River's lower rapids was impossible. In the novel, *The Heart of Darkness*, Conrad's self-insert character Marlow describes the Congo River as follows: 'But there was in it one river especially, a mighty big river, that you could see on the map, resembling an immense snake uncoiled, with its head in the sea, its body at rest curving afar over a vast country, and its tail lost in the depths of the land.'[90] Between Malebo Pool and Matadi, on the coast where Conrad imagined the head of the snake to be, are 200 miles of treacherous and unnavigable rapids. The resolute Leopold set to solving the overland problem. He envisioned an armada of steamboats hauling goods down the river a thousand miles from Kisangani to Malebo Pool, and then a locomotive from Malebo Pool to Matadi to bypass the rapids. He had forty-eight steamboats broken into sections (referred to as 'sectional steamers') and hauled inland by dismantling them in Matadi and reassembling them in Malebo Pool. Needless to say, the work was done by Congolese workers and overseen by the representatives of Leopold (Figure 8). The locomotive line was difficult and slow, taking eight years to build. And it was costly in human lives: about 132 whites died during the building of the railroad, and the number of Congolese who died is approximated to have been 1,800, but that estimate may have only related to the first two years. Eventually, in 1890, the railroad was in place for the lucrative flow of ivory and rubber to Europe.

Figure 8: The sectional steamer Le Stanley *leaving Vivi Beach, Congo.*[91]

The collection areas that Leopold devised were divided into two categories: the 'Domaine Privé' and the 'concessions'. The Domaine Privé region was intended to be Leopold's personal territory and extended along the main body of the Congo into the northeast. Although the income from this region was nominally to be used for general administration of the Congo Free State, Leopold fiddled with the figures. A claim by a later analyst was that the income was $10,000,000 more than Leopold had reported for a period of eight years. The concessions were parcelled off to companies which were headed by supporters and represented on the stock exchange. They were monopolies—each concession had territory that was theirs in exclusion, and there were no overseers (that were not associated with the concession) to appeal to for redress. Prominent among the concessions were the Société Anversoise and Abir in the north, Katanga in the southeast and Kasai in the southwest. Commissions set up local stations to procure the items; an armed 'Force Publique' ensured security and instituted a regime of brutality and hostage-taking to compel the indigenous Congolese to work. The Force Publique was made up of a tribe of cannibalistic Africans[xli] and orphaned children brought up in camps to serve as soldiers (Figure 9). They answered only to the agents at the station who, conveniently, did not ask many

xli 'The term "cannibal troops" has been used in reference to the Congo soldiers; I have used it myself. It is, perhaps, open to misconstruction. It is not suggested that the Congo soldiers are all active cannibals at the present time, and feed upon recalcitrant rubber-collectors, as well as mutilate them, or indulge in the same cannibal orgies as the Batetla allies of the State did in 1893-94, as graphically told by Dr Hinde. But a considerable number are recruited from tribes which are still notably cannibalistic, such as the Asandes, Batetla, Manyema, etc. Cannibalism clings, and if you stick a rifle into a cannibal's hand, and put a uniform on his back, you don't thereby convert him into a vegetarian. In the more accessible regions of the Congo, the troops of the State may have been drilled out of it, but that in districts further afield some of them still indulge in a human steak is not to be doubted.'–E.D. Morel, in *King Leopold's Rule in Africa*, p. 120.

questions. An incentive structure was also established where the rubber purchased at the lowest cost earned the highest commission. With such a structure, slave labour was inevitable.

Figure 9: Belgian Free Congo's Force Publique with a statue of King Leopold II.[92]

There is much written about, and much handwringing over, the ghastly events of the next twenty-three years from 1890–1913. Eyewitness accounts notwithstanding, few in any position of authority—least of all Leopold—took any action to halt the horrors. Witness reports began arriving almost as soon as Leopold's brutalities began. James Washington Williams was a prominent black American who sought Leopold's cooperation to bring emancipated black Americans to the Congo to contribute to the economy and also progress as a group in ways that were not possible in the United States even decades after the Civil War due to racial segregation and Jim Crow[xlii] laws. He arrived in Congo Free State in 1890 and was horrified by what he saw, writing an 'Open Letter to His Serene Majesty Leopold' that was distributed across Europe and also sent to President Harrison of the United States. In the letter, Williams reviled Stanley as a trickster who bamboozled the gullible natives. In addition, he condemned of the recruitment of excessively cruel Africans as overseers and the slave trade organised by Leopold's men. He was especially scathing of the lack of any facilities for the improvement of the natives such as schools and hospitals, and a corrupt judicial system that was quick to punish natives severely for the most trivial matter while exonerating whites. Indeed, Williams accused Leopold of 'a crime against humanity'. Conveniently, Williams died in 1891, sparing Leopold any amount of trouble to discredit and downplay these accusations. Around 1890, another black American missionary, William Henry Sheppard, travelled to remote areas along the Kasai River and befriended the native Kuba people. He had been there for eight years on a Presbyterian mission before Leopold's soldiers from the Concession Companie du Kasai arrived. Sheppard told his mission superiors in the United States of the massacre of resisting Kubas by the thousands and of the amputation and smoking of hands as trophies. Not much happened after Sheppard's report except that Leopold made it an offence to slander any Congo State official.

xlii Jim Crow was a pejorative term for black Americans and refers to laws and codes passed in the southern United States during the 'Reconstruction period' following the Civil War and emancipation of slaves. Jim Crow enforced racial segregation and limited the rights, autonomy and free movement of non-whites.

Rubber harvesting from rubber vines in the Congo was a brutal business. In bright sun, the plant takes the form of a bush but, when surrounded by tall trees, the plant becomes a liana, a climber which branches out and wraps around trunks and branches of supporting trees, reaching up to over 200 feet to obtain life-giving light. In time, the vine becomes woody with a trunk diameter that can be 'as thick as a man's leg'. When injured, milky white latex exudes from the cut, but quickly clots when exposed to air. Most commonly, to harvest latex, the tapper would constantly wipe off the fluid, smearing it on his own body until the vine stopped oozing. Then the latex was peeled off the body (presumably taking any body hair with it) and wound into a ball. Alternatively, the tapper climbed up into the tree and cut down the vine or dug up runners from under the ground. These were scored or the bark was stripped, and emerging latex collected after it coagulated. Another method was to cut the stem into about one-foot lengths and hammer it with a mallet until the plant fibre eroded away. The small amount of latex that remained was recovered. Boiling, the addition of salt, the hot infusion of the juice of the Diechia vine (*Strophanthus preussii*) or the leaves of *Bauhinia reticulata* trees caused latex to coagulate in a hurry. Complicating matters is that not all vine latex contains rubber, so tapping might yield latex, but it might be resinous or even contaminate previously tapped latex. All in all, the average yield would come to about 150 grams of rubber after about forty hours of work—not exactly copious quantities. The methods used by the Belgians also appeared counterproductive: In the one-year period from 1909 to 1910, every British, German, French and Portuguese colony in Africa showed increased production, barring Congo.[93]

What is obvious from this narrative is that Congo had a problem. The high pressure to obtain rubber meant that rough methods of draining were used, which meant that the plants often did not survive. As time went on, vines became harder to find and tap, and forays into the forest became longer and less productive. The agents administering the region devised a diabolical method to exert pressure on the tappers: their womenfolk and children were held hostage and corralled in stockades—and the only ransom accepted was rubber. Because of the indifference of the agents and the expense of feeding them, the hostages were starved (or worse), and the men who had gone to seek rubber came back to famished, mutilated, dead or missing family members. In their desperation to return quickly to release their families, rubber tappers would wrap rocks and debris within their rubber balls, which increased their weight and size to the acceptable dimensions. But the agents quickly got wise to this trick and sliced every ball open. If the ball contained debris, the hapless tapper was forced to eat it, and died a painful death from gut obstruction.[xliii] Alternately, the tapper could be tortured or killed. Whole villages were destroyed when the rubber quota was not met. But the atrocities inexorably came to light.

Edward Dene Morel was a clerk in the Elder Dempster shipping line that transported goods between Antwerp and the Congo Free State. In his accounting, Morel discovered that the value of ivory and rubber imported from the Congo was being under-reported. He was also struck by the shipments of guns and ammunition to the Congo Free State. This was especially perplexing since trading was supposedly carried out by barter rather than in the coin of the realm. His accounting showed that not enough goods equal to the value (often even below

xliii Rubber is insoluble in stomach acid and forms a plug when consumed in large quantities. I describe the mechanism in more detail in Chapter 8.

the value) of imports were shipped to the Congo for 'bartering purposes'. It quickly became obvious to him then that there was no barter, and that the natives were being forced to work as slave labour. After trying to rouse the chief executive of the shipping line to this obvious fraud and being rebuffed, Morel took matters straight to Leopold himself. He warned Leopold that atrocities were being committed in his name. Of course, Leopold was not surprised. Rejecting bribes to turn a blind eye, Morel resigned. He tried to publish his findings, only to find that the newspapers of the day would not carry his articles. So he started his own newspaper, *The West African Mail*, in which he recorded abuses using documents and letters and, crucially, photographs from missionaries who had been outraged by the treatment that they had witnessed being heaped upon the natives. He travelled to the United States and gained a reputation for his whistleblowing about the actual operation of the concessions that Leopold had authorised.

Reverend John Hobbis Harris and Alice Seely Harris were English missionaries; Alice was also a civil servant and a documentary photographer. The husband–wife team arrived in Congo Free State in 1898 and remained until 1905. Appalled at what they saw of the treatment of the Congolese by the Belgians, the pair made it their mission to expose the atrocities by taking and publishing photographs in the *Congo Balolo Mission*, a magazine, and then in pamphlets with wider circulation in Europe. Piteous photographs of young children with their hands cut off (Figure 10) or captioned: 'Nsala of Wala [...] with the hand and foot of his little girl of five years old [...] sentries killed his wife, his daughter and a son, cutting up the bodies, cooking and eating them.' (Figure 11) shocked readers.[xliv] The British government also took notice. In 1897,

xliv From the book *Don't Call Me Lady: The Journey of Lady Alice Seeley Harris*. Harris writes: 'He hadn't made his rubber quota for the day so

British Consul Pickersgill had written to British Prime Minister Lord Salisbury that 'the loss of life has been very great'.[94]

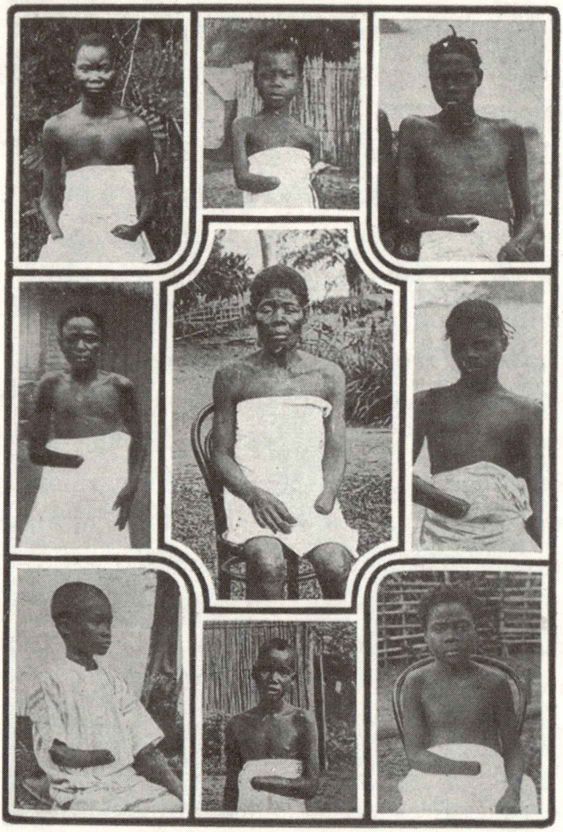

Figure 10: Civilian victims of mutilation by Free State authorities (1900–1905) in the privately owned territory of Belgian King Leopold. Rubber was produced at the cost of human rights abuses against the Congolese people, including amputations for unmet quotas and other colonial offenses.[95]

---

the Belgian-appointed overseers had cut off his daughter's hand and foot. Her name was Boali. She was five years old. Then they killed her. But they weren't finished. Then they killed his wife too. And because that didn't seem quite cruel enough, quite strong enough to make their case, they cannibalized both Boali and her mother. And they presented Nsala with the tokens, the leftovers from the once living body of his darling child whom he so loved. His life was destroyed.'

Figure 11: Nsala of Wala in the Nsongo district (ABIR concession) with the foot and child of his daughter, Boali, which was severed as a punishment for the father for having harvested too little rubber. The rest of her body and those of his wife, Bongingangoa, were eaten by cannibalistic overseers. The photo was taken in 1904 by John H. Harris, and the original caption notes that they also killed his son.[96]

When the Harrises returned to England they, along with H.R. Fox Bourne, set up the Anti-Slavery and Aborigines Protection Society[xlv] and engaged with the Congo Reform Association set up by Edward Dene Morel and Roger Casement. They met with George Herbert Ely and Charles James L'Estrange, who had established a portmanteau pseudonym known as Herbert

xlv Set up independently, these two organisations merged in 1909 to become the Anti-Slavery and Aborigines Protection Society, and J.H. Harris became its secretary. The Aborigines Protection Society was set up by Quakers in 1837 to 'to ensure the health and well-being and the sovereign, legal and religious rights of the indigenous peoples while also promoting the civilisation of the indigenous people who were subjected under colonial powers'. H.R. Fox Bourne became secretary in 1889. The Anti-Slavery Society was initially set up in 1839. The merged organisation persists today as Anti-Slavery International (www.antislavery.org).

Strang and embarked on writing stories for young adult men where the protagonist was a teenage boy. Their books fed a longing for adventure stoked by the exploits of intrepid explorers such as David Livingstone, Clements Markham, Richard Francis Burton, Edward Shackleton, Robert Falcon Scott and John Hanning Speake, but also exposed readers to contemporary events like wars and new methods of transport. Horrified by the events that were being revealed in Belgian Congo, Strang published *Samba: A Story of the Rubber Slaves of the Congo.*[97] The story is told from the perspective of seventeen-year-old Jack Challoner, who accompanies his uncle who has bought a concession to mine gold near a village in the Upper Congo, travelling with Nando, a Congolese guide. They hear of a massacre, then find a desolate village with burnt huts and the silence of death. They find a memorial with the possessions of the chief's wife strewn all around. On questioning if the chief's wife was buried there, Nando says yes: 'All dey find, sah. Bula Matadi[xlvi] come, make big bobbery; bang! Chief him missis lib for dead, sah. Bad man cut up, put in pot, only little bit left, sah.' But there they also find Samba—once a happy young boy who innocently brings a white man to the village where his grandfather is chief—it was his village. His story—the story of the Congo—was that the cruel white man demanded rubber. If adequate rubber was not forthcoming, then punishment would follow: the women carried away as hostages, the brutality and finally, the shooting. Samba's grandfather mourns: '*Botofé bo le iwa:* rubber is death!'

---

xlvi The villain of this story. Initially the name given to H. M. Stanley, but then used for anyone representing Congo Free State. Translates to 'crusher of rocks'. Bula Matadi later came to apply to any white man associated with the rubber trade.

Herbert Strang thanked the Harrises for 'revising proofs of the book, and for many most helpful suggestions and criticisms'. This indicates that the events of rubber collection and exploitation was authenticated by people who had spent years in the Upper Congo, witnessing the horror. Reverend Harris wrote to Leopold's chief agent in the Congo: 'I have just returned from a journey inland to the village of Insongo Mboyo. The abject misery and utter abandon is positively indescribable. I was so moved, Your Excellency, by the people's stories that I took the liberty of promising them that in future you will only kill them for crimes they commit.'[98] Random killings were rampant, after all. One of Leopold's agents, Luis Fievez, was quoted as saying: 'I called together the chiefs of the villages and ordered them to bring some manioc [cassava tubers]. On the agreed day, no manioc. Faced with such flagrant bad will, I declared war on them. One example sufficed. A hundred heads were cut off, and after that supplies were plentiful in the station. My aim was humanitarian. I ended a hundred lives, but that allowed five hundred others to live.'[99] This unbelievably barbaric incident is just one of the many countless acts of depraved butchery characteristic of that period.

In 1903, H.R. Fox-Bourne of the Aborigines Protection Society described the brutality of Leopold's regime in *Civilisation in Congoland.* He further petitioned that the Berlin Conference, initially convened to rubber-stamp Leopold's administration, be reconvened because of Congo Free State's violation of two principles of the Berlin Act of 1855: free trade and the welfare of the indigenous population of the Congo. Largely due to Fox-Bourne's persistence, British Prime Minister Lord Salisbury asked for the abuses to be documented 'for any time we may need it'. Despite widespread concern about the situation in the Congo, British law was not clear about how international intervention into the affairs of a sovereign state might be conducted. Sheppard and his co-defendant were represented by Emile Vanderwelde, a Belgian socialist politician, who later became an ally of Morel, one of the founders of the Congo Reform Association, an organisation which sought to abolish Leopold's reign and the abuses he had visited on Congo's population. Morel's reports and the documentation by various other travellers provoked a debate in the British Parliament and a resolution was adopted to accept his findings and state Britain's concern for Leopold's failure to live up to his idealistic plans for the AIC. In 1903, Sir Charles Dilke, a member of the British Parliament, raised the matter of abuses in the Congo during a parliamentary session. Ordered to investigate the many allegations was Roger Casement, then British Consul in Boma, Congo.

It is to be noted that, when these abuses were revealed, the British public was already unsympathetic to Leopold and his Congo Free State due to the Stokes affair in 1894. Charles Stokes was a British subject who had arrived in the Congo with a consignment of weapons which—as alleged by Captain Hubert-Joseph Lothaire of the Congo Free State—he was planning to sell to the Belgians' Afro-Arab enemies in eastern Congo. The Belgian judge ruled for Lothaire's side. Stokes was tried, summarily convicted and hanged from a tree. This peremptory treatment of a British subject caused outrage in Britain and damaged the Congo Free State's reputation there, though the Belgians tried to smooth the matter over by returning Stokes' body to his family and paying recompense. The general sentiment against Leopold's Congo was further stoked by Fox-Bourne's unremitting pleas and photographic documentation of horrific beatings, mutilation and starvation. Roger Casement's appointment reflected the British public's mood, and Leopold was going to find out just how sour that mood was. Interestingly, as Britain's representative in the Congo, Roger Casement had met Leopold in 1900 and impressed the king. He said afterwards: 'His Majesty, in bidding me farewell, asked me to write him privately at any time, and to write frankly, should there be anything of interest I could, unofficially, advise him of for the advancement of the general situation on the Congo.' Now Casement was ready to set pen to paper.

In 1903, Casement travelled to Belgian-administered Congo. His report 'On the Nile, near Kiro, January 21, 1903' begins thus: 'I have just visited the Belgian stations of Kiro and Lado, as also the station of Gondokoro in the Uganda Protectorate.' He continues: '... I noticed that, whereas there were numerous villages and huts on the eastern bank and on the islands, on the Belgian side not a sign of a village existed. Indeed, I do not think that any one of our party saw a single human being in Belgian territory, except the Belgian officers and men and the wives and children of the latter. Moreover, not a single native was to be seen either at Kiro or Lado ... The reason of all this is obvious enough. The Belgians are disliked. The people fly from them, and it is no wonder they should do so, for I am informed that the soldiers are allowed full liberty to plunder, and that payments are rarely made for supplies. The British officers wander, practically alone, over most parts of the country, either on tours of inspection or on shooting expeditions. I understand that no Belgian officer can move outside the settlements without a strong guard.'

Then, in a dispassionate voice, he provided detailed and wrenching descriptions of the wretchedness of the Congolese in the Congo Free State. The slim volume of eighty-six pages of text makes for harrowing reading. He describes cannibalistic overseers who ate their charges; the unreasonable demands for villages to supply stations with livestock, cassava and fish which were not paid for adequately, and testimonials of the savage beatings and murder that resulted when the supplies fell short. Workers who failed to collect their quota of rubber were shot, but each bullet used had to be accounted for by an equal number of severed hands taken from the corpses. If a bullet went off mark, or if an animal was shot for food, a hand was severed from a living human, and no questions were asked. Later, to allay the suspicion that women's hands were being substituted for men's, penises were demanded to keep count of bullets used. Women and children would be kept in stockades and starved so that their menfolk were sure to return from the jungle to ransom them with rubber. The despair of the population was such that, when they heard Casement might do something with their testimony, they willingly came to give personal accounts of their heartbreaking and enraging experiences. Casement recorded his thoughts: 'Of all the shameful and infamous expedients whereby man has preyed upon man ... this vile thing [rubber trade] dares to call itself commerce ... were I to touch on the subject of the treatment of the natives under the rubber regime, my indignation would carry me beyond the limits of official courtesy.' The specific horrors recorded by Casement have been documented time and again but to sum up: it is estimated that 10 million Congolese, half of the population before the Congo Free State was established, perished during Leopold's 'benign' leadership.[xlvii]

xlvii Not all died from Leopold II's Force Publique; some died from an epidemic of sleeping sickness. But there is no doubt that the brutality unleashed on the Congolese was the primary contributor to the numbers.

After their return from Congo, burning with indignation, Roger Casement and E.D. Morel set up the Congo Reform Association. Their efforts roused Europe and America to anger and brought Leopold a little closer to accountability. Authors such as Mark Twain and Arthur Conan Doyle expressed their horror in writing. Twain wrote *Leopold's Soliloquy*,[100] a scathing monologue in which Leopold casts himself as the injured, misunderstood philanthropist who was only bringing civilisation to the savages of the Congo. Doyle wrote a straightforward indictment in *The Crime of the Congo*[101] of the regime and its successor, the Belgian government. At these accusations, Leopold demurred and sent his own handpicked commission to investigate. But, hearing the testimony first-hand, one of the judges on the commission broke down in tears. Their scathing report authenticated Morel's and Casement's findings, and Leopold pivoted to suppressing his own commission's findings. Throughout this time, Leopold burnished his image within Belgium with a building spree, erecting beautiful edifices and earning the title of the 'Builder King'. Meanwhile, the abuses had not ceased. In 1908, American missionary William Henry Sheppard—who had previously reported the amputation and smoking of hands—described another instance of Kuba resistance and the brutality of the response by the Force Publique. The concession Companie du Kasai sued for libel. At the trial, the Belgian judge acquitted both the Companie and, lest it anger the United States, Sheppard as well. Following years of revelations, outrage and pressure, state of Belgium finally took charge of the administration of the Congo Free State from Leopold in 1908,[xlviii][102] and paid him 215.5 million francs for

xlviii Assessment of the 1919 Belgian government commission. Belgium administered until 1960. A timeline of the roiling early governance

renouncement of his title to his African territories. The state further undertook to pay his debts, assume control over his projects and threw in an additional 50 million francs payment. Today, streets in Belgium are named after him, although his statues, resplendent on horseback, came under attack in 2020 in Brussels, Ghent, Ostend and other cities following the Black Lives Matter movement. Many plinths now stand empty after the force of public opinion ruled. Leopold died quietly in 1909, causing barely a ripple. His actions were never investigated or punished.

The Amazon is the richest natural source of *Hevea* trees, and *Hevea* trees are the richest natural source of rubber. The trees are distributed over a wide area in their natural environment and isolation keeps them healthy. When planted at close quarters, they become susceptible to a fungus which causes SALB, the South American leaf blight. Where plantations of *Hevea* trees were established in the Amazon, they failed. The highest profile plantation failure came to the otherwise wildly successful industrial visionary, Henry Ford, who envisioned marching lines of rubber-yielding trees and an industrial efficiency in their harvesting and processing. Despite intense husbandry and the introduction of resistant *Hevea* clones from the East, plantations in the Amazon fell victim to SALB as soon as the tree crowns were close enough for it to spread. SALB levelled plantations in Guyana, Suriname and Panama, blighting estates across the region.[103] Even today, the Amazon

and long duration of the second President, Mobuto Sese-Seko, can be found in Reference 102.

struggles with SALB outbreaks, although it appears to not have spread to Asian or African plantations.

Rubber-yielding latex in the Amazon came from a variety of trees, each with slightly different properties: para rubber from *Hevea* trees, caucho rubber from *Castilla elastica*, manicoba rubber from *Manihot glaziovii*, mangabeira from *Hancornia speciosa*. Balata (a type of gutta-percha) from *Manilkara bidentata* also existed, but was not much desired. Sometimes, spotters called *matteiros* travelled around, identifying rubber trees or tracking exhausted or dead trees, but usually solitary tappers were turned out to set up a shelter and clear undergrowth for traveling from tree to tree. As in the Congo, their families were held hostage, so their running away was not a concern. But to obtain the requisite amount of rubber within the period of a month or so was an unpredictable business, given the environment. There were snakes, scorpions, disease-carrying insects, alligators and slashing thorns. And there were leeches. As Wolf and Wolf put it in their 1936 book, *Rubber, A Story of Glory and Greed*, 'In these swamps, then, men and leeches worked together, men tapping trees and leeches tapping men, ulcers on over-worked human trunks matching swollen, tumorous-looking masses of scars on overworked trees.'[104] Then there was the tree itself. Tapping without causing damage is a learned skill, and *guyaleros, chicleros, seringueiros*[xlix] and *heveleros* are terms for tappers who specialised in the identification and tapping of various species of rubber-producing plants in the Americas—guayule (*Parthenium argentatum*), chicle (*Manilkara zapota*), the Mexican rubber tree (*Castilla elastica*), and the para rubber tree (*Hevea brasiliensis)*, respectively. In the case of *Hevea* trees

---

xlix The term *syringeiros* came from the Maya method of making bottles from rubber which could be squeezed like a syringe.

which could be re-tapped, care had then to be taken to cut deeply enough into the latex-carrying laticifer tubes, but not so deeply as to damage the regenerative cambium layer. But when frantic, tapping was a matter of slashing and collecting what rubber was exuded, returning from time to time to make another gash. The wounds on the trees scarred over, making it harder to cut through the next time. Alternately the trees were cut down, drained. Then there was the need to coagulate and smoke the rubber to preserve it from microbial degradation, which took time and effort. The smoke had to be vertical and just hot enough. Inhaling smoke on top of all the other health-compromising conditions made for lives that were 'nasty, brutish and short' when they were not curtailed altogether by the whip or bullet.

Rubber also came in several grades. There was the gold standard, 'fine hard para' from *Hevea brasiliensis*, then 'weak fine' from *Hevea guyanensis*, 'medium coarse' and 'scrap'. The last two grades could incur punishment. Indiscriminate tapping or slaughter soon depleted the nearby large trees, necessitating deeper and longer forays. Besides being destructive to the trees themselves, the quantity of latex that was collected was often inadequate and the supply unreliable. Regardless, increasing rubber demand spurred various 'rubber barons' to divide up large areas in the Amazon for wild rubber harvesting and to establish *encomiendas*.[105] The *encomienda* had once been a convenient administrative practice of the Spanish Crown that allowed remote administrative districts a measure of self-governance. The Crown received a tribute of a fifth of the income, while preserving plausible deniability for the actions taken therein and freeing it from the pressures of providing for its emissaries. Considered unfair, the practice of *encomiendas* had been abolished by the New Laws enacted by Charles V in 1542. Now the practice was brought back, with additional virulence.

As vulcanisation and the pneumatic tyre facilitated Henry Ford's production of cars, the demand for rubber exploded and the Amazon joined the Congo in meeting the increase in demand. The overlords in the Amazon were citizens of Brazil, Colombia, Bolivia and Peru, usually of Spanish descent, who controlled millions of acres of territory. John Loadman writes in *Tears of the Tree*:[106]

> Manoel Carioca controlled much of the rubber coming down the Gregorio River – it would take a steamboat seven days to sail through his domain – whilst Luis de Silva Gomes had an estate on the Purus River which was estimated to be ten million acres in size. J. G. Araujo had half a million acres on the Negro. [...] Perhaps the biggest and most powerful of them all was Nicolas Suarez, who 'owned' sixteen million acres around the most southerly of the great rubber rivers, the Beni.' The barons spent much of their time in the large cities along the Amazon: Iquitos, Manaus, Santarem, and in Europe which allowed them, like the Spanish Crown earlier, plausible deniability about the methods used to collect rubber in their *encomiendas*.

Of particular notoriety were the Peruvian rubber baron Julio Arana and his compatriots Lizardo Arana, Pablo and Bartolomé Zumaeta, and Abel Alarco. From his beginnings as a pedlar in Yurimaguas, in the Loreto region of Peru, Julio Arana acquired land around Putumayo River on the western fringes of the Amazon. However, the rubber trees were spread out across in the forest, and required huge manpower to tap and process the latex. The tribes in the area included the Bora, Huitoto and Andoke, and they were enslaved by the simple expedient of terror. Unsurprisingly, the brutal methods employed in the Congo were used here too. Imported overseers from the sugar plantations of Barbados who had no shared history with their charges, and young boys from indigenous tribes hostile to the workers called the 'Muchachos de Confianza' were trained and encouraged to inflict unspeakable cruelty upon the workers. Besides working the men day and night, women were rounded up as whores and to populate 'stud farms' to produce a steady supply of workers. Starvation was a routine punishment. Dying men who had been flogged for inadequate harvests or who had had their genitals shot off for amusement were left to the mercy of maggots and dogs. The vastness and remoteness of the area meant knowledge of the abuses was contained. That is, until Walter Earnest Hardenburg decided to change jobs.

Walter Hardenburg was an American engineer working on a railroad in Colombia. He heard news about a railroad being built in the south of the Amazon, on the Bolivian border. In a situation reminiscent of the Leopold's railroad built to bypass the rapids of the lower Congo River, this railroad would circumvent the treacherous rapids on the Madeira River and link its navigable upstream route with the Mamore River. This would allow Bolivian rubber collected in the Suarez to be delivered to Manaus, a big metropolis in Brazil, from where it could more easily be transported to the Atlantic coast. Previously, rubber had been transported on the backs of the workers but it was inefficient, slow and dangerous; on the river, innumerable boat crews and rubber balls had been lost to the rapids, with the loss of the latter causing acute chagrin. Although the railroad was initially mooted in 1871, it was not built: living conditions were so unhealthy that one Brazilian disease expert supposedly said, 'There are no natives of this place; all children born there die.'[107] But the trials of the building of the Panama Canal provided lessons in managing tropical conditions, and work began again. In 1908, Walter Hardenburg and a colleague named Walter Perkins set off for the Bolivian border. They had both been offered work at the Madeira–Mamore Railway and they and two local boatmen canoed down the Putumayo River from Colombia into Brazil.[108] Along the way, they heard stories about Arana who supposedly ran a British company called the Peruvian Amazon Company (PAC) and was taking over the Putumayo, crushing dissent with gunboats and armed militia. Accurately enough, PAC was actually registered on the British Stock Exchange and had a British board of governors. Arana had been fêted by the British establishment, which was no doubt happy to see rubber from anywhere but the Congo. Slavery had been abolished in directly administered British overseas territories in 1833, so it was assumed PAC operated a slavery-free enterprise. But locals appraised them of the lawlessness of PAC, including a Colombian rubber collector called David Serrano who told them about his wife being raped in front of him by an PAC overseer called Miguel Loayza, and of both his wife and son being abducted.

Hardenburg and Perkins appear to have changed their plans, deciding to remain in the area, a mix of commerce—Hardenburg and Perkins bought a share of Serrano's rubber station 'La Reserva'—and high-minded necessity:

> …to call attention to the fact that owing to the oppressions of the Peruvian Amazon Company in whose service the greater part of the Huitotos, unfortunately, are the numbers of these Indians are diminishing to an alarming degree, and, unless something be done to protect them,

> this noble race of aborigines will, in my opinion, soon disappear completely, as have so many others in the region of the Upper Amazon.[109]

Hardenburg and Perkins appear to have fancied themselves equipped to negotiate the terms of purchase of La Reserva between the Colombians and Peruvians fighting over rubber-gathering territory. But fate intervened in the form of Loayza himself, who burned down La Reserva and took Hardenburg and Perkins captive on board his boat called the *Liberal*. Later, they heard that David Serrano had been killed. Somehow the Americans persuaded Loayza that Washington would get involved if they were both detained. They agreed that Hardenburg would travel with Loayza to Iquitos on the *Liberal* to negotiate the terms of sale (presumably because of their part ownership of La Reserva, although this is not clear).

Hardenburg then details his observations:

1. The Pacific Indians of the Putumayo are forced to work day and night for the extraction of rubber without the slightest remuneration except the food necessary to keep them alive.
2. They are kept in the most complete nakedness, many of them not even possessing a biblical fig leaf.
3. They are robbed of their crops and their family to satisfy the voracity, lasciviousness and avarice of the PAC and its employees, who live on their food and violate their women.
4. They are sold wholesale and retail in Iquitos at prices that range from £20 to £40 each.
5. They are flogged inhumanly until their bones are laid bare, and great raw sores cover them.

6. They are given no medical treatment, but are left to die and serve as food for the chiefs' dogs, and later, as food for maggots.
7. They are routinely castrated and mutilated, and their ears, fingers, arms and legs are cut off.
8. They are tortured by means of fire and water, and by tying them up, crucified head down.
9. Their houses and crops are burned and destroyed wantonly, and for mere amusement.
10. They are cut to pieces and dismembered with knives, axes and machetes.
11. Their children are grasped by the feet and their heads are dashed against trees and walls until their brains fly out.
12. Their old folk are killed when they are no longer able to work for the company.
13. Men, women, and children are shot to provide amusement for the employees or to celebrate the *sábado de gloria*, or, in preference to this, they are burned with kerosene so that the employees may enjoy their desperate agony.

He saw rubber tappers being beaten, starved and abused if they did not bring in their quota (Figure 12) and girls being used as sex slaves after their daytime job of domestic work was done. Their impunity was such that even Perkins barely escaped El Encanto with his life. Hardenburg resolved to meet Arana himself and tell him of the atrocities being carried out in his domains. When he finally met Arana after a lengthy wait in Iquitos, Arana professed ignorance and blamed Colombians for the abuses. Hardenburg was unconvinced. He could see that there were efforts to suppress the stories getting out. For example, the office of the local newspaper in Iquitos, run by Benjamin Saladaña Rocco who was just about to publish documented stories about Arana's PAC abuses, had been raided. Rocco had been pursuing justice for the victims of Arana through the courts to no avail.[110] Although the part-time American Consul in Iquitos professed to have heard about the abuses, he did not want to intervene in a problem outside of American jurisdiction. Rocco's son then approached Hardenburg with documentation of the abuses which his father had been unable to print. Word spread, and Hardenberg was then approached by several witnesses from whom he obtained sworn depositions. He then set sail for England to expose Arana's British company's abuses to the British board of governors and to the general public. It was July 1909.

Figure 12: An Indian woman condemned to death by hunger on Upper Putumayo. (The Peruvians stated that this was the work of Colombian bandits.)[111]

After arriving in Britain, Hardenberg could not initially find anyone to publish his story for fear of being sued for libel. But then he met Sydney Paternoster, the publisher of *Truth* magazine, through Reverend John H. Harris of the Antislavery and Aboriginal Protection Society (who had taken the photo of

Nsala of Wala in the Congo Free State). Paternoster published the story after separately confirming the facts through his contacts, and there was an outcry which was heard all the way to Parliament. The article and descriptions were particularly horrifying to the British because Julio and Lizardo Arana had travelled just a couple of years earlier in 1907 to London and raised £1,000,000 of capital for the PAC. Besides PAC being registered on the British Stock Exchange, there was a second British connection: the West Indians that Arana had imported as overseers. West Indians were considered to be British subjects—the British West Indies[1] were established in the seventeenth century as colonies for agriculture and to support the Atlantic slave trade—and therefore, the British government got involved. When questioned, PAC's British board of governors maintained their ignorance as to Arana's methods—some claimed they did not even speak Spanish, the language in which board meetings were held. The British decided an investigation was in order. Once again, Roger Casement was activated. It was 1910.

Casement was now the British Consul in Rio de Janeiro in Brazil. He had proved his mettle when investigating Leopold's Congo Free State's activities and now he was asked to investigate the allegations of abuse by Arana's PAC in the Putumayo. He

---

1 The British West Indies included the territories of Anguilla, Cayman Islands, Turks and Caicos Islands, Montserrat, the British Virgin Islands, Bermuda, Antigua and Barbuda, the Bahamas, Barbados, Dominica, Grenada, Jamaica, Saint Kitts and Nevis, Saint Lucia, Saint Vincent and the Grenadines, Belize (formerly British Honduras), Guyana (formerly British Guiana), and Trinidad and Tobago. They all remain within the Commonwealth of Nations, representing nations with British colonial history. Today, Bermuda, Anguilla, the British Virgin Islands, Montserrat and the Cayman Islands are still British overseas territories.

found it even worse than Hardenburg's shocking descriptions (which were later published in in the book, *The Putumayo, the devil's paradise*), and which came to be known as the 'Putumayo affair'.[112] The death toll was horrific. Casement calculated that 4,000 tons of rubber had cost 30,000 deaths, which he worked out to four pounds of rubber for a pound of human flesh. A parliamentary enquiry was duly set up by British Prime Minister Herbert Asquith, who no doubt knew the drill well by now. Following a damning report, Arana was censured, but he was a Peruvian and could not be imprisoned. He carried on producing rubber through his company, which got a boost with the start of World War I, and his PAC survived until 1920. Bartolomé Zumaeta had been killed years before by a man who had been forced to watch him publicly rape his wife; Pablo Zumaeta was generously thanked by a visiting American rubber survey commission in 1923: 'Among the many private individuals whose kindness we take pleasure in acknowledging are … Sr. Pablo Zumaeta of Iquitos.' The commission found no rubber-associated maltreatment of any Indians, but then they had not actually gone upriver from Iquitos. After much other political activity which included him, his son and daughter petitioning to reclaim his lost lands under a 'patriotic junta' and a full-scale war between Colombia and Peru, Julio Arana finally lost his lands to Colombia in a land settlement by Peru. He died in 1952, having served as Peruvian senator without paying any meaningful price for extracting countless pounds of flesh from humans in exchange for rubber.

Casement's life also took a strange turn. He became an anti-imperialist, demanding that people be given the freedom to govern themselves. In the case of Ireland, which was under

British rule, he made it his personal mission to support the cause of independence.

The British Empire had declared dominion over Ireland from the late twelfth century at the time of the Norman invasion and overthrow of the cluster of independent kingdoms that had existed previously. The Normans assimilated and, by the fifteenth century, British influence had been corralled into 'the pale', a fenced area encompassing the counties of Louth, Meath, Dublin and Kildare. The areas outside—beyond the pale—were under Irish control. In 1494, Poynings Law was passed, requiring any meeting of the Irish Parliament (established 1366) to be signed off by the British monarch's Privy Council. Notwithstanding the various hurdles to Irish sovereignty—Henry VIII crowning himself King of Ireland in 1584, Oliver Cromwell's Parliamentarians' defeat of the joint Royalist-Confederate Armies of Ireland in 1652 and the United Irishmen's Rebellion of 1798 followed by the Union Act of 1800 which re-merged Ireland as a dominion of the British Empire—Irish separatist sentiment burned brightly. The British Parliament further stoked the flames by settling English and Scottish planters in Ireland; seizing land from the indigenous Irish and granting it to loyalists; passing Penal Laws against Roman Catholics and erecting hurdles to Catholic landownership; transporting 50,000 people overseas as indentured labour; and causing two enormous famines—one after Cromwell's campaign 1652–1659, and the later *Drochshaol*, or the Great Potato Famine of 1845–1852—without lifting a finger to help.

Casement had been born in Dublin, Ireland, in 1864, within a decade of *Drochshaol*. The Irish held the British responsible in large part for the devastation that the failed potato crop caused because they had exported food from Ireland even as people starved. Casement went to Ireland in 1904 and again in 1905, when he joined the newly formed Sinn Féin party, which was focused on the cause for Irish independence. When Casement retired from British diplomatic service in 1913, he went back to Ireland and joined the cause of the separation of Ireland from British rule. He travelled to the United States and to Germany in 1914, looking for arms and volunteers for the separatists' cause. Britain and Belgium were at war with Germany at the time. Casement's emotions were complicated. He wrote: 'Sometimes I must confess when the present "Agony of Belgium" confronts me—and it cannot well be minimised it is in truth a national agony—I feel that there may be in their awful lesson to the Belgian people a repayment. All that they now suffer and far more, they, or their king, his government and his officers wreaked on the well-nigh defenceless people of the Congo basin.' Casement disapproved of imperialism anywhere; his sympathy for the cause of Indian independence was well known. He struck a deal with Germany during World War I for his self-declared 'one bold deed of open treason'—arranging an arms shipment for the Easter Rising of 1916.[113] The shipment was intercepted by the British and the boat carrying it was sunk. Casement was not on the arms shipment boat. He was ferried back to Ireland by a German U-boat on 21 April 1916, three days before the Easter uprising. He was found, arrested, accused of treason, transported to prison in England and on 29 June 1916, stripped of his knighthood. Documents alleging that he was also homosexual excited public sentiment against him and his 'deviant acts'. Celebrities jumped into the circus. Sir Arthur Conan Doyle and the US Senate pleaded for clemency; Joseph Conrad said he could not forgive Casement and neither could Casement's friend from his days in the Congo, the artist Herbert Ward, who had admired Casement enough then to ask him to be godfather to his youngest son. Ward's initial description of Casement in the Congo is almost breathless: 'The first name I would mention of all the European pioneers who were connected with the opening up of the Congo is the name of my friend and companion since 1884, Roger Casement. Imagine a tall, handsome man, of fine bearing; thin, mere muscle and bone, a sun-tanned face, blue eyes and black curly hair. A pure Irishman he is, with a captivating voice and singular charm of manner. A man of distinction and great refinement, high-minded and courteous, impulsive and poetical. Quixotic perhaps some would say, and with a certain truth, for few men have shown themselves so regardless of personal advancement.'[114] Ward had lauded Casement's report which brought down Leopold's control of Congo. But he could not tolerate Casement's treasonous act of reaching out to the Germans in wartime. To drive home the point, he changed Casement's godson's name from Roger Casement Ward to Rodney Sanford Ward.

The Treason Act of 1351 was unclear on whether the charge could be applied to Casement's case, and the hearing was contentious. In the act, the specific statute read that a person was guilty of high treason if they '… adhered to the king's enemies in his realm, giving them aid and comfort in his realm or elsewhere.' Casement's defence, led by Serjeant Sullivan was that the law could not apply as the activities that Casement stood accused of were carried out on German soil—and Germany was not in the king's realm. It was not elsewhere in the king's realm either. It was just elsewhere. The prosecution, led by Attorney General Sir Frederick E. Smith, founder of the Ulster Unionists, did not agree. They argued that the sentence should be read as if there was a comma between the words 'realm' and 'elsewhere' as in: '… adhered to the king's enemies in his realm, giving them aid and comfort in his realm, or elsewhere.' The wording 'or elsewhere' was the problem; the prosecution suggested that 'elsewhere' meant 'anywhere'. The prosecution prevailed. Casement was convicted and sentenced to death.

Roger Casement was thus 'hanged on a comma' at Pentonville Prison on 3rd August 1916. He was fifty-one.

Figure 13: 'Portrait of Roger Casement, (1864–1916), Patriot and Revolutionary' by Sarah Purser. National Gallery of Ireland.[115]

Outrages like the events in the Congo and the Amazon were not carried out in isolation. Leopold was inspired to use slave labour after observing forced labour in the Dutch East Indies during his journey as Prince Leopold, Duke of Brabant, through China via India and the Malay states, including Java (Figure 14). Forced labour was also employed where rubber was available in colonies run by the Netherlands,[116] Germany, France and Portugal. The Dutch were the last to actually abolish the trade in 1863, based on the passing of an 1848 law to do so. Such foot-dragging was made worse by even more delay—a ten-year 'transition' period which saw slaves freed only in 1873. But, at last, there was an end to slave trade across Europe. But Europeans still needed a substantial numbers of labourers for their colonies; they had to look for additional methods. Their response was to compel labour from the indigenous people.

The forced labour practices did not grow from nothing either. A practice called *corvée* was homegrown and prevalent in feudal systems across Europe where tenant farmers (*coloni*) were required to work for short periods without pay on their landlords' estates. The system was widespread in medieval Europe, but also in ancient Egypt and Sumer, the Incan civilisation, ancient Rome, the Russian Empire, Portugal's African colonies and even as recently as the early twentieth century in the United States where it masqueraded as statute labour and compelled unpaid work on public projects. Statute labour was abolished altogether only in 1913 when Alabama became the last state to strike down the law.

Unlike the penal system of Great Britain, which exported convicts to Australia and North America to provide *corvée* labour, the Vereenigde Oost-Indische Company (VOC; Dutch East India Company) merely modified the practice to force indigenous convicts to 'open up the frontiers of the colony'.[117] They established *gevangenissen* (prisons) for convicts where overseers were employed and the convicts made to work in mines or on infrastructure projects in areas as geographically disparate as Tuticorin (India), Robben Island (South Africa), Batavia (present day Jakarta, Indonesia) and the Banda Islands (near Java, Indonesia). When the Dutch state took over from the Dutch East India Company in 1799, the system was further developed into two types of *corvée*: *herendiensten* (or compulsory labour in mines and infrastructure building) and *cultuurstelsel* (the forced cultivation of cash crops from plantations). As such, more and more indigenous people were convicted for pettier and pettier offences, providing a pipeline from policing to the *gevangenissen*. Brutal beatings with rattan canes were used to maintain 'discipline' in mines, such as in the Ombilin Coal Mines in western Sumatra.

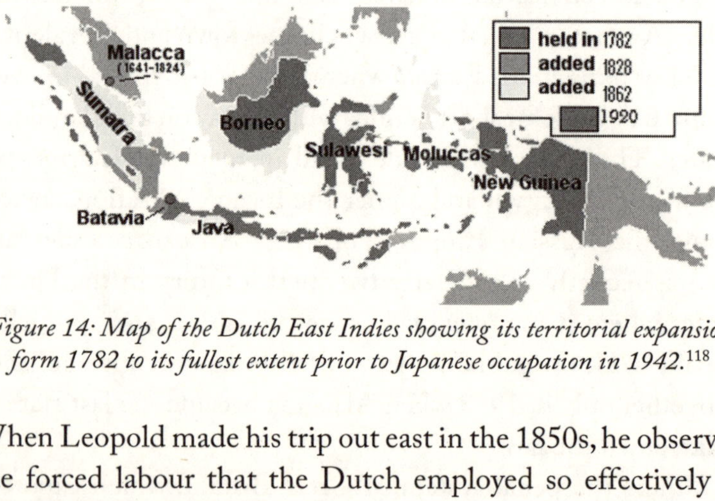

Figure 14: Map of the Dutch East Indies showing its territorial expansion form 1782 to its fullest extent prior to Japanese occupation in 1942.[118]

When Leopold made his trip out east in the 1850s, he observed the forced labour that the Dutch employed so effectively in their colonial pursuits, and his enthusiasm for the practice would bear torturous fruit in the Congo decades later. The conditions the Dutch imposed were such that in 1894, 176 convicts (19 per cent of the prison population) attempted desertion, of whom 146 were later recaptured. This led to a decision to use offshore islands such as Nusa Kambangen to house convicts, which successfully lowered desertion rates. By 1890, rubber plantations were established in Malaysia. By 1903, the Dutch were using mandatory convict labour for tending and harvesting rubber plantations on Nusa Kambangen. The number of convicts increased to 4,000 by 1920. Rubber from British and the Dutch East Indies would become a source of enormous wealth, and the lands that produced them would become strategically important in the build-up to (and throughout) World War II.

The decline of Brazilian and Congolese rubber was due to the stiff competition offered by eastern rubber, which derived from the offspring of the seeds sneaked out of Brazil by Henry Wickham and Robert Cross, and which were sent to British colonies in the Far East. There is quite a backstory to this biopiracy or entrepreneurship, as seen from the differing perspectives of the Brazilians or the British, respectively. Knowing rubber was their economic golden goose, the Brazilians would probably have declined to allow seeds to be exported, although no formal ban was enacted until 1918. Although Britain was one of the few countries privileged to trade with Brazil due to the *Decreto de Abertura dos Portos às Nações Amigas*, the British seethed at the lack of control, especially after Hancock's vulcanisation process caused the demand for latex to go through the roof. As demand continued to increase in the nineteenth century, the British realised that *Hevea* trees might do well in the moist tropical colonies in the Far East, such as Sri Lanka, Malaysia and Indonesia. Sir William Jackson Hooker, director of the Kew Gardens near London, tasked both Robert Cross and Henry Wickham with obtaining *Hevea* seeds that would be used to set up plantations.[119] The provenance of those seeds was quite a story and, like a fishing story, the story of obtaining the seeds grows with every telling.

In 1865, Clements Markham, a naval officer, visited India and Sri Lanka, and noticed something that he had previously observed in the Amazon: slaughter tapping—whereby wild trees were hastily cut down and thus killed—for rubber. The stocks of wild *Hevea* in the Amazon, and *Ficus elastica* on the Indian subcontinent were in decline, obviously presaging a time when there would be none left. Markham was a significant figure in the field of liberating plants from geographical confinement. He had previously had the brilliant idea of transporting another tree he had seen in the Amazon—the *Cinchona* tree which produces quinine—to India to treat malaria which was killing British expatriates. James Collins, a curator of Royal Pharmaceutical Society Museum quoted Markham's success with the *Cinchona* tree and suggested that the same principle would hold for *Hevea*. Markham was intrigued. Sir William Jackson Hooker requested the Foreign Office to ask the British Consul in Belem, the capital of Para state in Brazil, to send seeds to Kew Gardens. Of the seeds that were sent, only twelve plants were raised—on their journey to Calcutta, six perished en route due to cold, and the remainder did not survive for long. A second consignment of seeds in 1875 went rancid in storage and failed to germinate. Then, in 1876, Markham tapped his friend Robert Cross to go to the Amazon and collect the seeds of the *Hevea* from Para in Brazil, and *Castilla elastica* from Panama in Central America. Cross procured 1,080 seedlings late in 1876, but the swashbuckling Henry Alexander Wickham now enters the story.

Wickham was born in 1846 to well-off parents—his father was a solicitor—who lived on Haverstock Hill in a salubrious part of London, away from the pestilential cholera that raged around. In 1851, when Henry, the oldest, was four, his father unexpectedly contracted cholera and died, leaving his mother to take up millinery to raise her three children, two boys and a girl, with the youngest a son born a few months after his father's death. The following year was the year of the Great Exhibition of London which showcased the wonders of the world, of which one was Goodyear's Vulcanite Court on which Charles Goodyear spent £30,000 pounds to equip three rooms with walls, furnishings, decor and items as varied as inkpots and dolls all made of rubber. Other talk was about the new discoveries that were being made, and of the hardy men who made them: Sir Richard Burton who claimed to have discovered the source of the White Nile, David Livingstone's journey up Zambesi River, MacGregor Laird's travels in Sierra Leone and the celebrated Clements Markham who brought the *Cinchona* tree to Asia to treat malaria. Inspired by their exploits, Henry chose, at twenty, to travel to the Americas. He went to Central America and harvested feathers for British ladies' hats, returned to England in 1867 and set off again in 1868 for Brazil. He developed an enormous enthusiasm for the Amazon, writing a book on his trip: *Rough Notes on a Journey from Trinidad to Pará, Brazil, by way of the great cataracts of the Orinoco, Atababo and the Rio Negro*. He came back to England to marry, and then relocated his wife, his mother and his siblings to Santarem, where Tapajos River joins the Amazon.

Markham appears to have known of Wickham, and he requested the Foreign Office in Brazil to ask Wickham if he could obtain seeds. After some haggling, the Foreign Office offered Wickham £10 per 1,000 seeds for as many as he could collect. Wickham accepted, and periodically sent seeds, but they failed to germinate. Then something astonishing happened, in Wickham's telling. The ocean liner *Amazonas*, on its maiden voyage from Liverpool, arrived in Santarem, and Wickham was invited on board and enjoyed the hospitality of the captain. The liner departed upstream, but word came back that the merchandise they had brought from Liverpool to trade for rubber balls had mysteriously vanished from the hold. This meant that the *Amazonas* crew had nothing to barter with, and would have to return to Liverpool with empty holds. The rubber trees were just about getting ready to shed their seeds, and Wickham saw an opportunity. He chartered the *Amazonas* on behalf of the British government and set about quickly collecting thousands of seeds, drying them, packing them in wicker baskets weaved frantically for the purpose and loading them on the ship. Getting the seeds out of Brazil was trickier, since authorities were keeping a careful watch on exports to prevent another incident of *Cinchona*-type thievery. Somehow, Wickham charmed the customs officials, spinning them a tale of perishable academic specimens—the ship was allowed out of port. The rest is history. Wickham was a creative raconteur and may have embellished his story à la Henry Morton Stanley. What is not in doubt is that he arranged for 70,000 seeds to reach Kew on 14 June 1876. They were immediately planted; 2,397 of them germinated. The game was on. The seedlings were distributed to Sri Lanka, India and Singapore, and from there, seeds and seedlings went further east. Meanwhile, Robert Cross arrived in September with more *Hevea*, as well as *Ceara* and *Castilla* plants, which were also sent to eastern colonies. It is not clear whether it was Wickham's or Cross's plants that were the forebears of the plantations that sprung up, but they established remarkably successful and healthy plantations that were crucially free of SALB.

By 1910, rubber from the Far East was seen as superior in quantity and quality to that from Brazil and the Congo. Since these were also the areas undergoing investigations in Europe for brutal forced labour practices and abuse heaped on indigenous peoples, there was a stampede towards Asian rubber. Congo's rubber production had imploded after 1910 and the Casement report. Brazil tried to assert its geographical superiority with Fordlandia but that project failed. SALB was diminishing output across South and Central America while in the shiny new plantations of the Far East, vast acreages of healthy trees marched in rows twelve feet apart, and labour compelled by *corvée* and convict laws was easily available. Soon, the Far East was collectively producing 300,000 tons of rubber per year, which met up to 90 per cent of global demand.

And then, two major events changed the ever-increasing trajectory of rubber production from the Far East: the advent of World War II and the production of synthetic rubber from petroleum.

5

The War Machine

Napoléon famously quipped that armies march on their stomachs but, in the mechanised wars of the twentieth century and onwards, vehicles with rubber tyres transported soldiers and their supplies. The outbreak of World War I in 1914 lead to a colossal demand for rubber for tyres, casing for equipment, electrical sheaths, belts, gaskets and tubes; the use of chemical warfare also necessitated the mass production of gas masks containing rubberised fabric and seals.[120] But supply fell short of the explosive demand—the quantities of rubber available were inadequate, and the resulting shortage provided the impetus for the production of synthetic rubber.

Synthetic rubber had already been invented. The Frenchman Gustave Bouchardat made the first synthetic elastomer consisting of isoprene polymer in 1879. But isoprene units are difficult to polymerise, and the polymer strands were not long or sturdy enough to meet the standards of elasticity and strength of natural rubber. The efforts went on. In 1909, Fritz Hoffman and his team at Bayer created polymerised methyl isoprene, which was easier to synthesise than isoprene. Hoffman received the patent on 12 September 1909, and also won the cash prize that Bayer had offered in 1906 as an incentive for figuring out the process of synthetic rubber production. However, its synthesis was too costly for large-scale production. In 1910, the Russian Sergei Vasilyevich Lebedev prepared a synthetic rubber from butadiene. His process finally kickstarted the commercial synthetic rubber production, which began well before World War I. Synthetic rubber was now ready to supplement the demand for rubber in the war which was to follow in a few years. Germany used Fritz Hoffman's synthetic rubber process in its war effort, but the quantities were not adequate to meet its need, and the shortage sometimes resulted in tyres being mere metal wheels, which did the vehicles and the passengers little good. Because the British and France controlled rubber production in the Far East, and synthetic rubber was being supplied from the United States, the Allies had access to greater quantities of both natural and synthetic rubber. Victory was certain, especially once the United States joined the war.

After the Great War, efforts to make synthetic rubber continued in the USSR, Germany and the US with some competition and also some collaboration from US businesses despite concerns of German rearmament under the Nazis.[121] In 1923, priest and professor of botany and chemistry Julius Nieuwland synthesised a superior rubber-like material that could be vulcanised; it was named DuPrene. Waldo Semon, a prolific researcher with B.F. Goodrich produced polyvinylchloride (PVC), Ameripol, Koroseal and 5,000 other types of synthetic rubbers. The USSR had Sovprene, and the Germans subsequently made Buna; both were similar to

DuPrene. In 1931, two researchers, Hermann Staudinger (a German) and Wallace Carothers (an American who also created nylon), contributed to the synthesis of neoprene. In 1935, German scientists developed Buna rubbers (also known as nitrile rubbers) which contained two copolymers—acrylonitrile and butadiene—which showed increased resilience. There were three variations of this rubber: H (hard rubber), W (soft rubber) and B (Buna rubber). Buna rubber was of such high quality that it won the gold medal at the Paris Exhibition in 1937. In 1941, German tyres contained 37 per cent natural rubber but with the advances in synthetic rubber production, this lowered to 8 per cent by 1943.

Wartime Germany's synthetic and natural rubber manufacturing processes also heaped misery on unfortunate humans. In 1940, I.G. Farben opened a massive plant to make synthetic rubber and gasoline near Auschwitz and used concentration camp inmates to man them. In occupied Ukraine and the Baltic states, Heinrich Himmler ordered the mobilisation of women, children, Soviet prisoners and any able-bodied person to extract rubber from the Russian dandelion (*Taraxacum kok-saghyz*), but not very successfully, since very little production (a few hundred tons) of natural rubber could be derived.[122] Synthetic rubber allowed Germany to partially supplement the natural rubber shortage they experienced during World War II due to their lack of colonial outposts in the Far East. But natural rubber was still indispensable for some uses, such as aircraft tyres, and Germany looked eastward to its Axis ally Japan for a solution.

At the beginning of the war in 1939, Allied forces had control of 93 per cent of the world's rubber production, 77 per cent of it in Southeast Asia.[123] But Japan had begun flexing its muscle in Asia well before World War II—it had invaded Manchuria in 1931 and launched a full-scale invasion into China in 1937. In 1940, Japan obtained access to Vietnam, Laos and Cambodia through an agreement with the friendly Vichy government in France. Japan also signed agreements for territorial integrity with Thailand, and was looking covetously further afield. Concerned by the threat that Japan posed to Guam, the Philippines as well as the Indonesian and Malaysian rubber-producing areas that they depended on, US President Franklin Roosevelt declared a national emergency, froze Japan's US assets and stopped fuel supplies to Japan. On 7 December 1941, Japan invaded Malaysia, Guam, the Wake Islands, Philippines, Midway and Shanghai anyway, and bombed Pearl Harbor in Hawaii for good measure. Shocked and outraged, the US declared war on the Axis powers on 8 December 1941. China declared war on Japan the following day. But by then, Japan had occupied all the major rubber-producing areas of Southeast Asia, shutting off the spigot of natural rubber to the United States. However, Japanese mismanagement of rubber plantations slowed production to a trickle. Although some of this rubber was transported to Germany, there was not enough to meet its need and synthetic rubber had to plug the deficit.

The loss of the rubber plantations in Asia spelt potential disaster for the Allies' efforts in the war. The British had rubber coming in from its colony Ceylon (now Sri Lanka) and the US turned to Brazil and Liberia. Brazil was the only country in South America to enter World War II as a member of the Allied Powers. They provided soldiers to fight in Italy as well as 'rubber soldiers' who were recruited to tap the estimated twelve million *Hevea* trees in the Amazon. The US provided cash as an incentive for the recruitment, transport and support, including healthcare and religious education, of the tappers. As before, impoverished indigenous tappers were recruited with promises but they ended up with nothing, often also losing their lives. A total of 100,000 tappers were sought but, in the end, only 55,000 young and fit men (mostly from Ceara province) were forcibly recruited. These men were transported to the Amazon but, once there, they found that infrastructure was lacking. Rather than the production of rubber rising from the current 20,000 tons to 100,000 tons per year, it rose merely to 26,000 tons, failing dismally to meet Brazil's own expectations. After the war, the 'rubber soldiers' fared as rubber tappers through history have fared: poorly. Of the 55,000 sent to the Amazon, only 6,000 returned to Ceara. The fate of the remaining is unknown, but they were presumed dead. Those who returned did not see the promises they were made, of a lifetime pension and honour for their wartime efforts, kept.

Another country which got a raw deal in the rubber business was Liberia on the western coast of Africa. It was occupied by freeborn blacks and freed US slaves who had returned to Africa independently or via the offices of the American Colonization Society in the early nineteenth century. Liberia was a mass of contradictions. Despite being founded by slaves who had been denied representation in the United States, the constitution adopted in 1847 only permitted landed gentry to vote, and the specific section read as follows: 'All elections shall be by ballot and every male citizen, of twenty-one years of age, possessing real estate, shall have the right of suffrage.'[124] This was ironic, given that the majority of people who could afford to own land were wealthy Americo-Liberians who had experienced the same exclusion from suffrage in the US they were now imposing in Liberia. Further, though slavery was explicitly banned by the constitution, black plantation owners coerced and exploited indigenous labour. And most insidiously, a form of segregation was instituted in which Christian Americo-Liberians were at the top of the social order, and indigenous animistic Liberians at the bottom.[125]

In its quest to raise capital soon after declaring independence, Liberia had become indebted to Britain because the US had refused to recognise it as an independent country or support capital investment at the levels needed for a fledgling democracy to thrive. But being in debt to Britain was costly. The country limped along for a while, seeking opportunities for growth with little success. Things changed after the invention of the pneumatic tyre. Rubber became a desired commodity and Liberia had the climate to grow rubber trees that would benefit automobile industries in the US. At the same time, both the US government and the tyre company Firestone sought to secure its rubber supply chain. Despite the collapse of Fordlandia, Firestone was upbeat about the chances of a self-administered plantation in a distant land. Liberia was their choice, with the right climate for growing rubber trees, a cheap and plentiful labour force for harvesting it and a penurious government seeking investment. Liberia took a private loan of US$5 million at 7 per cent interest from the Finance Corporation of America (a subsidiary of Firestone Tyre and Rubber Company) for funding its impoverished government.[126] With the leverage of the loan and the backing of the US government, which was eager to secure an independent rubber supply stream, Firestone negotiated the ultimate sweetheart deal with Liberia in 1926[li]—a lease of a million acres at 6 cents per acre per

li This deal was to run out in 2025, but in 2009, Firestone negotiated an extension of sixteen years beyond the end of its ninety-nine-year lease, to include mining concessions. The new agreement ends in 2040. The terms are at: https://www.scribd.

year for a period of ninety-nine years, with an additional 2.5 per cent of rubber sales.[127] Indigenous Bassa people were cleared off the land—in their place, rubber trees flourished. On a plot of 90,000 acres split into forty-five divisions, trees were planted 12x15 feet apart, and a total of 850,000 rubber trees began producing high quality rubber. On the Firestone plantations, coercion and racial segregation were practiced, with indigenous labour being subjected to conditions close to slavery by Americo-Liberians and American overseers. In other words, the overseers did not share history or geography with the labourers. What could possibly go wrong? Firestone plantations, remarkably, had 'Whites only' areas to which even black Liberian diplomats were denied access but regardless, government officials were either complicit or complacent. The League of Nations accused the Liberian Government of 'systematically and for years fostering and encouraging a policy of gross intimidation and suppression' by [actions that would suppress] 'the native, prevent him from realizing his powers and limitations and prevent him from asserting himself in any way whatever, for the benefit of the dominant and colonizing race, although originally the same African stock as themselves'.[128] Several attempts were made to raise awareness about the 'virtual slaves' as Marcus Garvey put it, and as W.E.B Du Bois put it even more despondently: '... a body of local private capitalists, even if they are Black, can never free Africa; they will simply sell it into new slavery to old

---

com/document/152423546/An-Act-Ratifying-the-Amended-and-Restated-Concession-Agreement-between-the-Republic-of-Liberia-and-Firestone-Liberia-Inc. At this time, Firestone operates the world's largest rubber plantation in Liberia at 118,990 acres.

masters overseas.'[129] Nonetheless, rubber from Liberia shored up the Allies during World War II.

But, as usual, most of the benefits accrued to the top, leaving the indigenous indigent and resentful. Twenty-seven years of autocratic rule under President Tubman followed by another repressive leader, President William Tolbert, was too much. There was a revolt and rioting followed by a coup by the military in 1980. Coup after coup followed. Presidents were executed or assassinated. Through it all, Firestone ran its operations. In 1990, Charles Taylor's rebels occupied Firestone's premises and demanded the company pay taxes to him as rightful leader of Liberia. This Firestone did, despite the fact that Taylor's troops had terrorised and murdered workers on the plantation and then used it as a base for his assault on the capital Monrovia, triggering a civil war.[130] Charles Taylor's regime was briefly legitimised when he became president, but a second civil war followed and, beleaguered by internal and international pressure, Taylor resigned. Stability has returned to Liberia since 2005 and the first peaceful transfer of power took place in 2018 with former international soccer striker and Ballon d'Or winner George Weah and again in 2024 when Joseph Boakai was inaugurated.

In 2005, the International Labour Rights Fund slapped Firestone with a class-action suit on behalf of twelve Liberian workers and their twenty-three children. Suing under the Alien Tort Statute (ATS)[lii] in which the claimants alleged 'forced

lii The Alien Tort Statute was passed by US Congress in 1789 and states, 'The district courts shall have original jurisdiction of any civil action by an alien for a tort only, committed in violation of the law of nations or a treaty of the United States' (Title 28 USC 1350). In 2004, the US Supreme Court narrowed the action to suits against US entities by foreigners. On 5 May 2022, Senators Dick

labour, the modern equivalent of slavery' on the plantation. According to Dan Admonitis, a Firestone associate, each worker was required to tap 650 trees a day, spending two minutes at each tree, which works out to an unsustainable twenty-one hours per day per worker. When presented with this calculation, Mr. Admonitis walked it back as '2 minutes being a figure of speech'. Even if workers spent half that time per tree, that is still over ten hours of tapping alone, never mind the walk from tree to tree. Further, each tree had to be visited twice, once to place the collection cup and once to recover the latex. Thus, each worker had to recruit unpaid helpers, usually their children, to meet the quota. An Indiana District Court dismissed the case against Firestone, and the children appealed. Writing for 7th US Circuit Court of Appeals in Chicago,[131] Judge Richard Posner upheld the District Court's dismissal of the suit against Firestone, although he allowed that 'corporate liability is possible' under the Alien Tort Statute (ATS). His cautious judgement was that there was 'an inadequate basis to infer that Firestone violated customary international law in using the child labour'.[liii] A United Nations 2006 report 'Human Rights in Liberia's Rubber Plantations: Tapping into

---

Durbin (D-IL) and Sherrod Brown (D-OH) proposed an ATS clarification bill (S. 4155) to include suits against any defendant, citizen or not, who is present in the United States. It has not yet been brought to the full Senate for a vote.

liii In spite of the testimony of the children themselves, Judge Posner further wrote in his decision: 'Conceivably, because the fathers of the children on the plantation are well paid by Liberian standards, even the children who help their fathers with the work are, on balance, better off than the average Liberian child, and would be worse off if their fathers, unable to fill their daily quotas, lost their jobs or had to pay adult helpers, thus reducing the family's income. There is a tradeoff between family income and child labor; children are helped by the former and hurt by the latter; we don't know the

the Future' reported seven key failures to protect human rights on plantations, of which a few were: 'Concession agreements concluded with the Government of Liberia (GOL) impose very limited and vague obligations on plantation management to protect the human rights of individuals and communities living and working on the rubber plantations' and 'Child labour is frequently used on the plantations. Also many children are not registered at birth by plantation health facilities and cannot thus benefit from free education and health care.'[132] Quite far removed from the accusations of adverse environmental, health, and socio-economic impacts,[133] Firestone Natural Rubber Company (now a part of Japan's Bridgestone group) has an anodyne and uplifting website underscoring its sustainable environmental goals and broad social conscience, along with some self-congratulatory highlights touting its greater than two-billion-dollar investment in Liberia since 2003.[134] Of course, there is no doubt that this investment was badly needed by an impoverished country.

But at what cost?

Back to World War II, when the United States was staring down an impending rubber shortage. There were about a million tons of stockpiled natural rubber, although a consumption rate of 600,000 tons per year was going to quickly put a dent in it. President Franklin D. Roosevelt had seen this coming. He had established the Rubber Reserve Company (RRC) as a part of the War Production Board (WPB) to oversee supply mobilisation under the leadership of Donald Nelson, a former Sears Roebuck

---

net effect on their welfare of working on the plantation.' (*Flomo v. Firestone Natural Rubber Co LLC*, 2011)

executive. After the US joined the war, the rubber shortage was deemed critical. A rubber survey committee was launched under the leadership of financier Bernard M. Baruch, with members who included the presidents of Harvard University and the MIT. The Baruch Report was produced within the month with recommendations to appoint a rubber tsar to oversee the whole initiative, and emphasised the need to manufacture 1,037,000 tons of synthetic rubber. Roosevelt appointed William Henry Jeffers of the Union Pacific Railroad to the task, and Jeffers was determined to deliver.[135]

It is claimed that, but for the Manhattan Project, the rubber initiative would have been the most audacious and successful of the war programs. Known as 'Battling Bill' or 'Blunt Bill', Jeffers worked with dogged determination, making a lot of enemies in Washington in the process. Words were exchanged in the House of Military and Naval Affairs subcommittee where Jeffers 'roared again that Army and Navy factory expediters were "loafers" who made off with materials he could have used better'.[136] Jeffers' accusation was particularly biting because synthetic rubber production was for the war effort, and would have primarily benefited the army and navy (the US Air Force was not yet in existence). Then again, the infrastructure requirements for making synthetic rubber: boilers, pumps, valves and instrumentation, were also necessary for producing the military's other priorities: high-octane gasoline and components of escort ships which were in short supply at the time—and their need was more pressing. But Jeffers knew how to get things done by sheer determination and a thick skin. He started a vigorous recycling program which required citizens to save and turn in every scrap of rubber for the war effort. He instituted a nationwide speed limit of 35 mph and gasoline rationing in order to save tyre rubber. Synthetic rubber production in the US also increased from 3,721 tons in 1942 to 756,042 tons in 1944. Unsurprisingly enough, given Jeffers' uncompromising focus, the synthetic rubber initiative in 1945 outstripped worldwide natural rubber production.[137] Despite Germany's own successful synthetic rubber program helmed by I.G. Farben, the Allies won the war on the backs of their careful husbandry of existing supplies of rubber, their own successful production of synthetic rubber and by harnessing the power of the atom to make the most powerful bomb yet known.[138]

Figure 15: A selection of United States posters exhorting the public to save rubber scraps.[139]

The years after World War II in the United States saw the building of interstate highways under President Dwight Eisenhower and a huge spike in the number of personal automobiles—from 225 per 1000 people in 1945 to 775 per 1000 people in the year 2000,[140] tripling in a period of fifty-five years. The population, during the same time, grew from 150 million to 280 million,[141] nearly doubling. Add in commercial and government vehicles, and automobile growth and tyre rubber demand were growing inexorably. Tyre demand in the rest of the world also started growing, and the proportion of the middle classes who rated car ownership as a necessity went up as living standards increased. The tyre industry alone absorbed 76 per cent of rubber production and just this century, worldwide natural rubber production grew from 7 million metric tons in 2000 to almost 13 million metric tons in 2020.[142]

Rubber production in the twenty-first century is dominated by the Association of Natural Rubber Producing Countries (ANRPC)—Bangladesh, Cambodia, China, India, Indonesia, Malaysia, Myanmar, Papua New Guinea, Philippines, Singapore, Sri Lanka, Thailand and Vietnam, all in Asia—which produce 91 per cent of the supply. In 2021, the Côte d'Ivoire produced the fourth highest quantity of natural rubber after Thailand, Indonesia and Vietnam,[143] and Liberia's output was about a quarter of Côte d'Ivoire production levels. Central America, where it all began, does not feature in the top producing countries. Guatemala and Colombia export the largest quantity of rubber from South America, whereas Brazil produces about 200,000 tons and consumes most of it.[144] ANRPC estimates global demand (14.738 million tons) in 2023 to outstrip global supply of 14.672 million tons.

With a resurgence in the price of rubber, vast areas of Indonesia are being cleared for plantations with staggering damage to biodiversity, including to endangered orangutans that are endemic to the area, due to deforestation for palm oil or rubber tree plantations.[145] Allegations of labour exploitation in Liberia and land grabs in Cambodia[146] are familiar chronic problems.

What of consumption? China is the biggest consumer of natural rubber, hovering at 40 per cent of worldwide production. Other Asian countries with their rapidly expanding middle classes are huge consumers. With air travel taking off again after the COVID-19 pandemic, airlines are placing large orders. Aeroplane tyres use 100 per cent natural rubber for its high tensile strength, vibration dampening and tear resistance. Russia's war in Ukraine has also driven up demand as countries stockpile essential supplies. Europe has stopped importing Russian synthetic rubber, leaving more for the country's own needs, but the war is almost certainly imperilling Russia's import of natural rubber and the exit of tyre companies also has a detrimental economic fallout.[147]

Rubber has catalysed world economic growth. Table 1 below shows some correlations between world Gross Domestic Product (GDP) before and after rubber was discovered.

Table 1: Growth in population, GDP and rubber production over two millennia

Year	0	1000	1500	1913	1950	1973	1998
World population[148]	230,820	268,273	437,818	1,791,020	2,524,531	3,913,482	5,907,680
World GDP[149]	102,536	116,790	247,116	2,704,782	5,336,101	16,059,180	33,725,635
GDP increase per year from previous number		0.0011	0.0042	37,288.67	71,116.73	466,220.83	706,658.2
Total rubber production[150] in tons and (tonnes)*	Unavailable	Unavailable	Unavailable	120,000 (108,000)	2,000,000[151] (1,800,000)	9,500,000 (8,550,000)	15,000,000 (13,500,000)

*Includes natural and synthetic rubber production in tons (1 ton=907 kg) and tonnes (1 tonne=1,000 kg)

The Organisation for Economic Co-operation and Development (OECD) World Economy summary says in the introduction of *The Contours of World Development*:[152]

> Over the past millennium, world population rose 22–fold. Per capita income increased 13–fold, world GDP nearly 300–fold. This contrasts sharply with the preceding millennium, when world population grew by only a sixth, and there was no advance in per capita income.
>
> From the year 1000 to 1820 the advance in per capita income was a slow crawl — the world average rose about 50 per cent. Most of the growth went to accommodate a fourfold increase in population.
>
> Since 1820, world development has been much more dynamic. Per capita income rose more than eightfold, population more than fivefold.

Is there any doubt that rubber has accelerated the world's economy? Not at all. Rubber has undoubtedly raised global living standards. It has also caused enormous damage to its producing plants, to those who tap it, to the ecosystems and the surrounding flora and fauna destroyed by frenetic rubber harvesting or displaced by plantations and to those tainted by the environmental fallout of rubber disposal. The production of synthetic rubber has obviously helped with meeting demand, but its raw materials are petroleum by-products. With the gradual swivel underway towards alternative sources of energy in order to ameliorate global warming and climate change, forays into new sources implies exciting and innovative areas of research, and options range from recycling to biomass-based products. Any reduction in petroleum drilling will almost certainly reduce the availability of its by-products and consequently impact synthetic rubber synthesis.[153]

Another paradigmatic shift that is being considered is a new category of human diaspora: the push to colonise the moon and other planets in the solar system, and maybe even range beyond it within a few lifetimes. Would rubber be needed for the mission or for the longer-term? Almost certainly. It is hard to envision gaskets, tyres, tubing and other parts fundamental to operating machinery without rubber. Transporting natural or synthetic rubber will be expensive, but transporting its toxic and flammable precursors—styrene, butadiene and isoprene—would be dangerous; it seems pretty much a given that it will be prepared rubber that travels. Pound for pound, natural rubber is a more resilient and useful substance than synthetic rubber, so, as demand rises for extraterrestrial uses, the production of natural rubber is going to have to go up to meet that demand on top of the rising demand on our planet itself. Less destructive methods to obtain natural rubber and a new commercial source—the Russian dandelion, *Taraxacum kok-saghyz*—are being investigated so it is conceivable that rubber production could stretch to meet these new challenges. How resilient rubber will be in an oxygen-free environment, or in temperatures that may range beyond those on earth is also open to question. If a rubber item degrades, could it be recycled in the extraterrestrial location? Probably not; the energy needed would be prohibitive. So it would be discarded, and we know vulcanised rubber does not degrade readily. Therefore, we are going to export some of our existing problems to other places. Thinking through how refuse or recycling can be managed will benefit both extraterrestrial locations and this planet.

Rubber has fuelled human development. Like any technology, it has benefits and drawbacks. It has bettered the human condition, but at the cost of human lives and environmental degradation. But other developments tilt towards the positive side. There are signs that the less ecologically destructive source of natural rubber with the same characteristics as para rubber may be on the commercial horizon, obtained from *Taraxacum kok-saghyz*, which grows across temperate regions and even in slightly degraded soils. Combined with a less exploitative model than plantations, such as the smallholder farm (Chapter 10), it might reap benefits for pollinators as well for rubber production while also providing a supplemental stream of natural rubber. This is because dandelions support a wide variety of insect life at the bottom of the trophic pyramid and, being an annual plant with a quicker turnaround than *Hevea* trees, offers more rapid levels of production. It would also be significantly more possible to grow it for rubber production in temperate regions rather than bulldozing biodiversity-rich rainforests for *Hevea* plantations. It is crucial we preserve what is left of our tropical rainforests to mitigate climate change, and for this we will hopefully turn to plantations of rubber which include smallholders in tropical and temperate regions with fields of nodding yellow flowers buzzing with pollinators.

There is hope.

II
Gut Architecture

Preface

When life began to evolve on earth about 3.8 billion years ago, it consisted of single-celled bacteria-like organisms bound by a fat-based 'lipid' membrane which isolated the contents of their cell from the aqueous environment. They were poisoned by oxygen[liv] and needed to forage organic molecules from the environment or, in other words, 'eat' each other to survive. About 200 million years later, some bacteria generated chlorophyll, the lipid molecule that could harvest light energy, and convert it to chemical energy stored in carbohydrates.[lv]

liv Oxygen is highly reactive. In the absence of a biochemical pathway to convert oxygen into harmless products, like water, it can damage DNA and other essential molecules. Aerobic organisms have such a pathway, and anaerobic organisms do not. Early life forms were anaerobic because there was not yet any oxygen in the atmosphere.

lv The process of photosynthesis uses light energy to join up atoms originating from carbon dioxide and water to make carbohydrates. An example is glucose, which can be funnelled to make other molecules or broken down to release energy for metabolic processes.

By doing so, such 'photosynthetic' bacteria were freed from the need to eat but became even more attractive as food. To survive, they had to deter predators from feeding on them—and the arms race between photosynthetic prey and predators began. Lipids could be used not only to make membranes and chlorophyll, they could also be used to make antifeedants, like rubber, the subject of this book.

As tectonic plates shifted and the continents coalesced to form Pangaea in the period known as the Ediacaran, some animals were evolving into super-predators. Although relatively small in size compared to today's giants, evolution equipped them with a head bristling with sensors, muscles to pursue their prey, a mouth with teeth to rend this prey apart and a digestive system to break them down and absorb nutrition. As Pangaea broke up into Gondwanaland and Laurasia, early flowering plants evolved. They exploited animals' predatory interest in them by recruiting them to spread their pollen or seeds but first they had to deter predators from eating them. Latex was a particularly effective antifeedant and, as flowering plants diversified and spread with the help of pollinators, so did latex.

Chapter 6 describes the Amazon and Congo River basins where enormous herbivore diversity spurred the evolution of some of the most prolific latex-producing plants—*Hevea brasiliensis* and *Landolphia owariensis*. Millions of years later, these two areas would be linked by the shared tragedy of human exploitation in the pursuit of rubber. Geographically, these two regions had been connected when they were part of Gondwanaland, and they remain linked today by many parallels of flora, fauna and climate. These shared ecological and biological features set the stage for the discussion of the various threads that led to the evolution of latex-bearing plants.

Chapter 7 describes the purpose and mechanism of antifeedants. From their very naissance, herbivores and plants entered an evolutionary battle wherein the feeding strategies of animals were countered by the evolution of deterrent strategies by plants. The secretions plants produce, their varying structures, and the tactics creatures use to overcome them are described—for instance, caterpillars drain latex out of leaves before feeding, which demonstrates that latex is indeed an antifeedant.

Chapter 8 describes how animals respond to latex. Latex remains liquid when treated with alkali, but coagulates in acid. In this chapter, I will present a novel hypothesis that the presence of latex shaped the evolutionary divergence of digestive systems in herbivores. Browsing polygastric animals like goats, whose forage may contain abundant latex, have evolved a digestive system with multiple neutral-to-alkaline stomach chambers with symbionts where latex-rich foods are broken down before passing into an acidic chamber. Grazing monogastric herbivores like horses eat latex-free grasses and have acid-containing stomach chambers which could be blocked if latex is ingested with forage. The bacterium *Bacillus thuringiensis* (Bt) has exploited the alkaline guts of plant-munching larval insects to selectively target them with toxins, and these toxins have been further exploited to make genetically modified (GM) plants which are toxic to target pests. The impact of Bt on the environment and on non-target animals that encounter it in forage is explored.

Chapter 9 explores gutta-percha whose chemical structure[lvi] is the mirror image of natural rubber. It is produced by *Palaquium*

---

lvi Rubber and gutta-percha are related molecules. Both are made from isoprene units, but they are linked differently. This gives them quite different properties. For example, rubber is elastic, but gutta-percha is not.

trees from Southeast Asia and *Manilkara* trees from South America. Its resistance to salt water and cold temperatures makes it an ideal coating for undersea cables. This chapter describes the awe its properties evoked in a journalist.

Chapter 10 describes the negative impact of rubber on many aspects of the ecosystem, from large plantations of *Hevea brasiliensis* on biodiversity-rich moist tropical forests to the accumulation and impact of waste products. Although the large plantation model has made Southeast Asia a powerhouse of natural rubber production, the search is on for other options, such as smallholder plots and potential new sources of rubber.

Three appendices expand on the more technical aspects of this topic. Appendix A describes the evolution of the biochemical pathways for rubber synthesis. Appendix B describes the iterative changes in gene number and sequence that cause long-term evolutionary change using examples of molecules that have different properties but evolved from a common progenitor. Appendix C provides descriptions of plant-produced secondary metabolites with deterrent functions.

6

Continental Drift

Allan McDonald, the director of NASA's Space Shuttle Solid Rocket Motor Project at the aeronautical firm Morton Thiokol Inc., and his team are worried. They are fretful over the freezing temperature that is forecast for 28 January 1986, the date set for the launch of the Challenger space shuttle from Cape Canaveral, Florida. They were the manufacturers of the O-rings which sealed the Space Shuttle's solid rocket booster, and testing data had shown that the O-ring could fail in cold temperatures. NASA administrators are also worried. Launch has already been postponed three times. NASA has a lot riding on the publicity of this 'Teacher in Space' mission. The purpose is to generate public enthusiasm for the reusable space shuttle program and draw attention to the importance of education for producing the next generation of scientists. Congress is not happy with the expensive delays. NASA pressures Morton Thiokol to reconsider their decision to ground Challenger.

Morton Thiokol reiterates its no-launch assessment. They are overruled.

Launch day arrives. It is as cold as predicted.

The hundreds of students and their teachers gathered in the auditorium at Concord High School in New Hampshire are excited, and cheer the countdown to lift-off which is being screened on a giant television monitor.[154] They watch as Challenger, strapped to a massive orange external tank and two solid rocket boosters, rises from the launch pad. T+60 seconds after launch … T+65 seconds … T+70 seconds. The two solid rocket boosters, also made by contractor Morton Thiokol, and the subject of blow-by[lvii] concern from the engineers, are to detach at two minutes and fall into the Atlantic Ocean where they would be recovered and brought back to the Kennedy Space Center. But, at T+73 seconds, disaster struck. There is a burst of static as a starburst filled the screen where there had just seconds ago been a rising plume. There is a stunned silence.

Challenger had exploded.

Later, President Ronald Reagan gave a sorrowful speech where he paraphrased John Gillespie Magee Jr.'s poem *High Flight*, '[the astronauts] slipped the surly bonds of earth [to] touch the face of God', and appointed a commission to investigate the disaster. The commission recruited Nobel Laureate Richard Feynman—scientist, teacher, raconteur, musician and a gifted science communicator. Feynman understood the cause of the explosion was blow-by due to the failure of an O-ring seal. However, it was not just knowing of the O-ring's failure, but of explaining it to a largely lay audience.

In front of television cameras, Feynman picked up an O-ring at room temperature and squeezed it in a C-clamp. It flexed

lvii Blow-by is used to describe the unwanted leakage of combustion gases due to the failure of sealant rings between a piston and cylinder wall.

easily. He called for a glass of ice water, and placed the C-clamp with the O-ring in it. He waited for a few seconds for the ring to reach the new, lower temperature, and pulled it out. This time, the O-ring did not flex as much. Feynman explained: 'I took this stuff that I got from your seal, and I put it in ice water. And I discovered that when you put some pressure on it for a while, and then undo it, it doesn't stretch back. It stays the same dimension. In other words, for a few seconds at least—for more seconds than that—there's no resilience in this particular material when it's at a temperature of 32 degrees. I believe that has some significance for our problem …'

The O-ring seal that had failed, costing 7 lives and over 3 billion in US dollars, was made of rubber.

Well before humans were even dreamed of in evolutionary terms, never mind attempting space exploration, rubber was already going global. By the time plants evolved from algal progenitors, the motion of continental landmasses was imposing new pressures on living things, both because of the changing environment and because of one another reason—300 million years ago (Ma), in the Carboniferous period of the Palaeozoic era, all of the landmasses had collided into one massive supercontinent called Pangaea which resembled the letter 'C', stretching from the North Pole to the South Pole (Figure 15). The major ocean cradling the outer curve of the 'C' shape was called Panthalassa. Tucked into the inner curve of the 'C' was a smaller ocean called the Tethys. Vast forests of non-flowering gymnosperms—horsetails, club mosses, cycads and conifers—supported herbivores on land with leaf and seed and pumped out an atmosphere comprising 35 per cent oxygen. Responding to the high oxygen levels and plentiful food, animals of the time grew to unprecedented sizes. Human-sized millipedes, cat-sized scorpions and predatory flying insects with wingspans that were measurable in feet roamed the planet. Amphibians varied in size from six feet to six inches in length, but they were tethered to the water to lay their fragile eggs. These amphibians were the as-yet-unrealised ancestors of all other vertebrates because the major evolutionary step of laying leathery eggs that were impervious to drying out was just starting to occur. From this innovation, reptiles emerged. And as reptiles ranged further inland and began morphing some of their scales to feathers, birds with forelimbs modified into wings emerged as well, laying eggs with shells that were fortified with calcium carbonate.[lviii]

But continents were still on the move—Pangaea began splitting into Gondwanaland and Laurasia. The climate changed, becoming cooler and drier, and the shifting landmasses triggered the vast existing rainforests to collapse across today's Europe and America, burying them deep down to become coal and petroleum deposits in the future. The remaining forests changed composition and fragmented into islands, a bounty for speciation to occur. Oxygen levels plummeted, and the monstrous insects shrank in size. A short fifty million years later, around 250 Ma, on the cusp of the Permian–Triassic, volcanic eruptions in what is now Siberia cause stockpiled fossil fuels to burn, pumping out carbon dioxide in such vast quantities that the air became hellishly hot, reaching average daytime temperatures of 90°F/32.2°C.[155] By comparison, the average today is around 60°F/15.5°C. The surrounding seas turned acidic, with pH levels dropping to between 6.5 and 7, compared to between 7.5 to 9 today. This combination of inescapable heat, the high levels

lviii Mineral inclusions make flexible biomaterials stronger but brittle. For example, leathery eggshells are mineralised to make brittle eggshells and flexible cartilage is mineralised to make bone.

of carbon and sulphur dioxide and the acidic waters with low oxygen levels propelled the period of the first great extinction nicknamed 'The Great Dying'. It is estimated that seven in ten of land vertebrates and eight in ten of marine vertebrates vanished, among more than half of all forms of life. The major loss though was among marine invertebrates, with 87 per cent of all genera going extinct. The iconic trilobites[lix] which had diversified into 22,000 species—almost as many species as bony fish today—and which had hung on through climates thick and thin for 270 million years, were gone in the blink of a geological eye. The gaping niches left without occupants spurred the naissance of the reptilian archosaurs which predated dinosaurs, and the therapsids[lx] from which mammals evolved.

After a forty-million-year period of stability came the end of the Triassic, around 208 Ma. This included another period of extensive volcanic activity, which caused further extinctions. But a few small reptiles survived this upheaval into the next geologic period, the famous Jurassic era, evolving into the iconic dinosaurs of that period: the herbivorous sauropods, with their immense bodies and long necks and tails, and carnivorous theropods such as *Allosaurus* with their large, serrated teeth. As the Jurassic period was giving way to the Cretaceous, another birth occurred—insignificant at the time, but one with immense staying power and major repercussions for the future—that of flowering plants. Also emerging at this time were some shrew-

---

lix One of the earliest groups of arthropods—the class which contains insects, crabs, scorpions and spiders. Although incredibly abundant, widespread, and diverse, they all died out in this single extinction event.

lx Reptilian animals which gave rise to mammals and were distinguished by a distinctive skull structure and legs which projected vertically down.

like nocturnal therapsids which developed fur and nursed their young on nutritious secretions from their mammary glands.

The landmass of Gondwanaland, during the early Jurassic, had contained Africa's western skull-like projection nestled into the cavity on the eastern side of South America, creating a nexus between today's Amazon and Congo basins.[lxi] During the Cretaceous period, the breakup of Gondwanaland[lxii] caused Africa to drift away slowly eastwards towards its present-day location (Figure 16). South America shifted towards North America, which was then a part of the supercontinent of Laurasia. The Indian subcontinent was a massive triangular island and was just starting to drift from the western edge of Antarctica to begin its long journey northeast towards Asia, into which it would ram about 150 million years later, throwing up the Himalayas. Australia, attached to the other side of Antarctica from the Indian subcontinent, was moving away as well, preserving its marsupial species from the dominance of modern placental mammals that were abundant in Asia, Europe and Africa. Meanwhile, the plants were also hitchhiking to new areas on the moving continents and spreading abundantly using a novel reproductive structure: the flower.

A flower is just a modified leaf which contains the sex organs of the plants. Whereas the abundant gymnosperms[lxiii] proudly

---

lxi The Congo River has also been called the Zaire River, but in this book the name Congo will be maintained throughout.

lxii Thought to be due to a thinner earth's crust at this point, which allowed the upwelling of the asthenosphere under Cape Agulhas at the tip of Africa.

lxiii In Greek, *gymnos* means 'naked' and *sperma* means 'seed'. The gymnosperms are a major group of non-flowering, but seed-producing evergreen plants that including horsetails, conifers and cycads.

displayed their genitalia in cones which later harboured their seeds, flowering plants shyly (and slyly) sheathed theirs within a cavity, thereby also protecting their seeds from roving herbivores. This shielding is reminiscent of how placental mammals protect their unborn young within their bodies. These flowering plants evolved hard armour-like wood, but some also carried liquid defences on the inside: latex. Latex-bearing plants originated on the southern continent, Gondwanaland, and latex genes would spread through the evolving flowering plant clade, providing protection from browsing animals and plugging the structural damage that browsing caused.

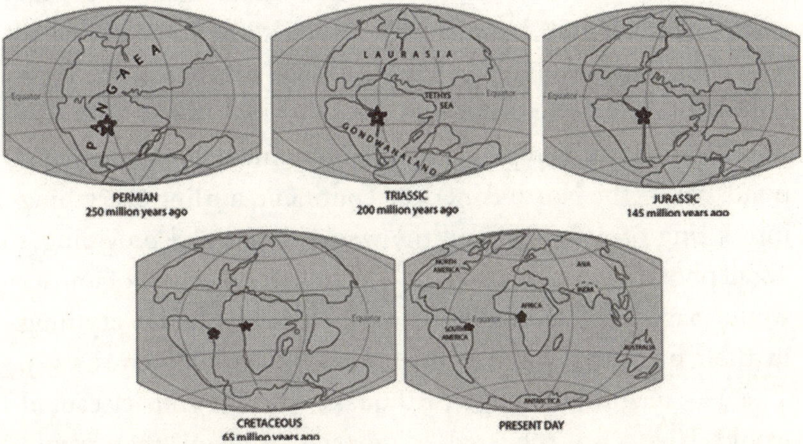

Figure 16: The making and breaking of continents over time. Supercontinent Pangaea over a span of 250 million years, from the Permian era to present-day Cenozoic era, the age of the mammal. The age of the dinosaurs lasted from 252–66 Ma (divided into the Triassic, Jurassic and Cretaceous periods within the Mesozoic era). The origin of flowering plants can be traced back to the Jurassic and they flourished in the Cretaceous period, during significant continental drift. The stars mark the location of the current Amazon and Congo rivers prior to, and after, continental separation in the Jurassic. Figure modified from US Geological Survey.[156]

By 66 Ma, Africa had already broken away from South America, India had slammed very slowly but spectacularly into the underbelly of Asia and a three-way split was occurring between Antarctica, Australia and South America—with the landmasses drifting southwards, eastwards and westwards, respectively. Then, unexpectedly, a twelve-kilometre-wide (around six miles) asteroid called Chicxulub slammed into what is now the Gulf of Mexico. At the instant of impact, the earth below the impact site would have liquefied and risen into the air, before falling as either melted rock to a depth of 130 metres at the site or strafing down as tektites (which are spherical glass bullets) up to 3,200 kilometres away in North Dakota. The crater that Chicxulub made measures 150 kilometres wide and 20 kilometres deep. The shockwave would have exploded living things in the blast radius. It would have triggered seiches—like the 'sloshing' of water in a bathtub only much more monumental—in lakes and ponds across the North American continent, hurling everything into a ring of debris around the water bodies and providing a 'fossil photograph' of the instant. The tremendous heat of impact would have triggered forest fires which obliterated everything in their path and raised temperatures 1,500 kilometres away. The 11+ magnitude mega-earthquake that the impact caused would have also triggered a monster tsunami that would have surged out to sea for thousands of kilometres over many days, causing a ring of flooding in Africa, Europe and South America bordering the Atlantic Ocean.[157] (By comparison, in 2004, the 9.1 magnitude underwater Banda Aceh earthquake touched off the tsunami which killed over 300,000 people from Southeast Asia to East Africa). Findings indicate that the planet continued to shudder for months after being slammed by the asteroid. The dust from the impact blotted out the sun for years and caused the widespread extinction of plants and animals alike, most significantly the dinosaurs.

The small, scurrying shrew-like mammals that had evolved in the Triassic survived the cataclysm, probably because they had huddled in caves underground which were somewhat protected from the climatic upheaval; these subsequently expanded, with range and diversity, into all the habitats that had been suddenly and tragically evacuated by their dinosaur occupants. The continents continued to drift. Latex-bearing flowering plants rapidly proliferated through the Amazon and Congo basins, even as the two regions shifted to new geographic and climatological locations.

The Amazon and Congo river basins share more than their origins in Gondwanaland. Both of them have gone through transitions from inland seas to rivers, and are the largest rivers in the world, draining massive catchment areas and emptying dizzying amounts of water into the Atlantic Ocean. The two regions show shared weather patterns. Both have three types of waters that are populated by fish with shared origins which have diversified to adapt to extreme local conditions. There is also high biodiversity among regional herbivores, which provided the selective pressure necessary for plants to produce formidable defences against predation. To set the stage, let's first examine these shared features.

The Amazon and the Congo are the two largest rivers by drainage area in the world. In first place, the Amazon basin drains 2.25 million square miles, discharging around 4 million cubic feet of water per second into the western South Atlantic. In second place, the Congo drains 1.5 million square miles, and releases 1.4 million cubic feet of water per second into the eastern South Atlantic. There is a seesaw of climatic conditions between the Amazon and Congo basins: floods in one basin coincide with droughts in the other.[158] The vast amount of transpiration and rainfall in the Amazon and Congo leads to another reciprocal climactic link with rising motions in one region causing subsidence in the other. These two great rivers also share the presence of three distinct types of water: clear water, white water (typically tan in colour) and black water. The main Amazon River, called the Solimões, upstream of the city of Manaus, rises in the Andes. Initially, its water is colourless and clear due to a lack of suspended material and organic colourants. Its pH range is broad, varying from 4.5 to 7.8. As the Solimões progresses downstream, it erodes its steep banks and the landslides that ensue introduce silt and minerals into the now tan-coloured 'white' water. Light does not penetrate far, and there are few plants in the river except for those that fall in or bob along the surface. It supports insect life such as biting mosquitoes, and the water has an alkaline pH between 6.2 and 7.2. The third main type of water, black water, is introduced by the Rio Negro, a tributary which encounters the Solimões at the *Encontro das Águas* or 'Meeting of Waters' near Manaus. Although transparent, the water is tinted brown from organic matter and contains little by way of minerals. Light does not penetrate far and there is little plant or animal life in this river. It is highly acidic, with pH ranging from 3.8 to 4.9, and it does not support insects: there are few biting mosquitoes around black water.[159]

The Congo River, similarly, has clear, white and black water. The upper Congo River includes Chambeshi River which originates in Zambia and flows north into the murky brown waters of the Lualaba, which becomes the main river, and reaches the Boyoma Falls, a series of seven large waterfalls over sixty miles south of Kisangani. The northern region is drained by tributaries of the Likouala-aux-herbes River with its black-water and acidic pH of 3.8 meandering through peaty swampland. The only white water is the nutrient-poor Ubangi River, with a pH of 7.4.[160] There are a few tributaries with clear water and the southern tributaries are mostly black water. The middle Congo River lies south of Boyoma Falls and is navigable for a thousand miles. The river slows down at Malebo Pool where, on the northern bank, is located Brazzaville, the capital of the Republic of Congo; on the southern bank stands Kinshasa, the capital of the Democratic Republic of the Congo. Downstream of Malebo Pool are the Livingstone Falls, over 200 miles of rapids marking the boundary of the lower Congo River until Matadi, heading out to the ocean[161] (See Figure 17).

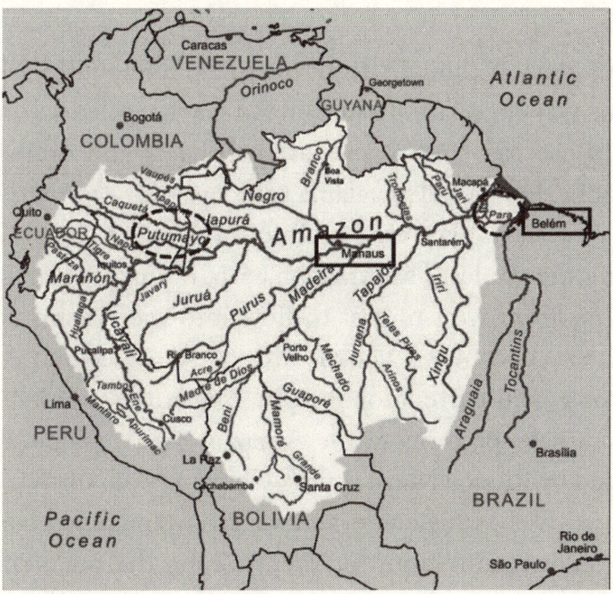

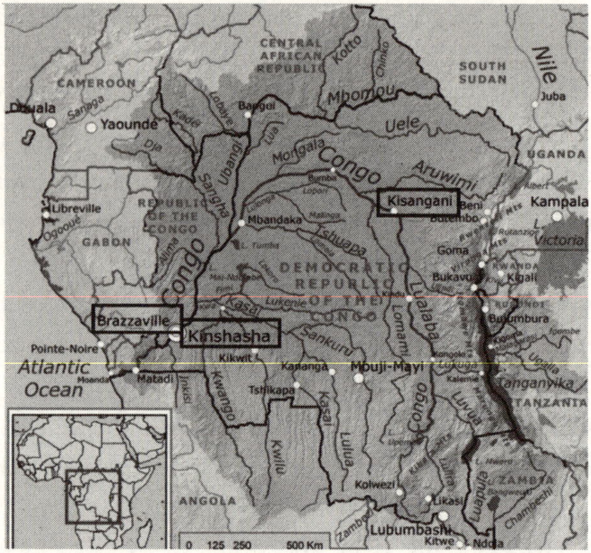

Figure 17: Locations of key cities along the Amazon River basin (top panel) and Congo River basin (bottom panel). Key cities are identified by black rectangles, and significant historical rubber tapping regions, the Para and Putumayo in the Amazon, by a broken oval line.[162]

The Amazon is thought to have emerged about 15 Ma. The Amazon was once part of a vast inland sea that filled a depression between the east and west coast highlands and drained into the Pacific. As Gondwanaland split up, the westward-bound South American plate crashed into the Nazca plate and began uplifting the Andes. The Amazon basin drainage then changed directions from west to east to flow into the Atlantic. By the end of the Miocene, ~5 Ma, the lifting had ceased and Amazon River took on its current topography. The process of establishing these drainage patterns in the Amazon over geologic time, as described by Russell Mapes of the University of North Carolina in Chapel Hill in his doctoral dissertation, included collecting 3,274 zircon grains from sediments along the main river and fourteen tributaries across the basin (no small task) and then measuring the ratio of lead to uranium ($^{206}Pb/^{238}U$) or two different isotopes of lead ($^{207}Pb/^{206}Pb$) to establish their age. The results were matched with geochronological maps of the basin to establish the zircon's provenance. The direction of flow of water in the basin during different geological times could thereby be inferred.[163]

The Congo's origins are murky. Drainage of the massive region has been in flux since about 800 Ma and appears to have switched directions and even primary river channels. Takemoto and colleagues used animal phylogeny[lxiv] and gathered geological evidence to suggest that the Congo has provided a stable geographical barrier which separated species since 34 Ma.[164] According to them, until about 34 Ma, the Congo and the other primary rivers, the Lualaba and Oubangi, appear to have flowed north into a sea which covered the upper portion of the continent but which later receded, leaving behind what is today the Congo basin. Subsequently, the uplift of the eastern portion and the splitting apart which begat the Rift Valley was accompanied by subsidence of the western portion of the continent, driving the movement of water from the basin to the Atlantic, and the waters of the Lualaba and Oubangi Rivers gained access to the Atlantic using the Congo's channel. Stankiewicz and de Wit, on the other hand, think that the drainage may have initially flowed east, not north. This hypothesis would imply that a major delta was located on the eastern side of the continent during the Cretaceous. Such a delta is thought to exist at the mouth of Rufiji River in Tanzania, but direct evidence by seismic studies have not been published, although they may exist. As Stankiewicz and de Wit delicately put it, 'Informal discussions with colleagues from a well-known energy exploration company have alluded to the

---

lxiv Phylogenies show evolutionary history, including lines of descent and relationships with other groups of organisms both living and dead. They are constructed using DNA, protein and morphological data.

fact that existing seismic data has revealed a large Cretaceous delta in the Rufiji region.'[165] The current topology of the Congo River is recent, dating to only about 2 Ma, significantly to a time when primates and hominids in Africa were undergoing divergence in central and western Africa. This is when bonobos and chimpanzees diverged from a common ancestor on different banks of the Congo River, and the *Homo* clade, from which modern humans evolved, was just emerging.[166]

Oriented and overlaid as they would have been while appended in the Jurassic, in 145 Ma, there is an interesting symmetry of the structure of the basins of the river, as if conjoined twins were separated (Figure 18). This is a curiosity rather than a fact, because the rivers are younger than the separation of the continents. However, the symmetry of the rivers foreshadows a symmetry of geography which may have exerted similar selective pressures, especially as the two regions remained tropical throughout. Biological parallels exist between the Amazon and Congo, harking back to both shared origins and shared pressures.

Figure 18: An imagined nexus between the Amazon and Congo basins in the Jurassic period.

Let's start with the fish. Characids are a group of laterally compressed diurnal (as in, active during the day) silvery fish, such as tetras, which are found in the Amazon and Congo basins. Although there are characids in Central America, they are thought to be recent invaders.[lxv] Their presence in both the Amazon and Congo basins point to a shared ancestry preceding the breakup of Gondwanaland.[167] They are unusual among fishes because they make no audible sound. For communication, they instead have a Weberian apparatus, which is a sensitive organ specialised for conducting vibrations made by the swim bladder to the inner ear. This is analogous to us using bursts of air expelled from the lungs, rather than making sounds using our larynx, for communication. The other linking feature is the extraordinary diversity of fish species contained in these basins.

Amazon's fish diversity is legendary; there are over 2,000 recorded species, some of which have successfully adapted even to the acidic[168] and nutrient-poor waters of the Rio Negro.[169] Many also have fearsome reputations. For example, piranhas are notorious for their ferocity and bloodthirstiness. When food is scarce, they are likely to attack en masse and strip to the bone anything that moves, even each other. Another infamous Amazon denizen is the slender, one-inch-long parasitic candiru fish which normally preys on the larger catfish, entering their gill cavity to feed on blood. It is feared for swimming up urine streams into penises or vaginas.[170] Once inside the body, trying to pull it out can cause it to flare its opercular spines and lodge itself into the cavity, after which it cannot be dislodged without

---

lxv Two species of dragon snakehead fish in the Western Ghats in Southern India were found to have diverged from the true snakeheads in the Chanidae family 120 Mya when Gondwanaland broke up, providing evidence for their antecedents being present across this continent.

causing a haemorrhage. The Congo is no slouch for housing peculiar fish either. With over 1,270 species exquisitely adapted to the diverse habitats that the Congo provides, and include the one-metre-long Goliath tigerfish (*Hydrocynus goliath*) with dagger-like teeth lining its fearsome jaws and the poisonous Congo pufferfish (*Tetraodon mirius*) which, like its more famous marine cousin, the Fugu porcupinefish, can inflate itself to several times its normal size when frightened. The weirdest of all of the Congo's fish may be the depigmented blind fish, *Lamprologus lethops,* which is presumed to live in the deepest parts of the river at depths of 220 meters (720 feet), which occur in the 320 kilometres of lower river. The rapids here are so fast and difficult even for fish to navigate that speciation has occurred due to the splintered microhabitats.[171] It seems the waters are roiling even at the depths at which these fish live. If a fish accidentally swims into an upwelling, it can be shot so rapidly to the surface that it dies due to the bubbling out of dissolved gasses from its blood and tissues, a condition called 'the bends'. This is an affliction sometimes seen in divers who ascend too rapidly from deep to shallow waters.[172]

Then there is the shared ancestry of flowering plants, which originated about 200 Ma in the Triassic, and diversified as the landmass broke up into Gondwanaland and Laurasia. Laurasia inherited most of the non-flowering conifers, whereas Gondwanaland contained what would become flowering tropical hardwoods.[173] The slow drift of the continental masses caused evolutionary radiation due to changing environmental conditions and migration into new ecological niches as landmasses made contact with other landmasses. The plant–animal relationships and arms races that followed led to an increased prevalence of latex as well as a variety of colourful chemical antifeedants that permeated the wood to make it unpalatable to animals or resistant to bacterial- or mould-mediated rotting. Some of the most visually spectacular and decay-resistant hardwoods have South American or African origins.

Flowering plants include towering trees, spreading shrubs and grasses. Pollination by air currents was adopted by grasses, but it necessitated the production of a vast amount of pollen, which is expensive to produce and a waste of energy, especially when only a small fraction of the pollen produced lands on the female stigma for fertilisation. Many grasses remain small (less than seven feet tall) for this reason, while others engage in vegetative reproduction using suckers or stolons[lxvi] to supplement their sexual reproduction capability. However, many other flowering plants leveraged predatory wasps which feasted on flower pollen, a rich source of protein as it happens, to carry additional pollen on their bodies to other flowers they visited, and thereby deliver pollen directly to flower stigmas for fertilisation. A wasp going from one flower to another could unintentionally deliver pollen directly to stigmas for fertilisation. Bees evolved from such wasps.[174] This pollinator-mediated targeting allowed flowers to waste less energy producing vast amounts of pollen that would just fall by the wayside. Some flowers even started providing a nectar reward for this service, and further advertised their presence with colourful petals and alluring scents.

But when insects find a source of free food, they lay eggs on it so their larvae can avail themselves of the food source as well. That was not part of the bargain the flowering plants were seeking when they attracted pollinators. Something had

---

lxvi Above- or below-ground horizontal stems by which some plants, such as grasses and bananas, reproduce.

to be done to put out the 'Trespassers Not Welcome' signs. The plants turned to what they already had—lots of terpenes[lxvii] that were used for scent and cell wall construction. By linking terpenes in long, long chains, these plants produced rubber which they enclosed in membrane vesicles and dispersed in an aqueous 'latex' solution. To this they could add other nasties, like poisons, and spread it throughout the plant through delicate tubes called laticifers, much like lymph is carried around animal bodies in lymphatic vessels. A caterpillar taking a bite of the leaf would damage these laticifers and ingest a mouthful of latex. The delicate vesicles would burst and release their rubber strands to form gummy tangles in the mouthparts of the larva, which, lacking hands, would vainly try to clear away the stuff. Give your dog a spoonful of peanut butter. Then imagine that the dog does not have a tongue—because larvae do not—and you will get the idea. The ooze also flows around the larva's body like quicksand, hardening as it dries out. The larva cannot feed or move. It dies. Problem solved.

But evolution does not produce traits to order. They are produced by genetic accidents—and plants that already had genes that produced unpalatable substances would have survived a little better than those that did not. Since the herbivory pressure was unrelenting, latex began to spread like wildfire. Terpenes, such as essential oils, volatiles and latex, are widely distributed in the plant clade testifying to their evolutionary value as deterrents to herbivory. Plants have a plethora—over 150 genes—for terpene synthesis, making these

---

lxvii Terpenes are ubiquitous lipids with the empirical formula C_5H_8 and constitute membrane molecules such as cholesterol. Plant terpenes are responsible for characteristic aromas (e.g., limonene of lemons), colours (e.g., carotenes of carrots), or bioactivity (e.g., cannabidiol of cannabis). Terpenes constitute many animal pheromones. Terpenes can also be linked into long chains to make rubber molecules.

chemicals remarkably widespread and versatile.[175] This really is significant—if terpenes had not continuously pulled their evolutionary weight by providing adaptive traits, they would not have diversified to this extent.

The plants and animals that had thus far evolved together were put under new selection pressures because new habitats were formed—such as lots of beachfront property—and they were filled rapidly through adaptive radiation. The evolutionary record shows that this process, dubbed vicariance-driven speciation, produced diverse offspring when a single population is separated into two by a newly erected barrier, such as a river.[176] Sarah McIntyre and colleagues examined biogeographical distribution and timelines with the molecular record for twenty-four different vertebrate species, such as closely related amphibians (those related by evolutionary origin from a single ancestral species) across continents. Their analysis showed that diversification resulted from post-separation radiation, rather than from species movement across barriers. It is reasonable to assume that vicariance-driven speciation—the pressure to adapt quickly to niches and stresses—applies to plants as well as to animals.[177] The biodiversity of flora supports both specialist fauna (herbivores that will travel far in order to rendezvous at their favourite plant café) as well as generalist predatory fauna (which will nibble on anything at hand). This incentivises geostationary plants to take evasive measures to avoid becoming that meal.

Latex is resoundingly successful in this regard. Tellingly, 70 per cent of all latex producing plants are tropical[lxviii] and all

---

lxviii Latex producers in Central America (such as *Castilla elastica*), North America (milkweed), Mediterranean (opium poppy) and

are eudicots[lxix] from regions that were part of Gondwanaland. Among these from the Asterids clade, are *Hevea* (euphorb family; Euphorbiaceae)*; Palaquium (*sapota family*;* Sapotaceae*)* and *Castilla* (mulberry family; Moraceae). *Landolphia* (dogbane family; Apocynaceae) and *Parthenium* (sunflower family; Asteraceae) are from the Rosids clade.[178] *Hevea* and *Castilla* originated in Central and South America, *Palaquium* in Southeast Asia, *Landolphia* in Africa and *Parthenium* in North America. Smaller amounts of rubber are made by a huge variety of plants, including *Asclepias* (milkweed), *Ficus* (fig) species and the Russian dandelion, *Taraxacum kok-saghyz*. If you are interested in the origins and diversification of the genetic and molecular precursors of latex which has underpinned the success of these plants, please see *Appendix A*.

Asia, such as *Ficus* species do not produce the huge volumes of latex as do plants in the Amazon and Congo.

lxix Flowering plants that have two cotyledons (seed leaves) within their seed, such as peas, beans, or mangoes. Contrasted with monocots which have one cotyledon, such as rice or corn.

7

With Patience, Arm Thyself

It is important to understand that organisms do not actually make a list of priorities such as predator deterrence, nor do they evolve in anticipation of future selection pressures. There is simply a cost-benefit ratio operating on an ongoing basis. If the costs of an adaptation are high and the benefits few, the organism will have low fecundity or will not survive. But, if the costs are balanced by a slightly better chance of survival, then the organism will outstrip its neighbours in offspring production. As the adage goes: 'When being chased by a bear, you only need to outrun your companions.'

The evolutionary imperative is to reproduce. But without life in the *here* and *now*, there will be no offspring produced and there will be no evolutionary future for the genes that hitchhike through time using physical bodies temporarily as a refuge.[lxx] These genes have a vested interest in your physical survival

lxx This was Richard Dawkins' insight, articulated in his revolutionary book, *The Selfish Gene*.

and reproduction. This calculation of survival odds would have operated as robustly for the earliest forms of life on earth—simple creatures made of just a single cell with no surplus energy for (or recourse to) fancy deterrents—just as it works for all life today. Our single-celled ancestors would have had to use what they already had in their genetic toolbox. At least 355 genes have been identified as being present in all living organisms, and must have been present in the hypothetical, single-celled, last universal common ancestor (affectionately termed LUCA) which lived about 4–3.8 billion years ago and gave rise to all life on earth.[179] The complement of genes that makes any organism successful in its habitat varies: the cholera bacterium has about 4,000 genes, and a human being has approximately 20,000. The smallest, fully synthetic, stripped-down version of life is a bacterium whose genome was artificially built by whittling away genes until the fewest needed for survival, i.e., 382, were identified.[180] Note that 382 is a pretty good approximation of the 355 genes that are thought to have been present in LUCA. Included in this collection are genes for structural and enzymatic proteins to make the building blocks that assemble the cell and then make it function.[181] These include genes that make enzymes for lipid processing and fatty acid breakdown[lxxi], which means that the genetic ingredients for rubber synthesis were

---

lxxi Lipids can be recycled by chopping them back into their component terpene parts and joining them up again differently. The breakdown and synthesis are done by enzymes. The important enzymes for this process are: phosphatidylserine synthase (*pssA-2*), acyl-CoA reductase (*paaZ*), isopentenyldiphosphate isomerase (*idi*), 3-hydroxyacyl-CoA dehydrogenase (*fadB2*), acyl-CoA dehydrogenase (*acd13*), heptaprenylglyceryl phosphate synthase (*pcrB*), pimeloyl-ACP methyl ester carboxylesterase (*ephE*), acyl-CoA thioesterase FadM (*ybaW*) and the thioesterase superfamily.

already present around 3.5 billion years ago. (For a description of the biosynthesis of terpenes, please see *Appendix A*.)

As time went on, changes to living organisms accumulated through duplications, mutations and structural rearrangements of genes. Modifications of palatability genes in an individual's body can do one of three things: a. it can have no effect; b. it can make the individual more palatable; or c. it can make the individual less palatable. If the first, the individual's chances of being eaten are the same as before. If the second, the individual's chances of being eaten increase. If the third, then the individual's chances of survival increase. For structural or metabolic genes that are necessary for life, mutational tinkering may occasionally result in a better product, but there is also a danger that the gene could be damaged, which would kill or hobble the carrier. It turns out that this existential risk can be mitigated by duplicating the gene and then making changes to only one of the two resulting copies. The original gene still performs its vital function, safeguarding the organism's survival. As for the copy—well, it doesn't matter if it doesn't work. But if it does work and enhances survival, it will be more adaptive, and the organism will thrive and reproduce. This duplicate-and-modify process has left its fingerprints all over the human genome, which is peppered with up to 18,000 non-functional 'pseudogenes' which arose by duplications.[182] If you are interested in learning more about this, please see *Appendix B*, where I dig a little deeper with examples of two proteins—haemoglobin and oxytocin—that exemplify the duplicate-and-modify process. This process happened over and over with terpene synthesis genes, giving not only latex with rubber particles or gutta-percha, but thousands of other odoriferous or bioactive chemicals such as papaverine from the opium poppy, camphor from the camphor laurel, thymol from thyme and azadirachtin from neem.

Latex is, without question, a biological marvel. It is an aqueous solution that resembles milk that is piped around the plant body in thin-walled tubes called laticifers. The solution appears milky because—like oil shaken up with water—it contains a dispersion of tiny fat globules inside which thin strings of rubber are packaged. When the plant is wounded, the delicate laticifers break and latex oozes out, releasing the rubber strands like freshly boiled spaghetti. It gums up the mouths or adheres to the bodies of attacking animals, who quickly retreat to look for something more palatable before they come to a sticky end. The exact composition of latex varies as widely as its origin. This variation, exemplified by opium, cannabis, rubber trees and milkweed, is linked, in its turn, to the wide range of selection pressures that plants in different ecosystems experience.

Plants exude a plethora of oozes: mucilage, gums, saps, resin and oils as well as latex. Since their functions vary, it is helpful to get a feel for the bigger picture to understand why.[183] Briefly, mucilages, gums and saps are carbohydrate-based and water-soluble, whereas resins and oils are not. Mucilages are sticky aqueous solutions of carbohydrates, and function in the normal physiology of plants for water storage and seed survival. They are found, for example, in okra fruit, marshmallow roots and the bark of the slippery elm. They are used as food or glue. Gums are also carbohydrates, but they are pathological products made when a plant is damaged. Gums swell by absorbing water and are used as thickening agents and stabilizers. Examples are agar, carrageenan and gum arabic.[184] Saps are aqueous sugar solutions carried in phloem tubes that redistribute nutrients around the plant, much like blood does in animals. Many plant syrups, such as maple, walnut and palm, are concentrated sap. Resins are formed from terpenes or phenolics[lxxii] and contain a high proportion of volatile compounds.[lxxiii] Their primary role in the plant is unclear, but many animals seek them out as beneficial compounds. For example, honeybees harvest resins to make propolis, which is a sticky substance with antibacterial properties. In the hive, it is used variously as a paint for brood cells, as grout to seal cracks or as concrete to entomb bodies of animals like mice which may enter the hives and die inside. Humans harvest resins such as frankincense, myrrh, balsam, asafoetida, hashish and camphor for ritualistic, psychoactive, aromatic or culinary purposes. Oils are triglyceride[lxxiv] fats, which serve as energy storage in seeds for embryo growth, such as sunflower oil, olive oil and coconut oil. Essential oils are distributed throughout the plant, have an odour and some are repellent or toxic to animals—sandalwood, lavender, clove, cedar and peppermint oils. You already know that latex is a dispersal of rubber-filled globules in an aqueous solution and circulates around the plant similarly to sap. However, sap attracts animals to plants, while latex repels them.

The word 'latex' derives from the Latin word which means liquid, which itself derives from a Proto-Indo-European root

---

lxxii Molecules that contain the aromatic benzene-based ring. These compounds have a characteristic pungent odour.

lxxiii Molecules that readily evaporate. Volatile compounds are responsible for the smell of substances because they enter the nose where smell receptors are located.

lxxiv Compound fats that are made of a carbohydrate and fatty acid and can be saturated or unsaturated. These are familiar molecules, like lard, butter and oils.

'*lat*' which means wet or damp. The term 'laticifers' probably stems from the term 'lactifers' for tubes that carry milk in the mammalian breast due to latex's resemblance to milk (latex comes in many colours, including orange, yellow, red and scarlet, but is usually white.) Latex synthesis is widespread in the plant world: 10 per cent of all flowering plants—a staggering 25,000 species—produce it. While latex from all origins has a common aqueous base and contains soluble and insoluble components, its composition varies hugely. Rubber strands are the primary insoluble particles, but a slew of other components that vary between species of latex producers may be present: terpenes in the para rubber plant, alkaloids (morphine, codeine and papaverine) in the opium poppy, phenolic glycosides in cannabis, cardiac glycosides in oleander, tannins in bananas, and additionally, proteins, starches, oils, sugars, resins, gums, alkaloids and inorganic compounds in the aqueous latex solution in which rubber particles are suspended.

To properly appreciate the structure and function of latex and laticifers, and how the natural synthesis of rubber relates to the health of a rubber tree, it is helpful to have a working understanding of its anatomy. A crosswise slice of a typical plant (Figure 19) yields concentric layers called annular rings, which are formed annually.[lxxv] Beneath the bark on the outside is a layer of living phloem tubes which transports the sugary sap made by photosynthesis around the tree; a deft mnemonic to remember this is that 'food flows through phloem'. Towards the pith of the tree are straw-like tubes called xylem, which move water up to the leaves. Xylem tubes can be reinforced or plugged with phenolics which confer strength and resistance to rotting. Both

lxxv The term 'annular' originates from the Latin word *annulus* (little ring) for the space between two concentric rings. The term 'annual' for yearly originates from the Latin *annus*, meaning year.

xylem and phloem are generated by stem cells called cambium, which are sandwiched in between (see Figure 19). As phloem is generated, the layers of new growth are infiltrated by laticifer cells which derive their energy from sugars in sap and use it to manufacture latex.

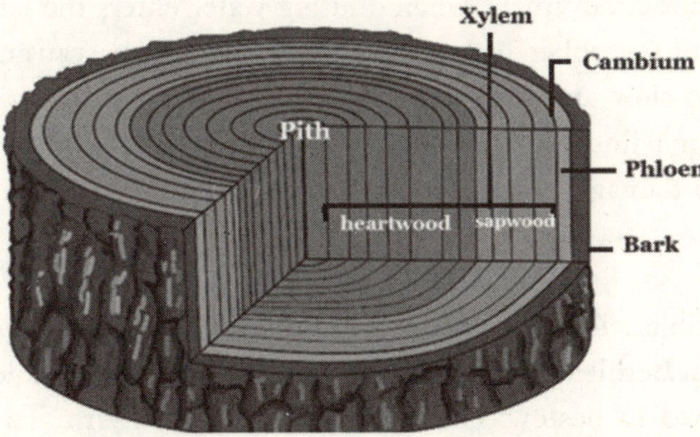

Figure 19: Schematic cross section of a tree. The pith in the centre is surrounded by heartwood, sapwood, cambium and bark. The oldest rings are located closest to the pith, whereas the most recently formed ring is located just beneath the bark, and the dark grey region immediately above the dead bark shows the living phloem layer.[185]

The tubes that produce and transport latex are annually generated by the cambium and join up into a three-dimensional net that pervades the region below the bark.[186] The proximity of the laticifers to phloem and xylem allows raw materials and water to diffuse into the cells for latex synthesis. Other tissues are also dispersed around the plant body to make, transport or store secondary metabolites such as resins, essential oils and gums.

Since laticifers are laid down in annual layers, there may be little or no connection between laticifers from one year's annular ring to another. By understanding the structure of the tree, it becomes obvious that tapping too deeply damages the essential phloem as well as severing the laticifer network beyond repair. Additionally tapping is only done on one side of the tree because cutting all around the trunk can kill it. When punctured, latex drains out of laticifers rapidly at first, and then slower as the mechanism of release moves from pressure to osmotic movement when diluting water enters the laticifer. Over time, rubber in latex solidifies into a plug, causing the flow to slow and then stop, much like how blood coagulates. This first line of defence protects the rest of the plant from further damage and prevents the entry of pathogens.

The Bible tells of the Magi who came to pay homage to baby Jesus in Bethlehem, bringing with them the most valuable gifts they had to bestow: gold, frankincense and myrrh. Two out of these three precious items were tree resins, valued for their aroma and their medicinal properties. Tree saps, gums, resins and other secretions and exudates[lxxvi] have been harnessed by animals including humans, but what purpose do they serve for the plants that make them? The answer is obvious: plants cannot run away from predators and therefore, for survival,

---

lxxvi Opium, guayule, chicle, para, gutta-percha, gutta balata, resins, frankincense, myrrh, camphor, tragacanth, asafoetida (gum oleoresin) are some plant products. The hardwood tree, *Guaiacum sanctum* (guaiacum) produces guaifenesin resin, used as an expectorant. Honeybees collect resin to fashion into propolis that they use to coat their cells and plug apertures. The US FDA has so far approved two botanical drugs for prescription. The first was Veregen (sinecatechins) sourced from green tea leaves and used as an ointment for the treatment of genital warts. The second is a proanthocyanidin derivative, crofelemer (marketed as Fulyzac) from the latex of sangre de drago or the dragon blood tree (*Croton lechleri*), which is an anti-diarrhoetic.

must decrease palatability. Thus, these secretions are survival tools—different defence mechanisms against different types of predators. There are mechanical barriers posed by woody stems, waxy leaves, sharp thorns, sticky secretions and irritating bristles; physiological barriers such as development-disrupting hormones; and chemical mechanisms such as the production of volatiles that attract predators of herbivores or alert nearby plants to mount guard to the presence of herbivores.

Plants can be just as deadly to animals as animals are to other animals, and this is not hyperbole. In order to not be eaten, plants abound with an alphabet soup of chemicals designed to make the predator so uncomfortable as to leave them alone, or to really make a point by killing them stone-cold dead. The hardwoods of the tropics are darker in colour due to the production of large amounts of chemicals such as tannins and phenolics, which resist rot caused by bacteria and fungi. Deterrence is produced by the presence of chemicals which may taste bad, smell strange or cause reactions like vomiting, nausea or hallucinations. Latex can incorporate these chemicals in addition to rubber. Ironically, these properties became so valuable to animals that they led to these plants being exploited for the very things that were meant to deter. For example, monarch butterfly larvae consume and sequester toxic cardiac glycosides present in milkweed latex to make themselves unpalatable to birds. A blue jay which eats a monarch larva or butterfly vomits it out and avoids it in the future.[lxxvii] Humans drink coffee, which contains caffeine, a

---

lxxvii Animals that have defence mechanisms display their toxicity with highly visible markings, usually in aposematic coloration: yellow, orange, black and white. In 'Müllerian mimicry', many unrelated but toxic animals, like bees, wasps, snakes and butterflies all adapt the same colour shorthand, and predators learn to avoid any prey with such discouraging coloration. Fascinatingly, some non-toxic

psychoactive drug. It is not mere coincidence that places with enormous biodiversity also contain flora representing the world's pharmacy because of their prolific evolution of deterrents—plants have been in an existential battle against an army that possesses incredibly diverse attack methods and weapons. Since these chemicals evolved secondarily for defence from molecules that were essential (primary) to life, they are termed 'secondary metabolites'. *Appendix C* provides an overview of secondary metabolites.

Plants were relative latecomers to terrestrial life. As they emerged on land, they encountered animals who had been heretofore snacking on algae that grew around ponds (as well as each other). The earliest plants were the mosses, which were quickly discovered and grazed on by microscopic animals. Even today, mosses are the best place for finding the ancient tardigrades, or moss piglets, famous as the most resilient life form ever known.[187] As plants evolved barriers, animals surpassed them with behavioural and physiological adaptations. Figure 20 shows these herbivore feeding strategies as they evolved with the diversification of plants. The earliest strategies were to pierce-and-suck and chew. These would be the exact behaviours that latex discouraged, as demonstrated in larva feeding experiments described later in this chapter. The takeaway is that latex was probably functioning as a deterrent as long as 400 million years ago.

---

animals, like the viceroy butterfly, mimic the markings despite being safe for birds to eat. This is called 'Batesian mimicry' and safeguards them from any animal that has experienced the unpleasant effects of any Müllerian mimic.

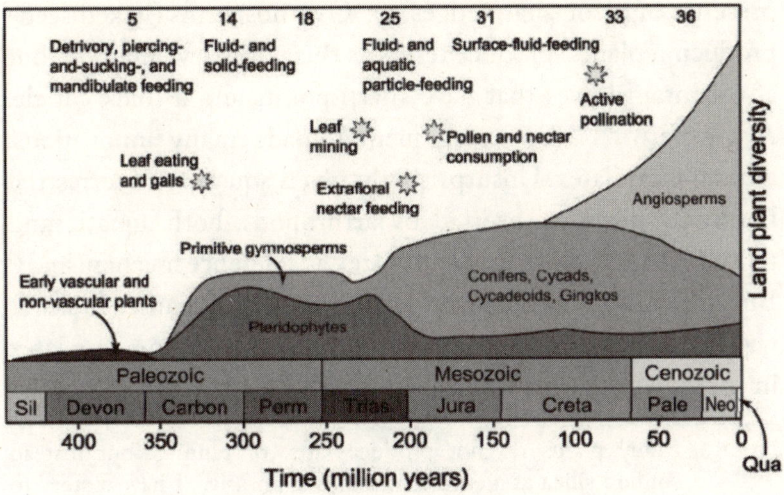

Figure 20: Origin of plant classes and insect feeding strategies over evolutionary time. The evolutionary developments of new classes of plants are shown accompanied by new feeding strategies due to the interactions between plants and insects. The numerals on top refer to the numbers of feeding strategies present. Below are the dominant feeding strategies, followed by the first occurrences of certain feeding modes indicated by a starburst. The geographic time scale and colours are obtained from the International Commission of Stratigraphy, where Sil—Silurian, Devon—Devonian, Carbon—Carboniferous, Perm—Permian, Tria—Triassic, Jura—Jurassic, Creta—Cretaceous, Pale—Paleogene, Neo—Neogene and Qua—Quaternary.[188]

Among the earliest animals that would have grazed on plants were aquatic and terrestrial arthropods (such as lobsters, spiders, mites, centipedes) and their larvae. Many plants, like ferns, do not produce latex or tannins, but instead contain silica and newly discovered chemicals as deterrents.[189] Silica is abrasive and can leave deep gashes in delicate oral tissue due to the presence of razor-sharp edges.[lxxviii] Gymnosperms (naked seed-producing plants) produce resins as their primary deterrent, but also contain leaves that have sharp points and a thick cuticle. Angiosperms[lxxix] (flowering plants) made many innovations, among them latex. Unsurprisingly, given aquatic and terrestrial herbivory pressures exerted by arthropods, both aquatic and terrestrial angiosperms produce latex as a defence mechanism.[190] But animals are also adaptable, and the next chapter looks at ways by which animals manage to evade or accommodate latex in their diet.

---

lxxviii Many plants do not produce latex or tannins, but instead contain silica as a deterrent. Silica is abrasive. I have a story to illustrate that. Many years ago, I took my two young sons to visit Scotland. We wandered through Edinburgh, crossed the Firth of Forth, and then went West to Glencoe. We first climbed Ben Nevis, and went from bright sunshine to frigid temperatures and falling snow at the top. For an easier day the following day, I picked Buachaille Etive Mor. The long path to the base of the mountain was overgrown with bracken, a type of fern, that grows to about 5 foot tall and was about a foot taller than my older son. We were laughing as we pushed our way through, me ahead, my children following. Suddenly my older son cried out. He had pushed a bracken frond with his hand, and the stem had ripped his small hand, opening a gash over an inch long and as perfectly straight as a paper cut. It was bleeding profusely. We blotted the blood as best we could, and I had him clench his fist. We drove to a doctor in Fort William to get some stitches in the gash. That was the end of the outing to Buachaille Etive Mor, but it was a demonstration of the razor-sharp edges that are conferred on the stem by the presence of silicates. Imagine that was your mouth. For animals that graze, avoiding bracken is imperative lest their mouths be similarly gashed open.

lxxix Angiosperms are flowering plants which contain their seeds inside a chamber. This protects the seed. Upon maturity, the chamber often becomes a fleshy fruit which encourages dispersal by animals: after consuming the fruit, the seeds are discarded away from the parents and grow into new plants.

8

Evolutionary Epicures

Latex solidifies when exposed to air, gumming up the mouth parts of chewing animals, particularly of larval insects. Back in 1905, a scientist named Kneip revived an 1887 hypothesis that latex was a deterrent after he fed leaves with intact laticifers and drained laticifers to slugs. The slugs rejected the intact leaves but ate ones from which the latex had been drained. This method was experimentally re-tested by Anurag Agarwal and Kotaro Konno in 2009, who also revived the earlier hypothesis that the presence of latex in so many flowering plants must indicate a commonality of function. Agarwal and Konno also noticed some flexible behaviours in caterpillars when dealing with latex-bearing leaves. The caterpillars severed the laticifers through which latex is transported under pressure from the main vein to the periphery in a manner that was adapted to the type of tubes that were present. In plants with 'non-articulated' laticifers (i.e., smaller laticifers branch out unidirectionally from a main vein) cutting the main vein disrupted latex flow to the tip of the leaf upon which they fed (Figure 21, left). In the case of articulated laticifers in which tubes interconnect in a network and latex can flow in any direction, caterpillars chewed trenches right across the leaves disrupting flow to all the branches (Figure 21, middle), leaving the leaf tip edible.[191] Related tactics included cutting across multiple veins supplying latex to regions of the leaf on which they planned to feed, or feeding on leaf tissue in between veins to avoid the largest laticifers (Figure 21, right).

Figure 21: Larval strategies to drain latex from leaves. Schematics (left and middle images) showing how leaf-munching larvae can tackle leaves by severing the main vein of a non-articulated laticifer (arrow; left) or cutting trenches across the lamina of the leaf to drain netlike laticifers (two arrows; middle). The black areas contain latex, and the grey areas show regions lacking latex. The photograph on the right shows the alternative strategy of interstitial lamina feeding.[192]

The second way latex impedes herbivory is by solidifying into a gummy ball in the presence of stomach acid. If you have ever eaten an unripe apple, banana, mango, papaya, sapota, persimmon or other latex-bearing fruit, you have experienced the unpleasant film that it forms in the mouth. If swallowed, the latex in unripe fruit coagulates in acidic stomachs like ours, glomming together undigested plant material and tannins to form a plug which can cause a painful and sometimes fatal blockage of the digestive system.[lxxx]

The ability to make food from light, water and air makes plants delicious sitting targets for animals who are compelled to live the precarious life of highway robbery of others' pantries to survive. Plants move a lot of material within their own bodies, just as animals do. Some plants—such as mosses—are tiny enough to diffuse food around their bodies; others are too big for water to overcome gravity without indoor plumbing (i.e., xylem tubes) to transport it up to the leaves where it is used to make sugars by photosynthesis. Xylem is made from elongated dead cells which link end-on-end to form pipes in the core of trees carrying water up to the crown. Living phloem cells surround the central xylem core and convey the sugary sap to the rest of the plant. Thus, every living part of the plant contains food, and every part becomes a target.

'Food' is the term used for the source of energy that powers life processes. The digestive system is really like an automobile's internal combustion engine. Food or gasoline molecules go in and get combusted, waste comes out and energy is siphoned to where it is needed. Unlike the 'burning' that occurs within the car's engine, however, the living organism has enzymes which allow it to break down molecules at lower temperatures. But other organisms are also looking for energy sources and naturally, the easiest way to obtain energy is by eating someone

lxxx Phytobezoars are masses of undigestible plant matter made of cellulose and lignin held together by glue-like substances. These are frequently tannins which are polyphenols which coagulate in acid, just like latex.

else and breaking down their molecules. Being a target for predation is inimical to survival for any type of life, especially for single-celled bacteria. To survive in order to reproduce, even early life forms had to first dissuade others from consuming them for energy. There are potentially two ways to defend against predators in this situation. One is by repurposing an existing material—analogous to how sharpening a stick at one end can transform it into a spear. The other is by creating a slew of new materials, some of which might fortuitously fulfil a defensive purpose.

Around 500 Ma, when most of earth's landmasses were collected together in the supercontinent Gondwanaland in the southern hemisphere, the waters were teeming with the staggering variety of animals born of the Cambrian explosion about 50 Ma before and high carbon dioxide levels were heating up land, plants emerged on land from aquatic algae. Despite the ever-present danger of predation, the benefit of aquatic life for algae was that their delicate flagellated gametes (eggs or sperm) could be released into the environment and were not vulnerable to drying out, allowing them to move around in the water to find a partner, mate, and settle down away from the parent. On land, they would encounter a dry environment where these delicate gametes could not swim around and would die from drying out. Despite the significant disadvantage of desiccation, land provided many advantages:

1. There was access to more sunlight. In water, sunlight only penetrates the first 650 feet, leaving the depths unconquerable by plants,
2. Varied habitats for specialisation, which minimised competition from other plants, and

3. Fewer animal predators—they were mostly confined to water because there was not much to eat (yet) on land.[lxxxi]

All plants originate from a specific type of algae,[lxxxii] and they quickly diversified. Primitive plants, such as mosses, ferns and cycads, still produce motile sperm, but they can only reproduce in soggy places. Terrestrial plants with little access to year-round water had to tackle two new problems (in addition to constant predation): a. they had to prevent the drying out of eggs, sperm and the resultant embryos, and b. they had to find a way to get eggs and sperm to meet in a common environment. The first problem was easily solved by retaining the eggs (ovules) within the mother's body, in the ovary, so that any embryo that formed would also be protected, even nourished. The ovaries became detachable 'fruit' with the seeds containing embryos inside. To solve the second problem, land plants made the sperm light enough to travel, but resistant enough to drying to get to the sedentary eggs. We now call this sperm 'pollen'. But now a new problem arose. The plants needed the fruit with their seed passengers to be dispersed far and wide to exploit other habitats, rather than become vigorous and plentiful competition to their

lxxxi Lichen are photosynthetic and were probably already present on land 500 Ma. Lichen are symbiotic organisms and contain algal and fungal partners in mutually beneficial relationships. The algal partner is capable of photosynthesis, and the fungal partner provides shelter and enzymes that break down rock as a step towards colonising new habitats.

lxxxii The earliest plant ancestor was a type of green algae in the group called charophytes. All plants are linked to this group: all have cellulose-synthesising machinery in their cell walls, chlorophylls a and b and a 'haplontic' life cycle. To make land accessible for colonisation, lichens (mutualistic algae and fungi) had to have first prepared soil by breaking down rock.

own parents. Plants could therefore either fling their seeds as far as they could throw them, or recruit animals who could range even farther as dispersal agents.

Of course, these animal helpers had to simultaneously be dissuaded from feasting either on the plants themselves or the precious and inconveniently nutritive seeds which were packed full of energy-rich molecules, like oils, for the embryo to draw on. Although plants had already inherited latex precursors from algae, these did not protect the seeds efficiently because seeds are typically desiccated and incapable of biosynthesis.[lxxxiii] So plants placed them inside fruits[lxxxiv] which were rendered inedible by latex—laticifer cells can acquire sugar from phloem and direct it towards latex production—but only while the seed was developing. As the embryo within the seed matures, latex production in the fruit is slowed down, the sugars accumulate and the fruit becomes sweeter. Some plants, such as apples, further laced the seeds with toxins such as cyanide to deter their consumption or, such as peaches, additionally hid the embryos in thick shelled cases. Animals would gather the fruit, carry it home and discard the seeds away from the parent after they ate it. Those seeds could then grow into new plants.

Can animals overcome the latex problem? Yes, and the evolution of digestive pathways to deal with latex is one of a slew of manoeuvres with which animals responded. As mentioned previously, caterpillars drain laticifers and eat the latex-free

lxxxiii 'Bio' = life; 'synthesis' = build; so, biosynthesis is the ability of living organisms to build molecules.

lxxxiv The fruit is really just the ovary, inside which the parent plant retained the egg. The egg becomes the seed. The ovary grows and, depending on the plant either produces latex and accumulates sugars, or develops into a hard causing. Many types of fruits exist, but all retain seeds inside for dispersal.

areas of the leaf, and monarch butterfly caterpillars leverage the unpalatable chemicals in milkweed latex by sequestering them in their own tissues. But the most remarkable adaptation relates to the structure and chemistry of the digestive system itself. The most familiar herbivores are mammals, and their feeding strategies inform their digestive system which are useful for understanding how animals evolved to deal with latex, which is what the following section will explore.

Herbivores are usually distinguished by the type of digestive system they possess and the type of plants they eat. In monogastric 'hindgut-fermenters', e.g. elephants and horses, food directly enters an anterior acidic stomach chamber, and symbiont-mediated cellulose breakdown occurs post-small intestine, in the hindgut (caecum or colon). In polygastric 'foregut-fermenters', e.g. goats and cows, multiple anterior chambers with cellulose-digesting symbionts precede an acidic stomach and the small intestine. These animals may also have additional hindgut fermentation in functional ceca or colons.[lxxxv] The terms monogastric and polygastric will be used from now on. Schematics of the two types of digestive systems are shown in Figure 22. The types of flowering plants[lxxxvi] eaten adds another layer of classification. This dietary specialisation is

lxxxv The word 'fermentation' relates to the presence of microbial symbionts which assist with breaking down cellulose. In polygastric foregut-fermenters, the symbionts are located anterior to the acidic stomach chamber, and in monogastric hindgut-fermenters, food passes through the acidic stomach before arriving in the caecum and colon where the cellulose-digesting symbionts live.

lxxxvi Flowering plants are divided into dicotyledonous plants (dicots), some of which make latex. These have seeds with two cotyledons or seed leaves, and examples are peas and beans. Monocotyledonous

indicated by use of the term 'browsers' or 'grazers'.[193] Browsers eat dicots which includes trees, shrubs and forbs, some of which make latex. Grazers eat monocot grasses which do not make latex, but may have silica and other antifeedants. Monogastric animals largely eat monocots (grasses lacking latex), but polygastric animals may browse and graze both dicots (shrubs and trees containing latex) and monocots.

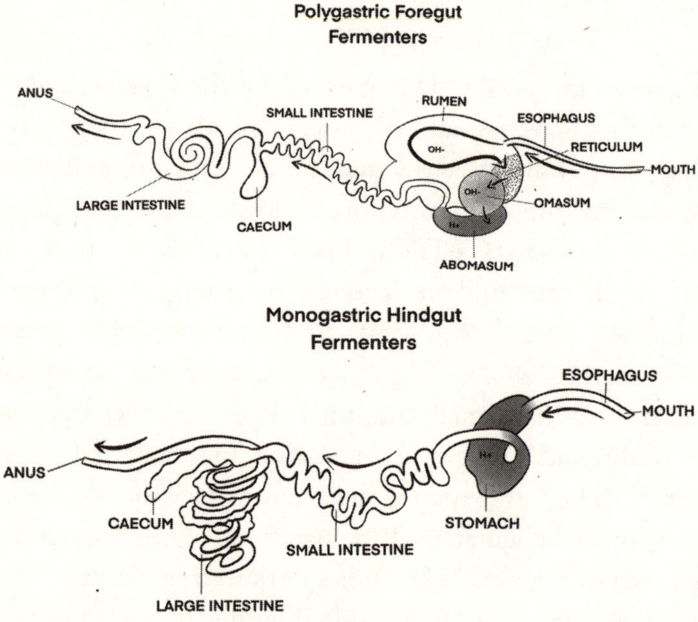

Figure 22: Schematic of mammalian herbivores' gastrointestinal tracts. Polygastric foregut-fermenters (goats, giraffes) are ruminants which have neutral-to alkaline-pH chambers (OH^-) anterior to the acidic stomach (H^+), whereas monogastric hindgut-fermenters (elephants, horses) have an anterior acidic (H^+) stomach. Both groups may additionally have hindgut fermentation in the caecum and/or colon with associated symbionts.[194]

plants (monocots) have seeds which have only one cotyledon and examples are rice and grasses. Most monocots do not make latex.

Recall that latex is a common antifeedant which coagulates in acid but remains liquid in neutral-to-alkaline pH. The takeaway is that if latex is present in the diet, it will quickly coagulate in animals with monogastric systems, but not in ones with polygastric digestive systems. Put together with the observation that latex is produced by dicots rather than by monocots, gut architecture takes on special significance. A monogastric animal will be made sick by latex in the diet, whereas a polygastric animal can tolerate small amounts (if the latex does not contain other poisonous substances). Thus, polygastric guts may have evolved as an adaptation to the presence of latex, a hypothesis that I have published in the peer-reviewed scientific literature.[195] Following is an explanation of how the pH of the gut correlates to feeding strategy.

There is a clear correlation between feeding strategy and the pH of the first chamber into which food arrives, usually the stomach (monogastric animals which include scavengers, carnivores, omnivores or herbivores) or rumen (polygastric herbivores). (Table 2). As shown in the table the order of decreasing acidity, we have: obligate scavengers (which eat carrion, such as vultures), specialist carnivores (which hunt a specific prey, such as dolphins), facultative scavengers (which hunt or scavenge meat, such as gulls), generalist carnivores (which eat a variety of meats, such as cats), omnivores (which eat both meat and plants), monogastric herbivores (which eat largely monocots) and foregut-fermenting herbivores (which browse dicots and monocots). This order recapitulates the dietary preferences with the more acidic stomachs being present in carnivores, and less acidic stomach in herbivores, with the lowest acidity being recorded in foregut-fermenting herbivores that encounter the highest levels of latex in their feed.

The data shows that the pH of the first chamber of the digestive system is acidic in monogastric animals which largely eat protein-based diets or grasses lacking latex. Polygastric herbivores are browsers which eat dicots and have a higher gut pH which slows latex coagulation. Most of data in this table was obtained from Beasley et al. (2015).[196]

Table 2: Average animal gut pH, classified by type of diet

Dietary lifestyle (type of gut)	Examples	First chamber pH*
Obligate scavengers which eat carrion (monogastric)	Wandering albatross, carrion crow, common buzzard, white-backed vulture	1.1 to 1.5
Specialist carnivores which eat a specific type of prey such as fish or insects (monogastric)	Gentoo penguin, bottlenose dolphin, great cormorant, common pipistrelle bat, common moorhen	1.4 to 6.8
Facultative scavengers which hunt but will eat carrion (monogastric)	Black-headed gull, bald eagle, opossum, barn owl, American bittern, peregrine falcon	1.3 to 4.5
Generalist carnivores which will eat multiple types of meat (monogastric)	Cat, snowy owl, great horned owl, ferret, common kestrel, common pied oystercatcher	1.2 to 3.6
Omnivores which will eat both meat and plants (monogastric)	Rat, baboon, common mallard, crab-eating macaque, domesticated pig, human	1.5 to 4.4

Dietary lifestyle (type of gut)	Examples	First chamber pH*
Hindgut-fermenting herbivores[197] which eat monocots (monogastric)	Shetland pony, horse, rabbit, beaver, porcupine, howler monkey, gerbil, hamster, rhino, guinea pig	1.7 to 4.7
Foregut-fermenting herbivores[198] which eat dicots and monocots (polygastric)	Hippo, sheep, ox, sloth, guanaco, llama, camel, giraffe, cow, colobus monkey, kangaroo, brocket deer	4.7 to 7.4

**pH is lower when starved but increases when an animal has just eaten. The feeding status of these animals was not recorded, so these values are for general information purposes.*

The polygastric clade includes: 1. cud-chewing ruminants with four gut chambers[lxxxvii] (deer, cattle, goats, sheep); 2. non-cud-chewing, three-chambered pseudoruminants lacking the rumen (camels, hippopotamuses); 3. The presence of salivary tannin-binding proteins and large livers[199] in browsers such as deer to deal with antifeedants which must be sequestered or detoxified; 4. an adaptive avoidance of latex-rich foods, preferring instead ripe fruits, nuts and tender leaves (monkeys). An unusually small leaf-eater (folivore) with foregut fermentation is the relatively tiny two-foot-long hoatzin, a bird from South America which

lxxxvii The four ruminant chambers are: 1. Rumen, which breaks down large food particles with symbiotic microbial action; 2. Reticulum, a honeycomb-like structure which filters out large pieces of food and moves them back to the rumen for breakdown; 3. Omasum, where absorption of water and nutrients takes place; 4. Abomasum, which is the true stomach with acid and enzymes.

is so special and odd that it occupies a taxonomic family all by itself. Their leafy diet and the space required by their foregut precludes big flight muscles, and the hoatzin is therefore an inadequate flier. Other polygastric animals are peccaries, colobus monkeys, kangaroos, llamas and sloths.

The presence of polygastric digestive systems in animals with a dicot browsing lifestyle implies gut evolution as a response to the selective pressure exerted by latex-bearing plants. Consider the following correlations for bovines: 1. The genetic diversity of cattle is highest in the forested Taurus Mountains of southern Turkey, indicating that woodland, not grassland, is where cattle emerged as a species; 2. The last wild Auroch, a type of European wild cattle, died in Jaktorów Forest in Poland in 1627, and these animals must have had a browsing lifestyle; 3. The historic bison herds across the Midwest in the United States were held responsible for converting forested landscapes to grassland, specifically because they ate growing tree shoots. Across many parts of the world, goats and deer are resented for their habit of reducing landscape trees planted at great expense down to nubs rather than staidly mowing the lawn. A new farming technique called 'silvopasture' (the deliberate integration of trees, forage crops and livestock on the same land) is recommended by the United States Forest Service and is being employed across many animal husbandry operations to combat heat stress as well as deforestation.[200]

The monogastric clade includes rhinos, elephants, tapirs, gerbils, Shetland ponies, pigs, quokkas, porcupines, wombats, koalas, hamsters, howler monkeys, guinea pigs, beavers, rabbits, humans and horses. These are mostly grazers who eat monocot grasses and have tougher teeth and tongues to withstand abrasive grass stems, and some are omnivores. Proteins, grass leaves and grain seeds are efficiently digested, but these animals are not adapted to substantial amounts of latex consumption—it would coagulate in their acidic stomachs. Because symbionts are housed beyond the main absorptive region of the small intestine (see Figure 22), a lot of the nutrients are inconveniently discarded in faeces. Two adaptations are present to compensate for this: 1. Several members of this group (e.g. horses, elephants and rhinos) are very large to accommodate the vast quantities of forage they must consume[lxxxviii] while 2. Smaller members are grass-eaters (lagomorphs such as rabbits, rodents such as hamsters, primates such as gorillas, and marsupials such as koalas) and some practice coprophagy—which means they eat their own faecal pellets. This 'second-pass absorption' allows the small intestines to properly absorb fermentation-generated nutrients by symbionts in the caecum and colon (see Figure 22). The takeaway is that monogastric herbivores are restricted to latex-free forage, but their superpower is to quickly adapt to diets of nutrition-poor monocot grasses or protein-rich seeds and meat. Such dietary flexibility in monogastric herbivores is associated with anatomical plasticity—as an experiment that was carried out over three decades ago demonstrated.

That experiment was set in motion in 1971. Five pairs of a largely insectivorous monogastric Italian wall lizard, *Podarcis sicula,* were introduced from a dry island to lush new habitat in the South Adriatic Sea where they foraged on fewer insects, but eight times as much vegetation as in their initial home. These lizards evolved a caecal valve (to slow down grass digestion and allow for its breakdown) in the incredibly quick timeline

lxxxviii It is my observation that dogs are much more inclined to eat horse manure than cow manure, probably because it is sweeter with more sugars since the cellulose-fermenting symbionts are located beyond the small intestine, although I could not find any direct measurements of sugar content in horse versus cow faeces.

of thirty-six years—a mere thirty generations—supporting the idea of the elasticity of the hindgut fermenter's digestive tract.[201] Anatomical plasticity extended to the head—the newly vegetarian lizards' head size and bite strength and musculature increased, presumably to tear at the resilient plant material. This anatomical plasticity provides dietary flexibility and the ability of monogastric animals to adapt as habitats change.

Although monogastric and polygastric gut functions seem cut and dried, the anterior gut chamber pH over an individual's lifetime varies in many animals. For frogs which undergo morphological as well as dietary metamorphosis gut length and pH also change accommodatingly: herbivorous tadpoles have neutral/alkaline gut pH and longer guts, whereas carnivorous tadpoles have acidic first chambers and shorter guts.[202] All adult frogs are carnivorous.

Plant-munching larvae of Lepidoptera (moths and butterflies), Diptera (flies, wasps and bees) and Coleoptera (beetles) have alkaline midguts, as would be expected. This physiology has been exploited by spore-forming soil bacteria such as *Bacillus thuringiensis* (Bt) and *Lysinibacillus sphaericus*. When these bacteria run out of food, they produce a resilient spore and equip it with a toxin which dissolves in alkaline pH. When the spore is ingested by a foraging caterpillar or mosquito larva, the toxin dissolves in its alkaline gut, gets activated, and inserts into the gut wall to cause leakage. The larva dies, giving the accompanying spore a nutrient-rich substrate of the dead body to germinate and grow in. Bt and related toxins are now widely used for the control of larvae of insect pests such as the Colorado potato beetle. This usage is not without risk since pest insect larvae, polygastric animals and even tadpoles possess alkaline guts, and may also ingest spores and toxin and may experience morbidity and mortality. For instance, *Leptodactylus* tadpoles are herbivorous and coexist with mosquitoes in ephemeral vernal ponds. Controlling mosquito larvae in such ponds using Bt may pose danger to amphibians. To test this hypothesis, researchers in Argentina fed *Leptodactylus* tadpoles with a Bt formulation (Introban®) and found that it was toxic.[203]

Another concern is that otherwise resilient polygastric herbivores may experience adverse effects from being fed transgenic plants expressing Bt since the active form of the toxin is engineered into the plant genome. In polygastric animals, alkaline rumens could become a site of action of the toxin, leading to the loss of gut integrity, whereas it would be broken down by stomach acid in monogastric animals. Morbidity and deaths are reported of sheep and cows which were fed Bt-corn and these can be attributed directly to the toxin, since there are no formulation ingredients to complicate the picture.[204] Since stalks and leaves of transgenic Bt plants can be used for animal feed, one option to avoid inadvertent toxicity is to break down the Bt toxin through a fermentative process called 'silaging', which is similar to the process of making yogurt. Both employ *Lactobacilli* bacteria to convert carbohydrates to lactic and acetic acids. Controlled experiments have shown that the feeding of silaged transgenic Bt-material was safe for dairy[205] and beef cattle.[206]

The takeaway is that polygastric animals are protected from latex toxicity due to their alkaline gut pH, but that exposing them to Bt-containing feed which is activated in alkaline pH may promote gut membrane leakage.

Among animals kept in zoos, polygastric animals like sloths and colobus monkeys should be better able to handle latex-rich food than monogastric animals like elephants, rhinos and howler monkeys. Captivity stresses animals but also constrains them from rejecting offered foods. These animals are particularly vulnerable to gastrointestinal discomfort manifesting as diarrhoea or failure to thrive, but these morbidities may be overlooked as the natural stress response of captive animals rather than as being due to unsuitable diets.

In summary, the ability to obtain energy through food is a key driver of reproductive success. In the herbivore's quest to wrest nutrition from plants, versus the plant's existential need to avoid being eaten, the simple and ancient biochemistry of producing and deploying latex shaped both sets of adversaries and has dramatically affected the evolution of guts of animals that browse latex-bearing dicots. On the plant side, a push for even more effective deterrents that could be added to latex further powered the evolution of a variety of intoxicants and toxins which, ironically, are exploited by animals as hallucinogens, perfumes and medicines.

The arms race keeps on going.

Ongoing.

9

Rubber's Alter Ego

Rubber is such a familiar substance that one assumes that it has been around in its present form forever. In fact, this now-ubiquitous material only became commonplace in the late 1800s. Its transformation from a tacky substance to any number of consistencies from pliable-soft to rock-hard and any number of uses, from waterproofing to shock absorption, were due to technological innovations to manipulate its resilience, some of which date back to times before recorded history.

The strength versus malleability of chemical bonds in materials produces two different types of polymers: those which are 'plastic' and can be reoriented structurally upon physical manipulation, and those whose bonds are permanent and whose shape cannot be reworked in a new way. Different systems use different tools for making or reworking bonds in manipulable materials. Living organisms use enzymes, some resins are set using ultraviolet light and iron rod recycling operations use heat. Other tools for reshaping bonds are by dissolving the material in solvents, or recovering them by evaporation and redepositing them.[lxxxix] When heat is used, the prefix 'thermo-' is added, as in 'thermoplastic'. A bonding analogy, albeit imperfect, is to compare the bonds in iron rods with those in concrete. Iron rods can be reclaimed, reshaped and reused, but concrete is not recoverable in an analogous way. Concrete can be pulverised, but it must be mixed with fresh cement for construction. Iron rods, however, can be melted and reshaped to a new conformation and purpose. In chemistry jargon, iron is 'plastic', concrete is 'set'. Glass is a material with high brittleness, but it is 'thermoplastic' and can be melted and reshaped. Bakelite, rubber tyres and fibreglass are 'thermosets' and cannot be recycled using heat. Rather than melt at high temperatures they will combust, that is, break down into volatile molecules and give off bond energy as heat.

Untreated latex from the rubber tree is a naturally thermoplastic substance. It freezes solid at cold temperatures and melts when warmed, as Charles Goodyear found to his chagrin. The resins frankincense and myrrh can be burned or carved into jewellery, but they cannot be reworked to a different shape by heating and moulding, so these are thermosets, i.e., their molecular structure breaks down on heating. By contrast, gutta-percha and resin from pine trees are thermoplastics, but their melting temperatures are so high (about 100°C and 85°C, respectively) that it is economically unfeasible to reshape them with heat.

---

lxxxix For reference, materials with bendy recycling arrows that can be reshaped are polyethylene (PET), high density polyethylene (HDPE), polyvinylchloride (PVC), polyvinyl chloride (PVC), Low density polyethylene (LDPE), polypropylene (PP), polystyrene (PS).

In this world of sets and plastics, rubber has a unique benefit. When it is raw, it behaves like a thermoplastic substance, but when vulcanised in the presence of sulphur and heat, it becomes a thermoset. That, really, is the reason that makes rubber such a valuable material. It behaves like a potato which can be cooked and mashed and moulded and modulated to yield different grades of resilience as needed. The absolute icing on the cake would be if those products could be returned to the form of the original potato.

That innovation is still awaited.

Gutta-percha is a remarkable material produced by trees of the *Palaquium* species indigenous to South Asia, of which the species *P. gutta* produces the highest quality. A molecular relative called gutta-balata is made by *Manilkara bidentata* species in South America, but its quality is lower than gutta-percha. As *Appendix A* shows, gutta-percha has more regular structure with the ability to stack and form intermolecular 'van der Waals'[xc] bonds than the tangled strands of rubber can, making it less elastic but more brittle. The brittleness can be modulated by the speed of cooling—faster cooling makes a less brittle product. It can be moulded into any shape after softening it with heat and is practically indestructible once set. It is also a superb sculpting material. Thomas Hancock's artist brother Charles recognised

xc A weak intermolecular interaction caused by short-lived fluctuations of electron distribution around atoms, which creates transient 'dipoles' (positive and negative charges on the same atom). This then leads to attraction between the negative dipole of one atom and the positive dipole of another atom. Also called 'London dispersion forces'. Each attraction is weak and brief but the abundance has a big effect.

its potential early and founded the Gutta Percha Company with Henry Bewley in 1845.[207] The company made bottle stoppers, tubing and insulated wires. David W. Bartlett gushingly describes it his 1852 book *London by Day or Night*:

> We made a visit one day to the 'Gutta Percha Company's Works', and as they are the only company in the United Kingdom holding the original patent, and first imported gutta percha from 'over the seas' and as a necessary consequence are at the head of the world in their manufactures, we will give a hasty sketch of what we saw on our visit. The manufactory is situated in the northern part of London, near a canal which runs into the interior of the country, and is large and commodious.
>
> We were introduced to the manager, who is a man of politeness and urbanity (qualities not too common in the business life of London), and sat down in his office for a few moments while he gave out orders for various and distant departments of the large manufactory without leaving his desk, by simply applying his lips to different mouth-pieces close at hand, the sound being carried through gutta percha tubes to the farthest corner of the vast building.
>
> In a few minutes, we repaired to the cutting department. Here the lumps of gutta percha are sliced into thin pieces by revolving knives, which cut six hundred slices per minute, propelled by steam. The gutta percha as it is imported from India is not fit for use—the collectors being careless—and it must undergo a process of purification here. The slices, when they drop from the revolving knives, are thin, and have the appearance of old leather. The manager next took us to the boiling and

> kneading-room. The slices are first put into enormous iron boilers, and boiled till of the consistency of tough dough, when they are thrown into a machine with rows of teeth, revolving eight hundred times per minute, and which tear the masses of gutta percha into infinitesimal shreds. The shreds are put into cold water, the gutta percha pure and unalloyed rising to the surface, while the dirt and refuse matter sinks to the bottom. It is then skimmed off, and put into lumps, to which a heat of 200 degrees is applied, and in this state the lumps, while plastic, are put into steam kneading-machines, to work out all the air and water that may exist in the pores of the substance. This process is a very curious and interesting one. After the gutta percha comes from the kneading-machine, it is by machinery moulded into the thickness of common leather, and is ready for use, or perhaps it is left in lumps, as occasion may require.

Bartlett goes on to describe their visit to the shoe sole manufacturing section: a tubing section with lengths of 400 feet being produced for fire hoses and electrical cable insulation; waterproof sou'wester hats, bonnet linings and stethoscopes; liquid gutta-percha band aids for wounds, golf balls (gutties)—and art. And what art! Bartlett goes into raptures:

> Next we visited the most interesting department of all—that where the nicer and more delicate articles are constructed. Here we first saw a beautiful frame, with the borders exhibiting every appearance of the finest carving, and with the inner portions exquisitely gilded. We were surprised that plain gutta percha could thus be made to resemble the choicest carved or gilded oak, rosewood, or

> mahogany. And not with the chisel, but merely by pressing the ungainly lumps into a mould, so that once a mould [is] constructed, hundreds and thousands of beautiful frames are turned out without the usual expense of artist-work. And they have a great advantage over wood in the fact that they never can be broken; dash them to the ground with all your strength, and it will not harm them. The manager took some delicate-looking flower-vases and threw them to the floor with violence; they bounded back into the air, but were not shivered. Here, too, we saw beautiful works of art—the head of a deer, with the ears falling, like real ears, the horns were slender and natural, but could not be broken.

Bartlett concludes his chapter: 'The first year of the discovery [1843] only two hundred weight [cwt.] were imported into England, while last year [1850] over 30,000 cwt. were entered at the docks.'[xci]

The overharvesting of gutta-percha to provide for novelty goods and undersea cables depleted the stock of trees. For a time, the South American relative, gutta-balata, was used instead. By the 1930's, petroleum-based polyethylene had replaced gutta-percha and gutta balata in most uses. But despite the progress in materials science, gutta-percha is still unmatched: it is chemically inert, non-toxic, minimally allergenic (even to most people with latex allergies), has good sealing properties and mixes well with other materials. For example, gutta-percha can be mixed with zinc oxide, waxes or resins and metal sulphates to produce gutta-percha sticks to seal tooth cavities to prevent

---

xci 1 cwt is equivalent to 50.80 kg in the Imperial system; so 200 cwt is approximately 10,000 kilos, and 30,000 cwt is approximately 1.5 million kilos, a 150-fold increase.

bacterial entry. If you've had a root canal, you are likely carrying gutta-percha around inside your mouth.

Gutta-percha has been known regionally from times immemorial. It was used for the production of large drinking bowls, called 'mazers' and the tree became known as the 'mazer wood tree'. A sample was collected in the seventeenth century by the British father–son team called the Tradescants for display in their museum. A booklet published in 1656 about the museum stated: 'The plyable mazer wood, being warmed in water, will work to any form.'[208] In 1843, William Montgomerie demonstrated its properties of non-shrinkage, chemical resistance and structural strength to the Royal Society of the Arts, further raising its profile. This was also the time period when undersea cables were being tested to carry news more quickly by telegraph. In 1843, Samuel Morse tested a wire coated in rubber and encased in lead to transmit messages across New York Harbor, which worked initially, but the rubber broke down in sea water. Michael Faraday suggested gutta-percha instead of rubber for coating the wire. He was right. Gutta-percha worked its insulation magic—its resilience in sea water actually improved with cold and pressure—on an immense scale. In 1851, the brothers John and Jacob Brett laid a cable with two layers of gutta-percha to successfully connect Dover, England, across the channel with Calais, France. Around 14,000 miles of gutta-percha for sixty-four coated cables had been supplied by 1865, including three Atlantic cables in 1857, 1858 and 1865.[209] Undersea cables laid across the world quickly brought news from distant shores, such as the eruption of Krakatoa in 1883.

In 2013, flat blocks of a rubber-like substance washed up on the beaches of England, Wales, the Shetlands, the Channel Islands, Norway, Sweden, Denmark, France and the

Netherlands. They were stamped TJIPETIR—the name of a nineteenth-century plantation in the Dutch East Indies. They probably came from the hold of a ship called the *Miyazaki Maru*, which was sunk by a German U-boat captained by Kapitänleutnant Walther Schweiger in May 1915. (Later on, in the same month, the Cunard liner *RMS Lusitania* was sunk by a U-boat under his command with the loss of almost 2,000 souls, which turned public opinion in the United States against Germany, and eventually resulted into its entering into World War I.)[210] The washed-up blocks were made of gutta-percha, apparently none the worse for their 100-year dip in salt water. It is precisely this extraordinary chemical and physical resilience that makes gutta-percha so very valuable.

On 20 May 1856, Massachusetts Republican Senator Charles Sumner gave a fiery speech on the Senate floor in the US Congress. Sumner was an intellectual. He had sponsored the Metric Act bill so that the 'confusion of Babel (in the systems of weights and measures then in use) may be overcome'. An abolitionist, he had railed against the institution of slavery and against the slavery-supporting southern Democrats. He named names, calling out South Carolina senator and slaveholder Andrew Pickens Butler. In addition to the opprobrium he heaped on Senator Butler, Sumner was targeting an 1854 law Butler had co-authored with Illinois Senator Stephen A. Douglas called the 'Kansas–Nebraska Act'. This act repealed the 1820 Missouri Compromise, which had been negotiated by anti-slavery northerners to prevent the spread of slavery above the 36°30' line, and the 'compromise' came from permitting Missouri to become the only slaveholding territory north of this latitude. By repealing the compromise, the 1854 Kansas–

Nebraska Act had returned the vast territories of the Louisiana Purchase to state control for deciding their own slavery status, eventually triggering the Civil War. In his speech, which he titled 'The Crime Against Kansas' Sumner said of Butler: 'Of course he has chosen a mistress to whom he has made his vows, and who, though ugly to others, is always lovely to him; though polluted in the sight of the world, is chaste in his sight—I mean the harlot, Slavery. For her, his tongue is always profuse in words. Let her be impeached in character, or any proposition made to shut her out from the extension of her wantonness, and no extravagance of manner or hardihood of assertion is then too great for this senator.'[211]

Two days later, three men entered the Senate chamber where Senator Sumner was at his desk, working on a document. They were South Carolina Representatives Preston Brooks, Laurence Keitt and Virginia Congressman Henry A. Edmundson. Preston Brooks, who was Andrew Butler's cousin, walked up to Sumner. 'Mr. Sumner, I have read your speech twice over carefully. It is a libel on South Carolina, and Mr. Butler, who is a relative of mine,' he said. As the forty-five-year-old Sumner began to stand, Brooks heinously began to hit him on the head with a gold-capped walking stick (Figure 23).[212] Sumner was soon blinded by the blood pouring from his wound. Keitt and Edmundson prevented other congressmen and senators from intervening—Keitt brandishing a cane and a pistol—as Sumner lost consciousness. Nevertheless, Brooks kept beating the unconscious senator up until his cane broke. Eventually, Brooks was pulled off and he exited the room without a word, leaving the cane behind.[213] That cane was made of gutta-percha. Had Brooks been in possession of a cane made from gutta-percha's cousin, natural rubber, he would have caused no less emotional, but certainly less physical, damage. However, despite its composition, the cane the infamous Preston Brooks used to thrash Charles Sumner did 'shiver'—only the half with the gold head is now on display at the Old State House Museum in Boston.

Figure 23: Lithograph of South Carolina's US Representative Preston Brooks attacking US Senator Charles Sumner of Massachusetts in the Senate Chamber with a gutta-percha cane in 1856. Although Brooks is shown holding the cane by the knob, eyewitnesses testified that he repeatedly hit Sumner with the gold knob end of the cane.[214]

10

The Good, the Bad

On 27 August 1883, news of the eruption of Krakatoa was carried around the world on gutta-percha undersea cables from Batavia (now Jakarta) in Indonesia. Sheltered from the pyroclastic fallout a few miles away, in the captain's cabin of the paraffin carrier ship the *Belem*, were seeds of gutta-percha's western cousin, the rubber-producing plant, *Hevea brasiliensis*.[215] These seedlings were destined for setting up plantations in Southeast Asia. They survived, and would go on to revolutionise the world's production of rubber.

In 2022, world natural rubber production stood at about 15 million kilotons,[xcii] a doubling of production from 2000, and a staggering five-fold increase from half a century ago in 1982. As mentioned earlier, south-east Asia is currently the largest natural rubber producer, with ten countries represented in the ANRPC. Among the top five producers outside the ANRPC

xcii 1 kt = 1,000 tons; 1 ton = 1,000 kg; 1 kg = 2.2 lbs

in 2022 are Ivory Coast, Nigeria and Ghana in Africa, Brazil in South America and Guatemala in Central America. (Figure 24).

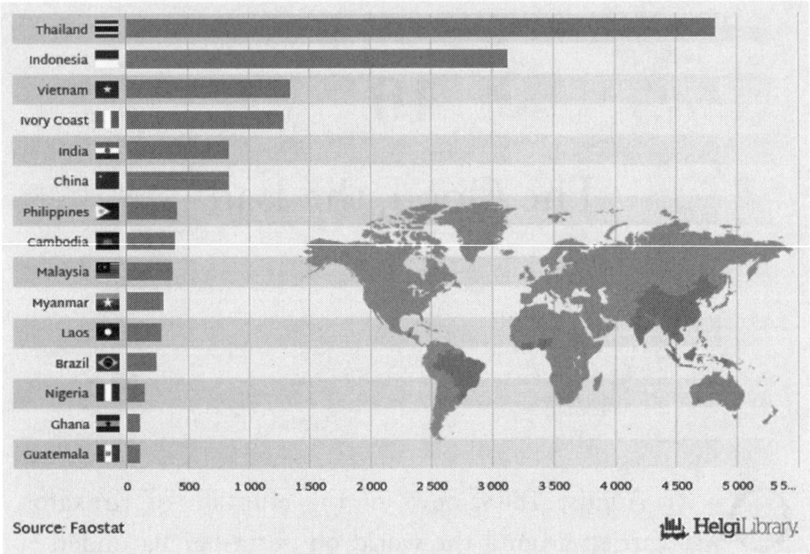

Figure 24: Natural rubber production in 2022 in kilotons (kt). The geographical locations of the top fifteen producers is shaded on the map.[216]

The consistently increasing demand for natural rubber · is causing significant and deleterious tropical forest impact. With a resurgence in the demand for rubber, vast areas across rubber-producing areas of Asia are being cleared with staggering damage to biodiversity. The ANRPC estimated that the demand for rubber would increase following the slowdowns caused by the pandemic in line with previous jumps in demand in 1922 following the flu epidemic, and in 1933, following the Great Depression. An increase of 250,000 hectares of land containing mature trees is expected, but the rise in rubber production is expected to be absorbed by the jump in demand.[217] Within just one decade between 2011 and 2021, two million hectares of additional land was transferred to rubber plantations in

Southeast Asia alone. In a survey of deforestation measured by decrease in tree canopy using satellite data, Jayathilake and team (2024) inferred that rubber plantations caused degradation of forest cover of the surrounding area of up to a kilometre on the island of Sumatra in Indonesia between 2000 and 2018. The intensity of degradation was proportional to plantation size, remoteness and market price. Nearer to protected areas, less intense degradation was noted. Plantations also degrade the quality of forest.[218] Where tropical forest had been converted to rubber plantations, plant richness decreased from 963 to 230, a 76 per cent loss.[219] Zhang et al. (2019) associated plantations with severe impacts on biodiversity and ecosystem effects and inferred that forest-to-rubber plantation conversion has more deleterious impact than timber logging.[200]

But it is not only the impact on biodiversity that rubber poses—it has exposed social and economic fault lines. In Brazil, the murder of Chico Mendes in 1988 rocked the region and the attentive world. His name is now immortalised in Brazil with the Institute for Conservation of Biodiversity—something he fought for along with worker rights at a time rubber planters were aggressively moving to expand. It was just another chapter in the struggles of the rubber industry. There is the ever-present danger of the agent of a fungal disease of rubber trees, South American leaf blight (SALB), making its way from South America to Southeast Asia and devastating the trees there, especially since the introduction of direct flights from Brazil (previously, to prevent this, direct travel had been resisted for decades prior). Concerns are also voiced that bioterrorists could cripple the industry with the release of pathogens. Climate change is a looming concern as well. There is much that is speculated, but there is little that is known about how hotter climates could affect rubber yield because trees produce latex in the cool, humid conditions of early mornings, but dry up as the day heats up. Rubber producers also face an economic battle. In 2024, rubber producers in India filed an application for intervention against cartel-like behaviour of tyre manufacturers, specifically MRF, Ceat, Apollo and JK Tyres, with India's Supreme Court.[221] The problems that attend natural rubber persist from plantation to product.

Yet there are some places where smallholders can contribute to the rubber crop without damaging the wild ecosystem. Some Asian countries have largely opted out of the industrial plantation model to empower smallholders who can eke out a living on as little as 3 acres of rubber trees.[222] An example is in the southern Indian state of Kerala, which contributes 90 per cent of the country's total natural rubber production.[xciii] Small holders with average of 1.23 acres make up 92 per cent of the land under rubber cultivation.[223] I spent some time in Kerala, visiting a rubber nursery and plantations in Palakkad and the Rubber Research Institute in Alleppey. Palakkad is lightly forested and is located between the Silent Valley National Park in Kerala and the Annamalai Tiger Reserve in Tamil Nadu. I rented a car and driver to explore the area. As we were leaving the city outskirts and driving towards Silent Valley, we stopped at a rubber plantation on the bank of the Malampuzha Dam Lake.

---

xciii India ranked #4 in the 2021 list of the world's top natural rubber producing countries with 749,000 metric tonnes. Above India in production were: Vietnam (1,271,474 metric tonnes), Indonesia (3,121,272 metric tonnes) and the world's top producer, Thailand (4,643,721 metric tonnes).

Jobi and his wife TJ, the farm owners, were friendly and welcoming. They showed me their marching lines of rubber trees planted 12 feet apart. Betel nut palms stood here and there (Figure 25). Jobi explained how rubber trees were in sections staggered by age so that, as older plants became unproductive, those sections could be replanted without disturbing the others. I noticed small polythene bag-umbrellas placed over the collecting cups so that dripping latex would not be diluted by rain. On another farm (owned by Jayan and located south-east of Palakkad), banana trees were planted in sections with young rubber trees since the canopy had not yet closed and adequate sunlight for other crops still reached the ground. As the trees mature, the intercropping practice is abandoned for easier access to the rubber tree trunks.

Figure 25: Rubber trees on Jobi and TJ's farm outside Palakkad, Kerala. Jobi presses rubber sheets previously coagulated by treating latex with formic acid while TJ collects the expressed liquid in carboys for biogas production. Photo credit: V. Rajan.

Jobi showed me how the latex he and TJ had collected in the morning had been treated with formic acid and left to sit for several hours in aluminium pans. The rubber had coagulated, and it was now time to press the liquid out and dry the sheets of rubber. At this point, the coagulated sheets were tofu-white and the texture and density was similar to raw chicken breast. As the sheet was passed through the wringer, the rubber sheet emerged, ribbed with little grooves. The liquid squeezed out was collected by TJ to be used for biogas production on the farm (Figure 25). After pressing, the ribbed rubber sheets are air-dried in the shade and then smoked. I observed the smoking process at Jayan's farm, where the smoker room had bamboo rods on which the rubber sheets were draped for several days until they had all turned dark. The slow, cool smoking provides a drying, preservative effect similar to smoked meat. The sheets are graded by cleanliness and appearance, then hauled to the rubber cooperative in town for sale. At the time I was visiting, a kilogram of high-quality rubber sheets would earn about INR 150 (approximately US $1.80) and crumb sold around INR 100 (US $1.20) in 2022. Jobi and TJ harvested around fourteen sheets a day during the high season and five sheets during the low season.

Figure 26: Top: Jobi presses rubber sheets through a wringer. Sheets awaiting pressing are stacked on the left wringer. Below left: Jobi holds up a pressed rubber sheet. Below right: A stack of rubber awaits pressing beside wringers. Photo credit: V. Rajan.

The following day, I visited a rubber nursery. It was a revelation. Rubber trees are not grown from seed to saplings. On the contrary, known high productivity rubber plant stems are grafted onto separately propagated rootstock, a process known as bud-grafting (Figure 27). The grafted plants are allowed to recover, tended until the grafting is judged to 'take' and then shipped to plantations. On the day of my visit, several thousand grafts were being loaded on a truck for the 2,000-mile trip to Assam, in the northeast of India, where rubber plantations are just starting up. In the late nineteenth century, twelve rubber seedlings, painstakingly coaxed to germinate from 1,000 seeds, had died of the cold in Calcutta (see Chapter 4). *Hevea* needs cool but moist mornings and warm daytime temperatures—climate change has warmed the higher latitudes, which were too cold for comfort 150 years ago, to balmy enough for the plants now.

Figure 27: Rubber rootstock with grafted high-productivity rubber tree stems. Photo credit: V. Rajan.

Two workers, Radhakrishnan and Rajan showed me around the nursery. Thousands of young plants were awaiting shipment in the shade of a large tent. Out back, one- or two-year-old trees were dotted around. They would be used as the rootstock for new grafts for high-yielding plants (Figure 28).

Figure 28: Radhakrishnan and Rajan, rubber nursery workers, with young rubber trees. Photo credit: V. Rajan.

I then visited the beautifully landscaped Rubber Research Institute in Kottayam, Kerala (Figure 29). The institute supports research into production of a variety of raw and vulcanised rubber products. There were several groups of students from local and national colleges who were visiting to learn new techniques in processing and production. They demonstrated the procedure for making pigmented latex gloves by stirring in different pigments into two separate beakers of latex, plunging hand-shaped moulds in and then steeping the lightly coated moulds in another solution. The rubber solidified, and could be peeled off and dried. There were also students working on mixing in carbon black, sulphur and other additives to give rubber resilience and tensile strength for use in car tyres and belts. The institute also develops high-yield rubber plants and interstitial methods like agricultural practices and parallel revenue streams.

Figure 29: Rubber Research Institute, Kottayam, Kerala.
Photo credit: V. Rajan.

The researchers at the rubber institute described a new initiative they were field testing—setting up beehives in rubber plantations to provide another revenue stream. Unlike regular dicots where the nectar-producing structure is located inside the flower, nectaries in rubber plants are located at the base of the leaf so the rubber honey season lasts all year long. Two of the rubber farmers I talked to about it were cautiously open to trying it out, and one other was not sure he wanted to be handling or hosting stinging insects. A rubber farm takes seven years to establish and lasts just over twenty-five more, but it can only be tapped during the cooler winter months. Although rubber wood can be sold to produce income when the plants have to be replaced every thirty years or so, there are revenue gaps seasonally, and having other revenue streams seems like a good idea. The options range from bees to intercropping with cash crops. During that time, as the trees are growing, there is plenty of sunlight available and plants such as bananas (as on Jayan's farm) are suitable. But, as the canopy develops, less sunlight is available and shade-loving plants fare better.

There are other constraints. The crops should not impede access to tree trunks by vining up the trunks or cause tripping hazards since tapping is done in the pre-dawn gloom. Their products should have high agricultural value and ideally not have a long lag time between planting and harvest. Following are some of the crops that meet these requirements.[224] The list is divided into 'initial intercrops' (banana, pineapple, groundnut, passion fruit, bamboo fungus, tobacco, hemp, yams, chilli peppers, cotton, taro, cucurbits, patchouli, mung bean, groundnut, pea, sugarcane, sorghum, maize, sweet potato and soy, among others) and 'permanent intercrops' (cocoa, cashew nut, custard apple, neem, mango, eaglewood, betel nut, papaya, cinnamon, coffee, mangosteen, macadamia nut, durian, konjac yam and valuable tropical hardwoods such as acacia, teak, rosewood, mahogany and padauk). Leguminous cover crops to suppress weeds and add nitrogen to the soil are also recommended. Some of these plants can additionally support honeybees or livestock.

The smallholder model allows this cottage industry to accrue benefits to farmers rather than corporations and many farmers belong to local cooperative societies which can negotiate better prices. The dispersed nature of smallholder farms also mitigates the spread of the potentially devastating diseases, such as SALB. Seasonal intercropping and livestock management on rubber farms additionally provides a steady revenue stream through periods when latex cannot be harvested. Finally, farmlands remain in the hands of farmers rather than corporations, which allows market prices to be maintained rather than undercut by volume producers at the cost of labourers. This is the least appreciated benefit of all. Owning the means of production also safeguards against exploitation for an industry whose track record has been quite woeful. This is a model that bears exporting to other countries where it is not already in place. Small-scale cultivation cooperatives could represent the win-win that the rubber industry needs to grow sustainably.

Rubber is indispensable for modern life, and the production of natural and synthetic rubber is projected to increase to meet demands. But there is also the matter of disposal.

- The worldwide market for automobile tyres is projected to grow at about 3.5% through 2028, but regional demand may be higher—the Asia-Pacific market, led by India, is expected to show 6.4% compounded annual growth rate (CAGR).[225] The markets project that 2.7 billion tyres will be sold in 2026 alone.[xciv] Shake that statistic and it disgorges

xciv Assuming each tyre weighs about 20 pounds and 2.7 billion tyres in 2026 alone, that is a total of 54 billion pounds. Projections are that there will be roughly 8.3 billion people on the planet in

6.5 pounds of tyre material for each of the projected 8.3 billion people who will be on the planet in 2026, several billion of whom will not own automobiles.

- Each year, about 1 to 1.8 billion tyres are discarded.[226] Discarded tyres are typically burned for energy rather than recycled. When recycled, they are used to make crumb for bulking asphalt, backfilling in landfills and construction sites and in Portland cement. Typically though, they are collected in tyre dumps where fires occasionally break out and are hard to put out. The biggest tyre graveyard in the world contains 7 million tyres and is in Al Sulaibiya in Kuwait; here fires in 2012 burned 5 million tyres, one in 2020 burned 1 million tyres, and a 2021 fire burned 7 million tyres.[227] Documentation by government agencies is hard to come by, but a list is maintained by Wikipedia which shows tyre fires happen everywhere.[228] Even this list is incomplete: the massive 2021 Al Sulaibiya fire is not on the list.
- Automobile tyres release millions of tons of rubber particles that wash into streams. A tyre stabiliser called 6PPD degrades into a substance known as 6PPD-quinone, which is toxic at the miniscule quantity of 95 nanograms per litre, or 0.095 parts per billion.[229] This chemical causes juvenile and adult Coho salmon to asphyxiate, crashing their numbers. The EPA has released an advance notice to protect salmon from this chemical[230] but the US is also changing administrations in 2025. Watch this space.
- Plastic and rubber microparticles are widely distributed in soil and water. They enter flesh and blood through the food we eat and the air we breathe, and into those of other

---

2026 (https://www.worldometers.info/world-population/world-population-projections/), so that will amount to 6.5 lbs of tyre per person, in 2026 alone.

animals also. *Plasticosis*[231] has recently entered the medical lexicon and maybe *caoutchoucosis* will too. Shredded rubber crumb obtained from recycled tyres in playgrounds has recently been associated with toxic additives; additionally, crumbs that shake loose can be ingested or breathed in by young children.[232] No doubt adverse health effects will be investigated if they emerge.

But there is also some good news.

A rubber-degrading organism, *Gordonia polyisoprenivorans,* was isolated, bizarrely enough, from an American cancer patient who developed pneumonia secondary to bacteraemia.[233] The surgeons speculated that it may have been consuming the rubber present in haematological catheters. This bacterium had previously been isolated from stagnant water in a rubber tyre and is ubiquitous in the environment, presumably feeding on the equivalently ubiquitous rubber particles. Rubber tyres are already being degraded by known microorganisms in the environment by bacteria in the *Corynebacterium-Nocardia-Mycobacterium* group, some *Actinomyces* (a type of filamentous bacteria),[234] *Delftia tsuruhatensis*[235] and less well characterised fungi in the genera *Penicillium* and *Aspergillus,* as well as several others. The enzymes they produce react with rubber and break it down.[xcv] The polluting results of our pathological love affair with rubber are already being mitigated by the unsung workhorses of the planet—degraders.

We are luckier than we deserve.

---

xcv Examples of rubber degrading enzymes are lipoxygenases, peroxidases and laccases. Lipoxygenases add two oxygen atoms to lipids like natural rubber, whereas peroxidases and laccases remove electrons from target molecules. Both of these mechanisms are referred to as oxidation.

III
Appendices

Appendix A

The Biosynthesis of Terpenes

Understanding how complex systems work can be accomplished by breaking them down into their component parts and examining each parts' contribution to the whole. In the same spirit of reductionism, latex can be studied by breaking it down to its simplest parts. Take a deep breath and let's dive in.

There are ninety-two naturally occurring atoms which represent the construction materials of the universe. Of these, living systems use only a handful, and only six—hydrogen, carbon, oxygen, nitrogen, phosphorus and sulphur—are used in abundance. Using the genetic code of the cell contained in the DNA, a class of proteins called enzymes is assembled in the cell. Enzymes are the toolkits of the cell and catalyse the formation of the other molecules the cell needs: proteins, carbohydrates, lipids and nucleic acids. In each generation, nature randomly modifies the inherited genetic code to build a few modified proteins and road-tests their function in a body which may be exposed to new challenges. It is an unstoppable process that has no pre-set destination but results in adaptation, because only successfully adapted bodies will accrue enough energy to reproduce—the big test—and pass on the modifications to their offspring. There are two 'secret sauce' ingredients to nature's success in building adapted bodies. One is having the time to implement an iterative *modify, build, and test* process. The other is the carbon atom.

Carbon is a familiar atom. In its simplest chemistry, carbon combines with itself in a variety of ways to make a large number of allotropes like coal, diamond and buckminsterfullerene (bucky balls). When linked to oxygen atoms, carbon makes gaseous carbon monoxide and carbon dioxide. Linked to hydrogen atoms, carbon is at its efficient best with added creative flair: it makes gaseous hydrocarbons like methane, liquids like gasoline, waxy or oily paraffins and a simple building block called isoprene. Necessary to the buildup or breakdown of isoprene is a dimeric carbon molecule, acetyl coenzyme A, shortened to acetyl CoA. The acetyl portion will be familiar to you—this is the stem for molecules like acetic acid (vinegar), acetone (nail polish remover) or the drinkable alcohol (ethanol) in beer. CoA is a molecular flag made from vitamin B5 that tells the cell that this acetyl molecule is primed and ready for chemical reactions. Primed acetyl groups are linked to make isoprene. Isoprene molecules can link up to produce larger molecules called terpenes which, in turn, produce chemicals whose structural and functional diversity is dizzying and include odour molecules, vitamin A and rubber.[xcvi]

---

xcvi Acetyl groups are linked together in different numbers to make a slew of fatty acids with different numbers of acetyl groups: lauric and palmitoleic acids with 6 acetyl units, myristic and oleic acids

Terpene (also called isoprenoid) biosynthesis occurs in bacteria and archaea, the two simplest life forms known.[236] Genes for their synthesis must have diversified early in evolutionary time because terpenes are ubiquitous even in ancient sediments, and they are so different and numerous—there are several tens of thousands of known structures.[237] Small terpene molecules are volatile and so have an associated fragrance, such as citronella and rose. Higher level terpenes are formed by sequential addition to make molecules with twenty, twenty-five and thirty carbon units and include essential fatty acids such as omega-3 and omega-6 oils. Catapulting way up, where constituent carbon atoms number in the thousands, we, at last, reach rubber and its cousin, gutta-percha. Their difference lies in the way the isoprene monomers are oriented (Figure 30). If the polymerising bonds (shown as a squiggle in the figure) are on the same side of the double bond, the molecule has cis-1,4 polyisoprene units and makes elastic rubber. If they are on opposite sides of the double bond, then the molecule has trans-1,4 isoprene units and makes rigid gutta-percha.

with 7 acetyl units, linoleic and palmitic acids with 8 acetyl units, stearic and linolenic acids with 9 acetyl units, and arachidic and arachidonic acids with 10 acetyl units. The reason for multiple acids with the same number of acetyl units is a function of the saturation or unsaturation of the fatty acid. Lauric acid is a saturated molecule, a fat which is solid at room temperature, and palmitoleic acid is an unsaturated molecule, an oil which is liquid at room temperature.

Natural rubber: cis 1, 4-polyisoprene

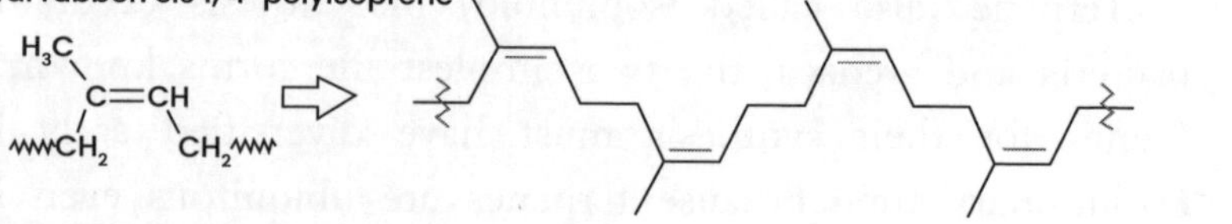

Gutta percha: trans 1,4-polyisoprene

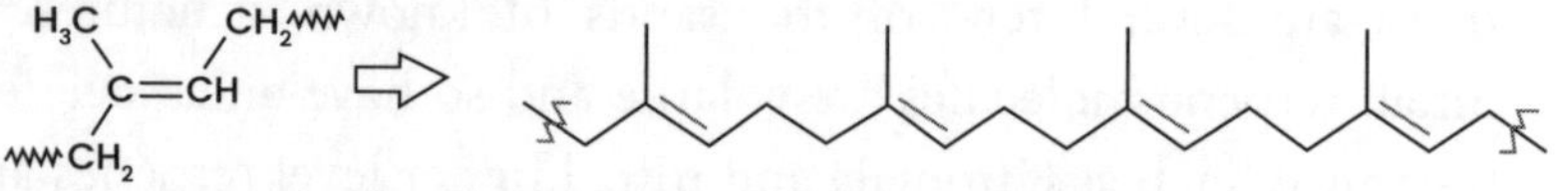

Figure 30: The chemical structures of natural rubber and gutta-percha. Natural rubber is a cis-1,4-polyisoprene with polymerising bonds (shown as a squiggle) oriented on the same side of the rigid double bond. Gutta-percha and balata have trans-1,4-polyisoprene with polymerising bonds oriented on opposite sides of the rigid double bond.[238]

As a consequence of the cis- or trans- units, bonding between strands varies. Gutta-percha has more bonds between strands and is rigid. Natural rubber has fewer bonds between strands and slides about like cooked spaghetti. But if sulphur is added and the mixture is heated up, vulcanisation occurs. Sulphur binds to natural rubber and forms strong sulphur-to-sulphur bonds between strands. This stops the strands sliding about as much and, when stretched and released, vulcanised rubber rebounds back to shape because of these anchoring bonds. This vulcanised rubber has an additional odd property: unlike most substances, rubber shrinks when heated and expands when cooled. This is beneficial when using belts to drive machinery: as the belts spin and heat up, they shrink to fit, rather than expand and fall off.

The C_5H_8 isoprene monomer is made in a series of biochemical reactions. One of these pathways, called the mevalonate pathway (MVA), is present in eukaryotes, archaea and some eubacteria and appears to be the original and ancient pathway for making terpenes, although some bacteria have a second pathway called the non-mevalonate pathway (MEP).[239] MVA's ubiquity implies that it is possible that the cenancestor[xcvii] had membranes containing isoprenoids.[240] What this means is that the enzymes engaged in this process are present in all life forms. Just think about that for a minute. Lurking in your body are genes that you share with lifeforms that evolved over two billion years ago!

Over time, the types and functions of isoprene-based molecules proliferated—5-carbon isoprenes linked to make 10-carbon monoterpenes, which are volatile and have aromas, such as limonene from lemons and geraniol from roses. Three 5-carbon isoprene units join together to make a 15-carbon sesquiterpene such as zingiberene from ginger. Diterpenoids have four isoprene units and twenty carbon atoms (e.g. taxol from yew and vitamin A), sesterterpenoids have five isoprene units and twenty-five carbon atoms (e.g. polygodiol from peppers) … the list goes on. Familiar molecules such as chlorophyll, vitamin D, steroids and prostaglandins are all terpenes. A famous triterpene is squalene, originally obtained from the liver of animals in the family Squalidae—the sharks. Squalene is used as a cosmetics ingredient and as an adjuvant (a chemical which stimulates the immune system) in many vaccines. The overharvesting of sharks—2.7 million sharks in 2023—for the beauty and pharmaceutical industries is causing their populations to crash. Other sources of squalene exist: sugarcane, olives and rice bran. Pressuring these industries to move to plant-based sources would help save some shark species from impending extinction.

Eventually we reach chain lengths of thousands and carbon atoms, which is where we find rubber and gutta-percha.

---

xcvii The cenancestor or LUCA is the ancestor of all life on earth.

Appendix B

Two Examples of the Duplicate-and-Modify Process

In Chapter 7, I touched briefly on how the 355 genes thought to be essential to life morphed to help their descendants adapt to new environments, but also the problem of messing with gene sequences. If the gene is important for survival, the animal will die if it is modified. But if the gene is first duplicated, then modifying the copy rather than the original allows new functions to emerge that may be adaptive. For example, the human genome has accrued around 14,000 pseudogenes which have no, or yet unknown, functions.[241] Many of our everyday genes arose from other genes that are still performing vital functions, for example genes belonging to the steroid family (cholesterol, estrogen, progesterone, testosterone, cortisol), membrane molecules (chlorophyll, haemoglobin, carotene) and the rubber synthesis enzyme superfamily. In this appendix, I will take a closer look at two examples of the 'duplicate-and-modify' process to show how new genes and functions emerge.

Haemoglobin is a member of the family of globin genes, and is a critically important protein in blood because it binds to and distributes oxygen around the body. There are three other globin genes in vertebrates: myoglobin (MB), neuroglobin (NGB) and cytoglobin (CYGB). NGB appears to be the ancestor of all these various globin genes; this gene has been dated back to 800 Ma, to the origins of the animal lineage itself. Besides binding to oxygen, NGB and MB also protect mitochondria when oxygen levels are low. This protective activity in cells provides an adaptive benefit: cells with the gene would have outperformed cells without, and the gene spread through the population. In adult vertebrates, haemoglobin consists of an α-globin and a β-globin subunit encoded by the HBA and HBB genes, and 2α and 2β subunits combine to make a large functional protein. But multiple versions of haemoglobin also exist, some which are expressed in embryonic or foetal stages, and some of which are nonfunctional pseudogenes (Figure 31).

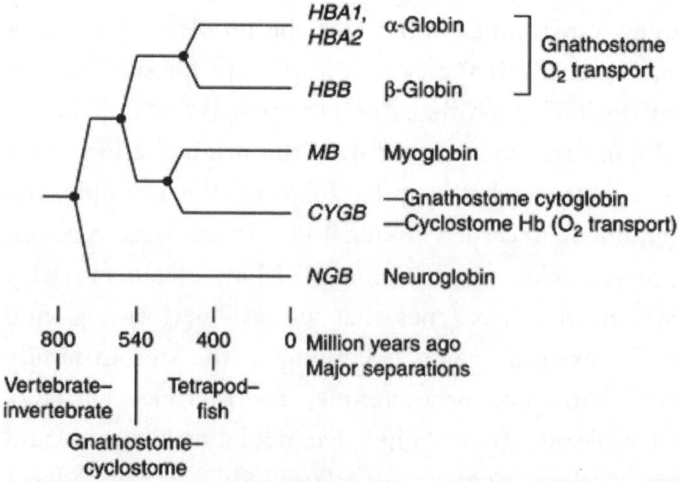

Figure 31: Model for evolution of vertebrate globin genes. The deduced times of duplication and divergence are shown along the horizontal axis, and contemporary human globin genes are shown on the right. Major duplication

events in globin gene evolution are noted along the tree, and time of origin of some major animal groups is indicated along the horizontal axis. For simplicity, only the gene tree is shown.[242]

Another example of this duplication-divergence in animals is the existence of related genes for the hormones oxytocin and vasopressin.[xcviii] Oxytocin is the famed 'love' hormone. It helps with childbirth, mother–child bonding and the establishment of trust between unrelated people. In an experiment, oxytocin recipients showed a greater willingness to overcome distrust and engage in a financial transaction despite a possible risk of betrayal than participants who received a placebo.[243] The amino acid[xcix] sequence of the hormone vasopressin (Cys-Tyr-Phe-Gln-Asn-Cys-Pro-Arg-Gly) differs in just two positions out of nine from oxytocin (Cys-Tyr-Ile-Gln-Asn-Cys-Pro-Leu-Gly). Vasopressin regulates a variety of social behaviours which may have arisen from its role as an antidiuretic hormone which regulates water levels in the body. Urination makes possible the practice of scent marking, which is used by many animals to establish their identity while claiming territory.[244] Identity is also tied to relationships. This links the (superficially unrelated) diuretic function of vasopressin with trust-bonding oxytocin, which arose by duplication and modification.

The evolutionary strategy of 'tweak and test' led to a variety of ways to modulate genes. Latex levels respond to the pressures of predation by herbivores and environmental stresses such as

xcviii These hormones are made in the supraoptic nucleus and paraventricular nucleus of the hypothalamus which project into the posterior pituitary gland where they are released.

xcix Amino acid sequences are encoded by genes. When the gene sequence is modified, the amino acid sequence may also change. The resulting protein may have a different structure and properties from the one it originated from.

drought. For example, well irrigated guayule plants accumulated less rubber than plants subjected to water stress.[245] One more way that molecules can diversify their functions: by combining functionally with another molecule to produce a physiological outcome. Some of these combinations are so familiar that one does not recognise them as being unusual. For example, diabetes is caused by the coordinated function of two molecules, insulin and the insulin receptor. If insulin is deficient, type 1 diabetes results. If the receptor is non-functional, it leads to type 2 diabetes. This is effectively like two separate entities that cooperate to function effectively, such as a car chassis and an engine. Together they can move you from one place to another, but independently, they are not functional for transport.

Appendix C

The Variety and Value of Plant Secondary Metabolites

Metabolites already present in the cell are also modified to fulfil secondary functions of deterrence. They may be metabolites that emerged from duplication-divergence, by co-opting existing pathways to combine molecule end products to a new function, or by tweaking a chemical reaction to make a different end product that is unpleasant to predators. Mutations do not cause these protective variations to show up fully formed or to emerge because it is helpful. Just as you cannot grow wings because you would like to fly, plants cannot wish into existence protective features like spines. Changes that occur are based on existing features that are tweaked a little, repurposing structures already present—spines are just leaves made pointy over time. Further, over a long period of time, a small spine can become a longer spine by increments, selected because a plant with a big spine deters more than a small spine, remains uneaten and reproduces to pass on long spine genes. Similarly, when a predator approaches, takes a bite and dislikes the taste, it may abandon that nasty plant for another nearby which is more palatable. The unpleasant-tasting plant survives to reproduce and pass on genes for unpleasant taste to its multiple offspring. Variations due to changes over time can iteratively hone the feature. Each change to the genetic code must be accompanied by a perceptible change in the interaction with herbivores. Without incremental increases in deterrent ability, the plant will simply get consumed and the change consigned to the dustbin of genetic history. If it survives, it joins the evolutionary arms race. And the evolutionary arms race is relentless—noxious-plant-munching pests have adapted by evolving resistance to toxins. The black-spined iguana eats poisonous manchineel fruit and lives on the deadly tree;[c] the monarch butterfly caterpillar not only eats but sequesters the toxic cardenolides in the latex of milkweed in its own body, thereby becoming unpalatable to birds.

Many deterrents are 'secondary' metabolites, which are not essential for life but have a significant role in adaptation. These include several made of terpene and their terpenoid derivatives as defensive and offensive weapons. The term 'terpenes' originates from turpentine, a secondary terpenoid that was distilled from the sap of the Mediterranean terebinth tree from prehistoric times. Although pine trees produce larger quantities, and commercial production is from petroleum, the name has stuck.

c The manchineel tree (*Hippomane mancinella*) is called the world's most dangerous tree. Every part of the tree including its roots and fruit are poisonous. It is native to Central and South America and produces a white latex containing a variety of noxious chemicals including phorbol esters.

Another familiar class of secondary terpenoids are the essential oils, which are aromatic and volatile with low molecular weight. They are called essential oils because they have a scent, an essence. These impart aroma to lavender, roses and citrus; add flavour to coffee, mint and bay leaves; and have buttery names that roll off the tongue: linalool, geraniol, citronellol. Although they are insoluble in water, they are generally soluble in alcohols or may be mixed in with resins and waxes. It is tempting to think that volatile terpene secondary metabolites are beneficial or benign. After all, these lovely perfumes and essential life molecules like chlorophylls and carotenes must be good for the animals drawn to them. Not so. These perfumes have multiple roles. Although they summon pollinators with a promise of nectar and pollen, they deter them from laying eggs (which would produce leaf-nibbling caterpillars) by tasting terrible and probably inducing a stomach-ache. Insects are repelled by some fragrances that are attractive to humans, such as camphor and citronella, which are now used as natural bug repellents.

Secretions are another defensive-offensive substance. The first is gum, which is a polysaccharide material soluble in water, producing a sticky and viscous jelly-like substance capable of entrapping small insects. The second is resin, a complex mixture of aromatic compounds which are heavy, non-volatile and insoluble in water. The term 'aromatic' comes from the presence of a benzene ring which is present in a slew of compounds that have a strong smell (like phenol), unpalatable bitter tastes and sticky, resinous textures. Some may even kill animals by interfering with cellular processes—this is the mode of action of artemisinin and taxol—or produce neurological disturbances such as tetrahydrocannabinol from cannabis. The third type of secretion is composed of enormous molecules of up to tens of thousands of terpene units, which ooze from cuts when the plant is damaged, serving as both deterrent and sticky band-aid for the wound. This substance, of course, is latex containing rubber. Table 3 provides a compilation of secondary metabolites with herbivory-deterrent properties.

Table 3: Classes of secondary metabolites that deter herbivory[246]

Class of secondary metabolite	Mechanism of action	Comments
Cyanogenic glucosides	R-CH-CN core, derived from amino acids. Molecules break down to release cyanide, which is a respiratory poison.	Wide distribution in all vascular plants, for e.g., cassava. Some insects, such as larvae of the southern armyworm have adapted to cyanide in their diet.
Glucosinolates	>100 variations, derived from amino acids. When released from special compartments, they produce 'mustard oils' which produce pungent taste. Breakdown of products in the gut may cause discomfort.	Present in radish, mustard, and cabbage families. Activated when plant cells are broken by the action of the enzyme myrosinase. Cooking inactivates the enzyme. Many pest insects have adapted to feed on plants containing glucosinolates.

Class of secondary metabolite	Mechanism of action	Comments
Non-protein amino acids	Derived from amino acids, these substitute for biogenic amino acids and get incorporated into proteins which then become non-functional. Their breakdown products may also be toxic.	Diversity of plants, and many legumes contain non-protein amino acids. Examples are canavanine (whose breakdown product is an analogue of ornithine) and mimosine, which is broken down by gut bacteria to toxic compounds. Resistant insects produce tRNAs that can discriminate against non-protein amino acids.
Alkaloids	Grouped together with true alkaloids, pseudoalkaloids and protoalkaloids. True alkaloids are derived from amino acids, are basic and have heterocyclic rings with nitrogen. Generally toxic, have psychedelic/ bioactive effects or are unpalatable. They are induced in response to microbial attack.	Over 15,000 types, produced by 20 per cent of plant species, including all of the poppy family of plants (Papaveraceae). Many alkaloids are bioactive and have been sought after for that activity. A slew of examples includes, caffeine (coffee), solanidine (potato), mescaline (cacti), strychnine (*Strychnos* seeds), nicotine (tobacco), cocaine (opium).

Class of secondary metabolite	Mechanism of action	Comments
Plant phenolics	Secondary metabolites originating from a variety of metabolites including aromatic amino acids, flavonoids, terpenes, tannins, lignin precursors. Deterrence mechanisms are through unpalatability, toxic effects, may be induced in response to microbial attack, cause complex formation with and inhibition of enzymes, induction of free radicals, or thickening of cells by deposition.	Phenolics are produced constitutively or induced in response to plant damage from a variety of pathogens including fungi, worms and insects. In some cases, phenolics, cellulose and latex form indigestible phytobezoars that cause alimentary distress.

Class of secondary metabolite	Mechanism of action	Comments
Plant terpenes	Act as antifeedants, toxins, and interfere with insect development. Wound-response volatile terpenes deter insects or recruit natural predators of herbivores. Sesquiterpenoids are induced upon microbial damage. Saponins are terpene glycosides and have antifeedant or toxic properties.	Diverse class with more than 40,000 known members built with isoprenoid (C_5H_8) monomer. Latex contains a variety of toxic terpenoids in addition to latex.

Epilogue

When I was in primary school, I was told that the rubber in the eraser on the end of my pencil came from the milk of a tree. Being somewhat literal minded, I seized on the two words I recognised and decided to make my own erasers. I put some wood shavings into a cup, added milk to it and stirred the mixture with the stubby end of a pencil for the rubber to coagulate on. It didn't happen immediately so I sat the cup on a windowsill and naturally … it festered. No rubber. No matter. Even if my early experiment was a bust, the poetry of the phrase 'the milk of a tree' stayed with me.

I went on to study biology. My doctoral thesis was on the mechanism by which a sporulation-associated bacterial toxin disrupted the gut membranes of mosquito larvae and caused their deaths. Antifeedants that had narrow spectrum activity, such as Bt, became popular and widespread as biological pesticides. They were formulated for various applications and some were engineered into crops to protect against insect damage during plant growth. I moved on to other research and eventually into teaching.

Through years of hiking, gardening and beekeeping, I became more attuned to nature. I noted that some plants like dandelions produced latex, that some plants were hosts to a large variety of caterpillars (oaks) and others tolerated only one or two species (milkweed). It got me wondering about the specific antifeedants in the plants. Along the way, I started writing a regular column on nature, which had me reading broadly, and helped me link latex as an antifeedant to its use to humanity in the production of rubber. I also began to wonder how come some animals could tolerate latex whereas others could not, and started to explore digestive system differences in herbivores. This opened up a whole new question about why the remarkably different digestive systems of ruminants and non-ruminant herbivores had evolved. This then threw up the question of whether antifeedants such as Bt might affect different digestive systems differently. I wrote up an academic paper, which was peer-reviewed and published. This information is what forms part of the second section of the book. I think that both the evolution of digestive systems and the effect of antifeedants based on type of digestive system merit more research interest.

Rubber re-entered my consciousness as I was writing a cheque for quite a lot of money for a set of new tyres for my car. With two cars in my driveway and eight tyres every three or four years to pay for, I got to wondering how many tyres were made and broken down each year. Well, the data (see Chapter 10) shows that about six pounds—roughly the weight of a brick—of tyre material is made per person per year. Thinking about it makes my head spin. That number does not count the tyres already in existence, just the new ones. It also does not count the numbers of bicycle tyres, motorcycle or three-wheeler tyres of the types popular in populous Southeast Asia. This brought me to another question: Where does all this material to make new tyres come from, and where do old tyres go? Historically, tyres were made largely of natural rubber. Although synthetic rubber has alleviated some of the demand in some applications, natural rubber is still in great and ever-growing demand, because of its flexibility and tensile strength, for uses as diverse as aeroplane tyres, belting and hoses. The natural rubber market is expected to grow by an annual compounding rate (CAGR) of around 5 per cent. How sustainable is this level of growth? What is its social impact?

Social impact of commercial activity is a broad and anodyne term that somehow gives the impression that it is restricted to the situation prevailing at the time of the event. However, impacts project into the future, as events shape society's structure and include cultural and socioeconomic outcomes. Societies whose administrative and environmental structures are shaped by commercial interests are likely to change profoundly if the commercial worth of the resource increases or decreases. In the case of decreasing value, desperation to maintain the income causes a push to further exploit the environment and drop the wages of the workers, leading to a downward spiral and a rapid exodus or degradation of the population. In the case of increasing value, environmental degradation may result, causing a downward spiral and an exodus of the population, but this exodus is noticeably slower as long as enough money comes in to sustain a populace. But eventually the resources get depleted, and there is widespread economic collapse and social unrest.

Although this story is about rubber, the same social impact can be seen for exploitation of natural resources from timber to mining to fishing to tourism. The story of rubber production is broadly applicable to the human condition. Hopefully, we can improve the story of both in parallel by knowing its social and natural history.

Acknowledgements

First, thank you to Professor Barry Holland, who supervised my doctoral thesis over thirty years ago, for lively discussions on science and politics ever since—your enthusiasm for this book gave me the confidence to persist. Barry, my husband Stephen, my friend and neighbour Krish and Westland Books' copyeditor Sanjana asked insightful questions to refine the narrative, caught omissions and errors and tightened up the prose. Working with them has been the best part of this whole process.

My thanks also to Dr John Loadman (author of *Tears of the Tree* and *The Hancocks of Marlborough*, both published by Oxford University Press) and to Professor James Goding (co-author of *Who Will Believe My Verse?: The Code in Shakespeare's Sonnets*, published by Australian Scholarly Press) who put time into reading a book by someone they had never heard of, and gave many helpful suggestions; to libraries and to online resources which curate information and make it available at low or no cost—the University of Delaware Library, the Delaware County Community College Library, Kennett Public Library, Google Scholar, Wikipedia, the Internet Archive, Helgi Library, and many dot-gov, dot-edu and dot-org sites—your value to independent researchers is incalculable; to the farmers and researchers in Kerala who generously shared information about growing and harvesting rubber, your helpfulness is gratefully acknowledged; to the scholars who answered questions or critiqued my reasoning—especially to the reviewers of the academic paper that arose out of my research for this book—you shaped a more robust work. And to Tarun, who went out of his way to help, thank you for your faith.

To Karthika, who accepted this book for publication, thank you for your trust. To Sanjana who copyedited the book, the process was streamlined and made so enjoyable because of you; thank you also for the pert chapter titles! To Saurabh, who designed the cover, and to Mukul, who typeset the manuscript, I appreciate your creativity and attention to detail. To other members of the Westland team, thank you for your work on this book.

To my family: Steve, Ashish, Samir, Maggie and Mandi, thank you for being willing sounding boards and enduring the process with good grace. To my beloved border collies, Bach and Coda, who were so simpatico that I could ponder when we went for our 'walkies'—I miss you so much. To my father and to my mother, who read an early version of this manuscript but passed away before seeing the book in print, your encouragement remains with me.

Finally thank you to you, the reader. Without you, all this is for nothing. I hope you find this book is worth your investment of time and money.

Endnotes

Chapter 1: The Mesoamerican Ballgame

1 Dupey García, Élodie. "The materiality of color in the body ornamentation of Aztec gods." *RES: Anthropology and Aesthetics* 65, no. 1 (2015): 72-88.

2 "BBC - a History of the World - About: Transcripts - Episode 38 – Ceremonial Ballgame Belt." n.d. www.bbc.co.uk. https://www.bbc.co.uk/ahistoryoftheworld/about/transcripts/episode38/.

3 Ehrenwald, Jan. "The Return of Quetzalcoatl and Doctrinal Compliance: A Case Study of Cortes and Montezuma." *American Journal of Psychotherapy* 14, no. 2 (1960): 308-321. doi: https://doi.org/10.1176/appi.psychotherapy.1960.14.2.308.

4 Hassig, Ross. 2016. "Combat and Capture in the Aztec Empire." *British Journal for Military History* 3 (1). https://journals.gold.ac.uk/index.php/bjmh/article/view/683/805.

5 Townsend, Camilla, and John Graham. 2009. "Burying the White Gods: New Perspectives on the Conquest of Mexico the Feathered Serpent Deity at Teotihuacan, a Major Urban Center in the Valley of Mexico Predating the Aztec Civilization. Photograph." https://www.studythepast.com/376_spring10/conquest_of_mexico/burying_the_white_gods.pdf.

6 Jaime-Riverón, O. L. A. F., and Christopher Pool. "The impact of volcanic hazards on the ancient Olmec and Epi-

Olmec economies in the Los Tuxtlas region, Veracruz, Mexico." *The political economy of hazards and disasters* (2009): 133-154 PDF available at: https://www.academia.edu/download/71234935/THE_POLITICAL_ECONOMY_OF_HAZARDS_AND_DIS20211003-9352-36jaiy.pdf#page=148

7 Figure 1 modified from https://sco.m.wikipedia.org/wiki/File:Mesoamerica_topographic_map-blank.svg © Sémhur/ Wikimedia Commons / CC-BY-SA-4.0. The area and dates are approximate and for information purposes only.

8 Bower, Jessica. "The Mayan Written Word: History, Controversy, and Library Connections." *International Journal of the Book* 14, no. 3 (2016). DOI:10.18848/1447-9516/CGP/v14i03/15-25

9 Clendinnen, Inga. *Ambivalent Conquests: Maya and Spaniard in Yucatan, 1517-1570.* Vol. 61. Cambridge University Press, 2003. https://archive.org/details/ambivalentconque00inga/page/68/mode/2up [Accessed 1 Nov. 2023].

10 Vail, Gabrielle. "The maya codices." *Annu. Rev. Anthropol.* 35, no. 1 (2006): 497-519. https://doi.org/10.1146/annurev.anthro.35.081705.123324

11 Maffie, James. "Aztec Philosophy: Understanding a World in Motion." United States: University Press of Colorado, 2014. https://www.google.co.uk/books/edition/_/yYbgCwAAQBAJ?hl=en&gbpv=1

12 Blomster, Jeffrey P., and Víctor E. Salazar Chávez. "Origins of the Mesoamerican ballgame: Earliest ballcourt from the highlands found at Etlatongo, Oaxaca, Mexico." *Science Advances* 6, no. 11 (2020): eaay6964. doi:https://doi.org/10.1126/sciadv.aay6964

13 Charlton, Thomas H. "The Olmecs: America's First Civilization." *American Anthropologist* 108, no. 3 (2006): 581. Available from: https://archive.org/details/olmecsamericasfi0000dieh/page/n3/mode/2up p.108

14 Figure 2 Olmec colossal head from San Lorenzo Tenochtitlan, Veracruz, Mexico. Image credit: Gary Lee Todd. Olmec and Gulf Coast Gallery, INAH, National Museum of Anthropology, Mexico City. From: https://commons.wikimedia.org/wiki/File:Olmec_Colossal_Head,_San_

Lorenzo,_Veracruz,_1200-600_BC_-_side.jpg Licensed under CC0 1.0 Universal Public Domain Dedication.

15 Wolf, Howard, and Ralph F. Wolf. *Rubber: a story of glory and greed.* 1936.

16 Pérez, Nora A., Víctor Hugo Guzmán, José Luis Ruvalcaba, Oscar G. de Lucio, Miguel Pérez, Alan Nagaya, Nathael Cano et al. "Unraveling the Olmec rubber balls from El Manatí, Mexico: a technological and compositional analysis." *Archaeological and Anthropological Sciences* 16, no. 2 (2024): 27. https://doi.org/10.1007/s12520-023-01930-1

17 Figure 3 image credit: Bobak Ha'Eri - English Wikipedia, https://commons.wikimedia.org/w/index.php?curid=682685; Licensed under https://creativecommons.org/licenses/by/2.5/deed.en

18 Figure 4 image credit: Madman, https://commons.wikimedia.org/w/index.php?curid=3257613; Licensed under https://creativecommons.org/licenses/by/2.5/deed.en

19 Bitto, Robert (n.d.). *The Mesoamerican Ballgame – Mexico Unexplained.* [online] Available at: https://mexicounexplained.com/the-mesoamerican-ballgame/

20 Figure 5 image credit: Thomas Aleto, https://commons.wikimedia.org/wiki/File:El_Tajin_Ballcourt_Mural_(Tom_Aleto).jpg Licensed under https://creativecommons.org/licenses/by/2.0/

21 *BBC News.* 2022. "Maya Rulers' Ashes Turned into Pelota Balls - Expert," August 2, 2022, sec. Latin America & Caribbean. https://www.bbc.co.uk/news/world-latin-america-62391543.

22 Demarest, Arthur A., Chloé Andrieu, Paola Torres, Mélanie Forné, Tomás Barrientos, and Marc Wolf. "Economy, exchange, and power: new evidence from the late Classic Maya port city of Cancuen." *Ancient Mesoamerica* 25, no. 1 (2014): 187-219. DOI:10.1017/S0956536114000121

23 Maffie, James. Aztec Philosophy: Understanding a World in Motion. United States: University Press of Colorado, 2014. https://www.google.co.uk/books/edition/_/yYbgCwAAQBAJ?hl=en&gbpv=1

24 Santana, A. (n.d.). Available at: http://ijp.tamu.edu/blog/wp-content/uploads/2021/05/Santana.MaffieReview.pdf

25 Hosler, Dorothy, Sandra L. Burkett, and Michael J. Tarkanian. "Prehistoric polymers: rubber processing in ancient Mesoamerica." *Science* 284, no. 5422 (1999): 1988-1991. https://doi.org/10.1126/science.284.5422.1988

26 Tarkanian, Michael J., and Dorothy Hosler. "America's first polymer scientists: Rubber processing, use and transport in Mesoamerica." *Latin American Antiquity* 22, no. 4 (2011): 469-486. https://doi.org/10.7183/1045-6635.22.4.469

27 Cook, Ron O. "Rubber Olmec Balls." n.d. Blog.world-Mysteries.com. https://blog.world-mysteries.com/strange-artifacts/rubber-olmec-balls/.

Chapter 2: The Fruits of Discovery

28 "Columbus Returns to Spain." n.d. www.chroniclesofamerica.com. https://www.chroniclesofamerica.com/spanish-conquerors/columbus_returns_to_spain.htm. https://www.chroniclesofamerica.com/spanish-conquerors/columbus_returns_to_spain.htm

29 Griffenhagen, George B. "The materia medica of Christopher Columbus." *Pharmacy in history* 34, no. 3 (1992): 131-145. https://www.jstor.org/stable/41111458

30 Symcox, Geoffrey, and Blair Sullivan. *Christopher Columbus and the Enterprise of the Indies*. Boston and New York (2005).

31 "The Story of Rubber." n.d. www.chroniclesofamerica.com. http://www.chroniclesofamerica.com/invention/story_of_rubber.htm.

32 "Tlachtli." n.d. Pslc.ws. http://pslc.ws/macrog/exp/rubber/aepisode/tlachtli.htm.

33 sabre0link. 2013. "Trachtenbuch by Christoph Weiditz, Ca. 1530–1540." Adelaide's Artistic Attempts and Endeavors. June 21, 2013. https://adaloden.wordpress.com/2013/06/20/trachtenbuch-by-christoph-weiditz-ca-1530-1540/.

34 Figure 6: Image in the public domain. Obtained from: https://commons.wikimedia.org/wiki/File:Weiditz_Trachtenbuch_010-011.jpg

35 Tandy, W. A. "The history and development of rubber coatings." *Progress in rubber and plastics technology* 13, no. 1 (1997): 1-16. https://doi.org/10.1177/147776061997130100l
36 Loadman, John. *Tears of the tree: the story of rubber-a modern marvel.* OUP Oxford, 2005.
37 "Charles-Marie de La Condamine - Biography." n.d. Maths History. https://mathshistory.st-andrews.ac.uk/Biographies/La_Condamine/
38 Figure 7 by Tomruen. https://en.wikipedia.org/wiki/Spheroid#/media/File:Spheroids.svg. Licensed under: https://creativecommons.org/licenses/by-sa/4.0/
39 Ulrich, L.T. (2009) "Erasing History | Perspectives on History | AHA." n.d. www.historians.org. https://www.historians.org/perspectives-article/erasing-history-may-2009/
40 Zerbi, Tommaso. "Playfair and the City." (2018): 236-238. doi: https://doi.org/10.1525/jsah.2018.77.2.236
41 Sempa, Francis P. "A New Take on General MacArthur's Warning to JFK to Avoid a Land War in Asia." *The Diplomat* (2018). https://thediplomat.com/2018/10/a-new-take-on-general-macarthurs-warning-to-jfk-to-avoid-a-land-war-in-asia/
42 Boje, David. "Empire Reading of Manet's Execution of Maximilian: Critical Visual Aesthetics and Antenarrative Spectrality." *Tamara Journal of Critical Organisation Inquiry* 4, no. 4.3/4.4 (2005): 118. https://www.proquest.com/scholarly-journals/empire-reading-manets-execution-maximilian/docview/204418637/se-2

Chapter 3: Patent Battles

43 Kline, David, and David Kappos. 2021. "1.2 the Weakness of Early Patent Systems - Introduction to Intellectual Property | OpenStax." Openstax.org. February 22, 2021. https://openstax.org/books/introduction-intellectual-property/pages/1-2-the-weakness-of-early-patent-systems.
44 Administrator, UTRF. 2012. "America Invents Act Explained." University of Tennessee Research Foundation.

February 24, 2012. https://utrf.tennessee.edu/america-invents-act-explained/.

45 "Charles Goodyear Receives Patent for Vulcanized Rubber." 2014. *https://www.massmoments.org/moment-details/charles-goodyear-receives-patent-for-vulcanized-rubber.html*

46 "Personal Narrative of the Origin and Progress of the Caoutchouc or India-Rubber Manufacture in England: Hancock, Thomas, 1786-1865." 2014. Internet Archive. 2014. https://archive.org/details/personalnarrati00hancgoog/page/n132/mode/2up?q=1844.

47 Anderson, Gregory, Caryn Fahey, Adrienne Richards, Samantha Sullivan Sauer, David Wegman, and Jen Booth. 2024. "27.5 Rubber and Other Elastomers." Pressbooks.pub. Pressbooks. February 16, 2024. https://ecampusontario.pressbooks.pub/orgbiochemsupplement/chapter/rubber-elastomers/.

48 Korman, R. (2002). *The Goodyear story: an inventor's obsession and the struggle for a rubber monopoly*. Encounter Books.

49 Hayward, N. (1839) (Assignor to C. Goodyear) Improvement in the mode of preparing caoutchouc with sulphur for the manufacture o[f] various articles. U.S. Patent 1,090 Available at: https://patents.google.com/patent/US1090A/en]

50 Somma, Ann Marie. 2014. "Charles Goodyear and the Vulcanization of Rubber | Connecticut History | a CTHumanities Project." Connecticuthistory.org. 2014. https://connecticuthistory.org/charles-goodyear-and-the-vulcanization-of-rubber/.

51 Ferguson, Joe. 2010. "Massachusetts History Timeline: Massachusetts Important Dates." Ereferencedesk.com. 2010. https://www.ereferencedesk.com/resources/state-history-timeline/massachusetts.html.

52 Loadman, John, and Francis James. *The Hancocks of Marlborough: Rubber, Art and the Industrial Revolution-A Family of Inventive Genius*. Oxford University Press, 2010.

53 "Thomas Hancock | Science Museum Group Collection." 2024. Sciencemuseumgroup.org.uk. 2024. https://collection.sciencemuseumgroup.org.uk/people/ap30249/hancock-thomas.

54 "Choate's Famous Sentence | Dartmouth Alumni Magazine | January 1953." n.d. Dartmouth Alumni Magazine | the Complete Archive. https://archive.dartmouthalumnimagazine.com/article/1953/1/1/choates-famous-sentence. The sentence is reproduced below:

> Consider the work he did in that life of 40 years the range of subjects investigated and discussed; composing the whole theory and practice of our organic and administrative politics, foreign and domestic; the vast body of instructive thought he produced and put in possession of the country; how much he achieved in Congress as well as at the bar, to fix the true interpretation, as well as to impress the transcendent value of the Constitution itself, as much altogether as any jurist or statesman since its adoption; how much to establish in the general mind the great doctrine that the government of the United States is a government proper, established by the people of the States, not a compact between sovereign. communities, that within its limits it is supreme, and that whether it is within its limits or not, in any given exertion of itself, is to be determined by the Supreme Court of the United States the ultimate arbiter in the last resort—from which there is no appeal but to revolution; how much he did in the course of the discussions which grew out of the proposed mission to Panama, and, at a later day, out of the removal of the deposits, to place the executive department of the government on its true basis, and under its true limitations; to secure to that department all its just powers on the one hand, and on the other hand to vindicate to the legislative department, and especially to the Senate, all that belong to them; to arrest the tendencies which he thought at one time threatened to substitute the government of a single will, of a single person of great force of character and boundless popularity, and of a numerical majority of the people, told by the head, without intermediate institutions of any kind, judicial or senatorial, in place of the

elaborate system of checks and balances, by which the Constitution aimed at a government of laws, and not of men; how much, attracting less popular attention, but scarcely less important, to complete the great work which experience had, shown to be left unfinished by the judiciary act of 1789, by providing for the punishment of all crimes against the United States; how much for securing a safe currency and a true financial system, not only by the promulgation of sound opinions, but by good specific measures adopted, or bad ones defeated; how much to develop the vast material resources of the country, and to push forward the planting of the West not troubled by any fear of exhausting old States by a liberal policy of public lands, by vindicating the constitutional power of Congress to make or aid in making large classes of internal improvements, and by acting on that doctrine uniformly from 1813, whenever a road was to be built, or a rapid suppressed, or a canal to be opened, or a breakwater or a lighthouse set up above or below the flow of the tide, if so far beyond the ability of a single State, or of so wide utility to commerce and labour as to rise to the rank of a work general in its influences another tie of union because another proof of the beneficence of union; how much to protect the vast mechanical and manufacturing interests of the country, a value of many hundreds of millions after having been lured into existence against his counsels, against his science of political economy, by a policy of artificial encouragement from being sacrificed, and the pursuits and plans of large regions and communities broken up, and the acquired skill of the country squandered by a sudden and capricious withdrawal of the promise of the government; how much for the right performance of the most delicate and difficult of all tasks, the ordering of the foreign affairs of a nation, free, sensitive, self-conscious, recognising, it is true, public law and a morality of the State, binding on the conscience of the State, yet aspiring to power, eminence, and command, its whole frame filled full and all on fire with American feeling, sympathetic with liberty everywhere how much for the right ordering of the foreign affairs of such a State aiming in all his policy, from his speech on the Greek question in 1823, to his letters to M. Huslemann in 1850, to occupy the high, plain, yet dizzy ground which separates influence from intervention, to avow and promulgate warm good will to humanity, wherever striving to be free, to inquire authentically into the history of its struggles, to take official and avowed pains to ascertain the moment when its success may be recognised, consistently, ever, with the great code that keeps the peace of the world, abstaining from every thing which shall give any nation a right under the law of nations to utter one word of complaint, still less to retaliate by war the sympathy, but also the neutrality, of Washington how much to compose with honor a concurrence of difficulties with the first power in the world, which any thing less than the highest degree of discretion, firmness, ability, and means of commanding respect and confidence at home and abroad would inevitably have conducted to the last calamity a disputed boundary line of many hundred miles, from the St. Croix to the Rocky Mountains, which divided an exasperated and impracticable border population, enlisted the pride and affected the interests and controlled the politics of particular States, as well as pressed on the peace and honor of the nation, which the most popular administrations of the era of the quietest and best public feelings, the times of Monroe and of Jackson, could not adjust; which had grown so complicated with other topics of excitement that one false step, right or left, would have been a step down a precipice this line settled forever the claim of England to search our ships for the suppression of the slave-trade silenced forever, and a new engagement entered into by treaty, binding the national faith to contribute a specific naval force for putting an end to the great crime of man the long practice of England to enter an American ship and impress from its crew, terminated forever; the deck henceforth guarded sacredly and completely by the flag how much by profound discernment, by eloquent speech, by devoted life to strengthen the ties of union, and breathe the fine and strong spirit of nationality through all our numbers how much, most of all, last of all, after the war with Mexico, needless if his counsels had governed, had ended in so vast an acquisition of territory, in presenting to the two great antagonist sections of our country so vast an area to enter on, so imperial a prize to contend for, and the accursed fraternal strife had begun how much then, when rising to the measure of a true, and difficult, and rare greatness, remembering that he had a country to save as well as a local constituency to gratify, laying all the wealth, all the hopes, of an illustrious life on the altar of a hazardous patriotism, he sought and won the more exceeding glory which now attends which in the next age shall more conspicuously attend his name who composes an agitated and saves a sinking land recall this series of conduct and influences, study them carefully in their facts and results the reading of years and you attain to a true appreciation of this aspect of his greatness his public character and life.

55 "Morey Charles." 2014. Fiddlebase. 2014. https://www.fiddlebase.com/biographical-sketches/morey-charles/.

56 "A Centennial Volume of the Writings of Charles Goodyear and Thomas Hancock." *(Souvenir of the Centennial Meeting of the American Chemical Society in Commemoration of the Discovery of the Vulcanization of Rubber by Charles Goodyear in 1989)* HathiTrust. 2023. https://babel.hathitrust.org/cgi/pt?id=mdp.39015016043740&seq=7.

57 Loadman, John. *Tears of the tree: the story of rubber-a modern marvel.* OUP Oxford, 2005.

Chapter 4: Dying for Rubber

58 "The Volcanic Explosivity Index: A Tool for Comparing the Sizes of Explosive Volcanic Eruptions | U.S. Geological Survey." n.d. Www.usgs.gov. https://www.usgs.gov/observatories/yvo/news/volcanic-explosivity-index-a-tool-comparing-sizes-explosive-volcanic.

59 Osipov, Sergey, Georgiy Stenchikov, Kostas Tsigaridis, Allegra N. LeGrande, Susanne E. Bauer, Mohammed Fnais, and Jos Lelieveld. 2021. "The Toba Supervolcano Eruption Caused Severe Tropical Stratospheric Ozone Depletion." *Communications Earth & Environment* 2 (1): 1–7. https://doi.org/10.1038/s43247-021-00141-7.

60 Clarsen, Georgine. 2008. "Eat My Dust." *Johns Hopkins University Press EBooks*, January. https://doi.org/10.1353/book.60154.

61 Ikeda, Yuko, Atsushi Kato, Shinzo Kohjiya, and Yukio Nakajima. "Pneumatic Tire Technology." In *Rubber Science: A Modern Approach*, pp. 167-220. Singapore: Springer Nature Singapore, 2024.

62 "Michelin Heritage | Michelin." n.d. Www.michelin.com. https://www.michelin.com/en/group/heritage.

63 Winchester, Simon. *Krakatoa: The day the world exploded*. Penguin UK, 2004.

64 Sobel, Dava. *Longitude: The true story of a lone genius who solved the greatest scientific problem of his time*. Macmillan, 2005.

65 Bird, Michael I., Scott A. Condie, Sue o'Connor, Damien o'Grady, Christian Reepmeyer, Sean Ulm, Mojca Zega, Frédérik Saltré, and Corey JA Bradshaw. "Early human settlement of Sahul was not an accident." *Scientific Reports* 9, no. 1 (2019): 8220. https://doi.org/10.1038/s41598-019-42946-9

66 Ioannidis, Alexander G., Javier Blanco-Portillo, Karla Sandoval, Erika Hagelberg, Juan Francisco Miquel-Poblete, J. Víctor Moreno-Mayar, Juan Esteban Rodríguez-Rodríguez et al. "Native American gene flow into Polynesia predating Easter Island settlement." *Nature* 583, no. 7817 (2020): 572-577. doi:https://doi.org/10.1038/s41586-020-2487-2

67 "The Treacherous and Productive Seas of Southern Africa." 2017. Earthobservatory.nasa.gov. January 27, 2017. https://earthobservatory.nasa.gov/images/89535/the-treacherous-and-productive-seas-of-southern-africa.

68 "Slav | Etymology, Origin and Meaning of the Name Slav by Etymonline." n.d. Www.etymonline.com. https://www.etymonline.com/word/slav.

69 Internet Archive. 1913. *The Cambridge Medieval History. Vol. 2, the Rise of the Saracens and the Foundation of the Western Empire. Internet Archive.* Cambridge: University Press. https://archive.org/details/cambridgemedieva0000unse_m6m6.

70 "A Letter to the Soldiers of Coroticus." n.d. Www.ancienttexts.org. https://www.ancienttexts.org/library/celtic/ctexts/p02.html.

71 Jeal, Tim. *Explorers of the Nile: The triumph and tragedy of a great Victorian adventure.* Yale University Press, 2011.

72 Diamond, Jared M. *Guns, germs, and steel: The Fates of Human Societies.* W.W. Norton & Company. New York.1999.

73 "Article I | the National Constitution Center." n.d. Constitutioncenter.org. https://constitutioncenter.org/interactive-constitution/interpretation/article-i/clauses/761.

74 UK Government. 2015. "Modern Slavery Act 2015." Www.legislation.gov.uk. 2015. https://www.legislation.gov.uk/ukpga/2015/30/contents/enacted.

75 global slavery index. 2018. "Maps | Global Slavery Index." Global Slavery Index. 2018. https://www.globalslaveryindex.org/2018/data/maps/#prevalence.

76 Hancock, Thomas. 1857. *Personal Narrative of the Origin and Progress of the Caoutchouc or India-Rubber Manufacture in England. Google Books.* Longman, Brown, Green, Longmans, & Roberts. https://play.google.com/books/reader?id=zTQNAAAAYAAJ&pg=GBS.PR8&hl=en.

77 Galenson, David W. "The rise and fall of indentured servitude in the Americas: An economic analysis." *The Journal of Economic History* 44, no. 1 (1984): 1-26. PDF available at: https://masculinisation.wordpress.com/wp-content/uploads/2015/05/galenson_the_rise_and_fall_of_indentured_servitude_in_the_americas.pdf

78 Tomlins, Christopher. "Reconsidering indentured servitude: European migration and the early American labor force, 1600–1775." *Labor History* 42, no. 1 (2001): 5-43. PDF available at: https://library.fes.de/libalt/journals/swetsfulltext/11116561.pdf

79 Smith, Katrina M., and David Luis-Brown. "1619: The First Africans in Colonial Virginia." PDF Available at: https://www.academia.edu/download/61303254/Katrina_Smith-_Essay-_Final_Draft20191122-92123-18faqfb.pdf

80 Coelho, Philip RP, and Robert A. McGuire. "Biology, diseases, and economics: an epidemiological history of slavery in the American south." *Journal of Bioeconomics* 1 (1999): 151-190. https://doi.org/10.1023/A:1010034830415

81 Aishwariya, Sachidhanandham. "Interesting dimensions of vegan/ahimsa silk." *The Indian Textile Journal* 108 (2020): 112.

82 CNN, Sugam Pokharel and Tom Page. 2021. "Silk Slaves: India's Bonded Laborers Are Forced to Work to Pay off Debts." CNN. March 13, 2021. https://edition.cnn.com/2021/03/13/asia/silk-slaves-india-the-freedom-project-spc-intl/index.html.

83 "11.3: Cotton and Slavery." 2019. Humanities LibreTexts. March 11, 2019. https://human.libretexts.org/Bookshelves/History/National_History/Book%3A_U.S._History_(American_YAWP)/11%3A_The_Cotton_Revolution/11.03%3A_Cotton_and_Slavery.

84 Morel, Edmund Dene. *Red Rubber: The Story of the Rubber Slave Trade Flourishing on the Congo in the Year of Grace 1907*. TF Unwin, 1907. Available at: https://archive.org/details/dli.bengal.10689.3510/page/n7/mode/2up

85 Blake, Stephen, Samantha Strindberg, Patrick Boudjan, Calixte Makombo, Inogwabini Bila-Isia, Omari Ilambu, Falk Grossmann et al. "Forest elephant crisis in the Congo Basin." *PLoS biology* 5, no. 4 (2007): e111. https://doi.org/10.1371/journal.pbio.0050111

86 Loadman, John. *Tears of the tree: the story of rubber-a modern marvel*. OUP Oxford, 2005.

87 Jeal, Tim. *Stanley: Africa's Greatest Explorer*. Faber & Faber, 2011.

88 Hochschild, Adam. "King Leopold's Ghost: A Story of Greed, Terror, and Heroism in Colonial Africa." *The Wilson Quarterly* 23, no. 1 (1999): 103-105. https://erenow.org/modern/kingleopold/
89 "The Project Gutenberg EBook of the Casement Report." n.d. Www.gutenberg.org. https://www.gutenberg.org/files/50573/50573-h/50573-h.htm. No.3. Dec 11, 1903.
90 Conrad, Joseph. 1899. *Heart of Darkness*. Gutenberg.org. 1899. https://www.gutenberg.org/files/219/219-h/219-h.htm.
91 Figure 8: Image in the public domain. "The Congo and the Founding of Its Free State; a Story of Work and Exploration: Stanley, Henry M. (Henry Morton), 1841-1904: Free Download, Borrow, and Streaming: Internet Archive." 2014. Internet Archive. 2014. https://archive.org/details/congofoundingofi02stan/page/264/mode/2up?q=sectional+steamer.
92 Figure 9: Image in the public domain. BCPA. 1950. "Pictures from Belgium"S Colonial Army, the Force Publique." Internet Archive. 1950. https://archive.org/details/pictures-from-belgiums-colonial-army-the-force-publique/peterverlinden-standbeeldvanleopoldiiinbelgisch-kongojpg.jpg.
93 Brown, Harold. *Rubber: its sources, cultivation, and preparation*. J. Murray, 1914. (p.8)
94 Pickersgill to Salisbury, 25 Jan. I897, F.O. 63/ cited in William Roger Lewis: Roger Casement and the Congo. https://www.jstor.org/stable/179771
95 Figure 10: Image in the public domain. Available at: https://en.wikipedia.org/wiki/Atrocities_in_the_Congo_Free_State
96 Figure 11: Image in the public domain. Available at: https://commons.wikimedia.org/wiki/File:Nsala_of_Wala_in_Congo_looks_at_the_severed_hand_and_foot_of_his_five-year_old_daughter,_1904.jpg
97 Strang, Herbert. n.d. *Samba: A Story of the Rubber Slaves of the Congo*. https://www.gutenberg.org/cache/epub/39061/pg39061-images.html
98 "BBC NEWS | Africa | King Leopold's Legacy of DR Congo Violence." 2009. Bbc.co.uk. 2009. http://news.bbc.co.uk/2/hi/africa/3516965.stm.

99 courts, UZA-people's, forums, and Tribunals Says. 2016. "HIDDEN HISTORY: The Belgian Genocide and the Slave State in the Congo – 10,000,000 Deaths from 1885-1908 (Archive)." RIELPOLITIK. March 23, 2016. https://rielpolitik.com/2016/03/22/hidden-history-the-belgian-genocide-and-the-slave-state-in-the-congo-10000000-deaths-from-1885-1908/.

100 "Twain, Mark. *King Leopold's Soliloquy*. n.d. Www.gutenberg.org. https://www.gutenberg.org/files/62739/62739-h/62739-h.htm

101 Doyle, Arthur. *The Crime of the Congo*. gutenberg.org. 2024. https://www.gutenberg.org/cache/epub/37712/pg37712-images.html

102 BBC News. 2018. "Democratic Republic of Congo Profile - Timeline." *BBC News*, November 2, 2018. https://www.bbc.com/news/world-africa-13286306

103 "*Pseudocercospora ulei* (South American Leaf Blight of Rubber (SALB))." 2022. *PlantwisePlus Knowledge Bank* Species Pages (January). https://doi.org/10.1079/pwkb.species.33893.

104 Wolf, Howard, and Ralph F. Wolf. *Rubber: a story of glory and greed* (1936). First published ©1936, 2009 J.J. Little and Ives Company, New York. Reprinted 2009 Smithers Rapra.

105 Minster, Christopher. 2019. "Colonial Spain and the Horrors of the Encomienda System." ThoughtCo. 2019. https://www.thoughtco.com/spains-american-colonies-encomienda-system-2136545.

106 Loadman, John. *Tears of the tree: the story of rubber–a modern marvel*. OUP Oxford, 2005.

107 Wolf, Howard, and Ralph F. Wolf. *Rubber: a story of glory and greed* (1936). First published ©1936, 2009 J.J. Little and Ives Company, New York. Reprinted 2009 Smithers Rapra.

108 Goodman, Jordan. *The Devil and Mr Casement: One Man's Struggle for Human Rights in South America's Heart of Darkness*. Verso Books, 2020.

109 "Hardenburg, W.E. *The Putumayo, the Devil's Paradise. Travels in the Peruvian Amazon Region and an Account of the Atrocities Committed upon the Indians Therein*.

110 "The Putumayo Affair." n.d. Www.bouncing-Balls.com. http://www.bouncing-balls.com/timeline/putumayo.htm.

111 Figure 12: Image in the public domain. From Hardenburg, W. E. (1913) The Putumayo, the devil's paradise; travels in the Peruvian Amazon region and an account of the atrocities committed upon the Indians therein. p.53. The photo legend states it was reproduced from the "Veridades" in Lima, Peru

112 Survival International. 2019. "Death in the Devil's Paradise - Survival International." Survivalinternational.org. 2019. https://www.survivalinternational.org/articles/3282-rubber-boom.

113 Mitchell, Angus, ed. *One Bold Deed of Open Treason: The Berlin Diary of Roger Casement 1914-1916*. Merrion Press, 2016. Available at: https://archive.org/details/onebolddeedofope0000case

114 Ward, Herbert. *A Voice from the Congo: Comprising Stories, Anecdotes, and Descriptive Notes*. 1863-1919: Free Download, Borrow, and Streaming: Internet Archive." 2014. Internet Archive. 2014. https://archive.org/details/voicefromcongoco00ward.

115 Figure 13: Image in the public domain. Available at: https://commons.wikimedia.org/wiki/File:Portrait_of_Roger_Casement_P557.jpg

116 "'The World's Oldest Trade': Dutch Slavery and Slave Trade in the Indian Ocean in the Seventeenth Century | History Cooperative." 2020. June 19, 2020. https://historycooperative.org/journal/worlds-oldest-trade-dutch-slavery-slave-trade-indian-ocean-seventeenth-century/.

117 Rossum, Matthias van. 2018. "The Carceral Colony: Colonial Exploitation, Coercion, and Control in the Dutch East Indies, 1810s–1940s." *International Review of Social History* 63 (S26): 65–88. https://doi.org/10.1017/s0020859018000226.

118 Figure 14 image credit: Noseycjr. Available at: https://en.m.wikipedia.org/wiki/File:Territorial_Evolution_of_the_Dutch_East_Indies.png. Reproduced under https://creativecommons.org/licenses/by-sa/3.0/deed.en

119 Jackson, Joe. *The Thief at the End of the World*. Gerald Duckworth & Co, 2010.

Chapter 5: The War Machine

120 "WWI: The Development of Synthetic Rubber." 2020. Blogs. November 6, 2020. https://www.coruba.co.uk/blog/wwi-the-development-of-synthetic-rubber/.

121 Kolko, Gabriel. "American Business and Germany, 1930-1941." *Western Political Quarterly* 15, no. 4 (1962): 713-728. https://doi.org/10.1177/10659129620150

122 Clarence-Smith, William G. "The battle for rubber in the Second World War: Cooperation and Resistance." In *Global histories, imperial commodities, local interactions*, pp. 204-223. London: Palgrave Macmillan UK, 2009. https://doi.org/10.1057/9781137283603_11

123 Tully, John. *The devil's milk: A social history of rubber*. NYU Press, 2011.

124 "1847 Constitution of Liberia (Original)." 2010. Web.archive.org. January 17, 2010. https://web.archive.org/web/20100117084908/http://onliberia.org/con_1847_orig.htm.

125 Clair MacDougall, Glenna Gordon. 2016. "These Abandoned Buildings Are the Last Remnants of Liberia's Founding History." Smithsonian Magazine. https://www.smithsonianmag.com/history/liberia-created-former-slaves-fading-into-history-180959503/

126 Robtel Neajai Pailey. 2023. "Stopping Firestone and Starting a Citizen 'Revolution from Below': Reflections on the Enduring Exploitation of Liberian Land and Labour." *Third World Quarterly* 45 (1): 1–18. https://doi.org/10.1080/01436597.2023.2240729.

127 John Ort. 2022. "How Firestone Exploited Liberia — and Made Princeton as We Know It." n.d. *The Princetonian*. https://www.dailyprincetonian.com/article/2022/12/firestone-library-rubber-exploitation-princeton.

128 "Report of the International Commission of Inquiry into the Existence of Slavery and Forced Labor in the Republic of Liberia. Monrovia, Liberia, September ..." 2023. HathiTrust. 2023. https://babel.hathitrust.org/cgi/pt?id=uiug.30112059732252&view=1up&seq=7.

129 Everill, Bronwen. n.d. "When the Rubber Hits the Road." Foreign Policy. https://foreignpolicy.com/2021/11/06/liberia-firestone-rubber-capital-us-war-review-gregg-mitman/.

130 "Firestone and the Warlord: The Untold Story of Firestone, Charles Taylor and the Tragedy of Liberia." n.d. FRONTLINE. https://www.pbs.org/wgbh/frontline/article/firestone-and-the-warlord/.

131 "FLOMO v. FIRESTONE NATURAL RUBBER CO LLC." 2022. Findlaw. 2022. https://caselaw.findlaw.com/court/us-7th-circuit/1573873.html.

132 "Alien Tort Claims Act Lawsuit Alleges Slavery and Child Labor on Liberian Firestone Plantation." 2009. Global Labor Justice-International Labor Rights Forum. July 18, 2009. https://laborrights.org/in-the-news/alien-tort-claims-act-lawsuit-alleges-slavery-and-child-labor-liberian-firestone.

133 "Ej Atlas." n.d. Ejatlas.org. https://ejatlas.org/conflict/firestone-bridgestone-rubber-plantations-liberia.

134 "Firestone Liberia." n.d. https://www.firestonenaturalrubber.com/.

135 "U.S. Synthetic Rubber Program - National Historic Chemical Landmark." n.d. American Chemical Society. https://www.acs.org/education/whatischemistry/landmarks/syntheticrubber.html.

136 Times, Russell B. Porterspecial To the New York. 1943. "JEFFERS ASSAILS FACTORY 'LOAFERS' from ARMY, NAVY; He Declares Officers Serving as 'Expediters' Impede the Rubber and Other Plans TALK CRITICIZED by OWI Not Cleared, It Says, but He Retorts That He Was Telling Facts 'to Get Job Done' JEFFERS ASSAILS FACTORY 'LOAFERS.'" *The New York Times*, January 26, 1943, sec. Archives. https://www.nytimes.com/1943/01/26/archives/jeffers-assails-factory-loafers-from-army-navy-he-declares-officers.html.

137 Rudner, Martin. "Rubber strategy for post-war Malaya, 1945–48." *Journal of Southeast Asian Studies* 1, no. 1 (1970): 23-36. http://www.jstor.org/stable/20069844

138 Provost, Nyla. "The development of synthetic rubber and its significance in world war II." *History in the Making* 15, no.

1 (2022): 8. Available at: https://scholarworks.lib.csusb.edu/cgi/viewcontent.cgi?article=1262&context=history-in-the-making

139 Figure 15: Images in the Public Domain. From: Government & Geographic Information Collection, Northwestern University Libraries. World War II Posters Collection. https://dc.library.northwestern.edu/

140 Shoup, Donald. *High cost of free parking*. Routledge, 2021. Available at: https://escholarship.org/content/qt4vz087cc/qt4vz087cc.pdf

141 Macrotrends. 2024. "U.S. Population Growth Rate 1950-2024." Macrotrends.net. 2024. https://www.macrotrends.net/global-metrics/countries/USA/united-states/population-growth-rate.

142 "Natural rubber production worldwide from 2000 to H1 2023 Statista. https://www.statista.com/statistics/275387/global-natural-rubber-production/.

143 "Natural Rubber Leading Producers Worldwide in 2023." n.d. Statista. https://www.statista.com/statistics/275397/caoutchouc-production-in-leading-countries/

144 Castellanos, Daniel Salazar. 2022. "Latin America's Rubber Industry Looking to Bounce onto the World Stage." Bloomberg Línea. March 8, 2022. https://www.bloomberglinea.com/2022/03/05/latin-americas-rubber-industry-looking-to-bounce-onto-the-world-stage/.

145 Platt, John R. 2016. "Bornean Orangutan Now Critically Endangered." Scientific American. July 11, 2016. https://www.scientificamerican.com/blog/extinction-countdown/bornean-orangutan-critically-endangered/.

146 Eco-Business. 2022. "Cambodian Indigenous Community Suffer Years of Harassment by Rubber Barons." Eco-Business. December 8, 2022. https://www.eco-business.com/news/cambodian-indigenous-community-suffer-years-of-harassment-by-rubber-barons/.

147 Schunk, Andrew. 2023. "Dealing with War, a Year In: 4 Impacts from Russia's Attack on Ukraine." Rubber News. January 10, 2023. https://www.rubbernews.com/news/4-major-impacts-russias-war-ukraine.

148 Maddison, A. (2006), *The World Economy: Volume 1: A Millennial Perspective and Volume 2: Historical Statistics*, Development Centre Studies, OECD Publishing, Paris, https://doi.org/10.1787/9789264022621-en.

149 Maddison, A. (2006), *The World Economy: Volume 1: A Millennial Perspective and Volume 2: Historical Statistics*, Development Centre Studies, OECD Publishing, Paris, https://doi.org/10.1787/9789264022621-en.

150 Frank, Zephyr, Musacchio, Aldo. "The International Natural Rubber Market, 1870-1930." Eh.net. https://eh.net/encyclopedia/the-international-natural-rubber-market-1870-1930/.

151 Loadman, John. *Tears of the tree: the story of rubber–a modern marvel.* OUP Oxford, 2005

152 Maddison, A. (2006), *The World Economy: Volume 1: A Millennial Perspective and Volume 2: Historical Statistics*, Development Centre Studies, OECD Publishing, Paris, https://doi.org/10.1787/9789264022621-en.

153 Mori, Ryohei. 2023. "Replacing All Petroleum-Based Chemical Products with Natural Biomass-Based Chemical Products: A Tutorial Review." *RSC Sustainability.* https://doi.org/10.1039/d2su00014h.

Chapter 6: Continental Drift

154 Pettinato, Tony. 2019. "On This Day: Students Stunned as Space Shuttle 'Challenger' Explodes." GenealogyBank Blog. 2019. https://blog.genealogybank.com/on-this-day-students-stunned-as-space-shuttle-challenger-explodes.html.

155 Scott, Michon, and Rebecca Lindsey. 2020. "What's the Hottest Earth's Ever Been?" Www.climate.gov. June 18, 2020. https://www.climate.gov/news-features/climate-qa/whats-hottest-earths-ever-been.

156 Figure 16: Image in the public domain. USGS. 2019. "Historical Perspective [This Dynamic Earth, USGS]." Usgs.gov. 2019. https://pubs.usgs.gov/gip/dynamic/historical.html.

157 Gulick, Sean P. S., Timothy J. Bralower, Jens Ormö, Brendon Hall, Kliti Grice, Bettina Schaefer, Shelby Lyons, et al.

2019. "The First Day of the Cenozoic." *Proceedings of the National Academy of Sciences* 116 (39): 19342–51. https://doi.org/10.1073/pnas.1909479116.

158 Eltahir, Elfatih AB, Brian Loux, Teresa K. Yamana, and Arne Bomblies. "A see-saw oscillation between the Amazon and Congo basins." *Geophys. Res. Lett* 31 (2004): L23201. https://doi.org/10.1029/2004GL021160

159 Roberts, Tyson R. "Ecology of fishes in the Amazon and Congo basins." *BULL MUS COMP ZOOL, VOL 143, NO 2, P 117-147, 1972.* (1972). Available at: https://ia601304.us.archive.org/5/items/biostor-699/biostor-699.pdf

160 Dargie, Greta C., Simon L. Lewis, Ian T. Lawson, Edward TA Mitchard, Susan E. Page, Yannick E. Bocko, and Suspense A. Ifo. "Age, extent and carbon storage of the central Congo Basin peatland complex." *Nature* 542, no. 7639 (2017): 86-90. https://doi.org/10.1038/nature21048

161 Secon, Holly. 2020. "The Congo River Basin: Home of the Deepest River in the World." *Live Science*, August 5, 2020. https://www.livescience.com/congo-river.html.

162 Figure 17 (left panel) Modified from Amazon River Basin https://en.wikipedia.org/wiki/Amazon_basin#/media/File:Amazonriverbasin_basemap.png under Creative Commons CC.BY-SA 3.0 license. Figure 17 (right panel) Map showing the Congo River drainage basin modified from https://en.wikipedia.org/wiki/Congo_River#/media/File:Congobasinmap.png under Creative Commons CC.BY-SA 4.0 license

163 Mapes, Russell (2009) Past and Present Provenance of the Amazon River. Ph.D. Dissertation. University of North Carolina at Chapel Hill. https://core.ac.uk/reader/210596990

164 Takemoto, H., Kawamoto, Y. and Furuichi, T., 2015. "How did bonobos come to range south of the Congo river? Reconsideration of the divergence of Pan paniscus from other Pan populations. *Evolutionary Anthropology: Issues, News, and Reviews*, *24*(5), pp.170-184. https://pubmed.ncbi.nlm.nih.gov/26478139/

165 Sta Stankiewicz, Jacek, and Maarten J. de Wit. "A proposed drainage evolution model for Central Africa—did the Congo flow east?." *Journal of African Earth Sciences* 44, no. 1 (2006):

75-84. Available at: https://pubs.ecgs.lu/publications/jacek/publications/Stankiewicz_Jacek_publication_7.pdf

166 Flügel, Tyrel J., Frank D. Eckardt, and Fenton PD Cotterill. "The present day drainage patterns of the Congo river system and their Neogene evolution." In *Geology and resource potential of the Congo basin*, pp. 315-337. Berlin, Heidelberg: Springer Berlin Heidelberg, 2014. doi.org/10.1007/978-3-642-29482-2_15

167 Britz, Ralf, Neelesh Dahanukar, V. K. Anoop, Siby Philip, Brett Clark, Rajeev Raghavan, and Lukas Rüber. "Aenigmachannidae, a new family of snakehead fishes (Teleostei: Channoidei) from subterranean waters of South India." *Scientific reports* 10, no. 1 (2020): 16081. https://doi.org/10.1038/s41598-020-73129-6

168 "Amazon Fish Project | Home." n.d. Www.amazon-Fish.com. https://www.amazon-fish.com/.

169 Jézéquel, Céline, Pablo A. Tedesco, Rémy Bigorne, Javier A. Maldonado-Ocampo, Hernan Ortega, Max Hidalgo, Koen Martens, et al. 2020. "A Database of Freshwater Fish Species of the Amazon Basin." *Scientific Data* 7 (1): 96. https://doi.org/10.1038/s41597-020-0436-4.

170 Breault, J. L. "Candirú: Amazonian parasitic catfish." *Journal of Wilderness Medicine* 2, no. 4 (1991): 304-312. Available from: https://journals.sagepub.com/doi/pdf/10.1580/0953-9859-2.4.304

171 Stiassny, Melanie LJ, and S. Elizabeth Alter. "Evolution in the fast Lane: diversity, ecology, and speciation of cichlids in the lower Congo River." *The behavior, ecology and evolution of cichlid fishes* (2021): 107-133. https://doi.org/10.1007/978-94-024-2080-7_4

172 Weisberger, Mindy. 2020. "Dying Fish Revealed Congo Is World's Deepest River." Livescience.com. https://www.livescience.com/congo-river-fish-with-bends.html

173 Thomas, Peter A. *Trees: their natural history*. Cambridge University Press, 2014.

174 Branstetter, Michael G., Bryan N. Danforth, James P. Pitts, Brant C. Faircloth, Philip S. Ward, Matthew L. Buffington, Michael W. Gates, Robert R. Kula, and Seán G. Brady. "Phylogenomic insights into the evolution of stinging

wasps and the origins of ants and bees." *Current Biology* 27, no. 7 (2017): 1019-1025. DOI:https://doi.org/10.1016/j.cub.2017.03.027

175 Chen, Feng, Dorothea Tholl, Jörg Bohlmann, and Eran Pichersky. "The family of terpene synthases in plants: a mid-size family of genes for specialised metabolism that is highly diversified throughout the kingdom." *The Plant Journal* 66, no. 1 (2011): 212-229. doi: 10.1111/j.1365-313X.2011.04520.x

176 McIntyre, Sarah RN, Charles H. Lineweaver, Colin P. Groves, and Aditya Chopra. "Global biogeography since Pangaea." *Proceedings of the Royal Society B: Biological Sciences* 284, no. 1856 (2017): 20170716. http://dx.doi.org/10.1098/rspb.2017.0716

177 Maron, John L., Anurag A. Agrawal, and Douglas W. Schemske. "Plant–herbivore coevolution and plant speciation." *Ecology* 100, no. 7 (2019): e02704. https://doi.org/10.1002/ecy.2704

178 "Latex." n.d. Www.fs.usda.gov. https://www.fs.usda.gov/wildflowers/ethnobotany/latex.shtml

Chapter 7: With Patience, Arm Thyself

179 Weiss, Madeline C., Filipa L. Sousa, Natalia Mrnjavac, Sinje Neukirchen, Mayo Roettger, Shijulal Nelson-Sathi, and William F. Martin. "The physiology and habitat of the last universal common ancestor." *Nature microbiology* 1, no. 9 (2016): 1-8. https://doi.org/10.1038/nmicrobiol.2016.116

180 Glass, John I., Nacyra Assad-Garcia, Nina Alperovich, Shibu Yooseph, Matthew R. Lewis, Mahir Maruf, Clyde A. Hutchison III, Hamilton O. Smith, and J. Craig Venter. "Essential genes of a minimal bacterium." *Proceedings of the National Academy of Sciences* 103, no. 2 (2006): 425-430. https://www.pnas.org/doi/full/10.1073/pnas.0510013103

181 Weiss, M., Sousa, F., Mrnjavac, N. *et al.* The physiology and habitat of the last universal common ancestor. *Nat Microbiol* 1, 16116 (2016). Supplementary Table 2 https://doi.org/10.1038/nmicrobiol.2016.116

182 Poliseno, Laura. "Pseudogenes: newly discovered players in human cancer." *Science signaling* 5, no. 242 (2012): re5-re5. DOI: 10.1126/scisignal.2002858

183 Abarca, Luis Francisco Salomé, Peter GL Klinkhamer, and Young Hae Choi. "Plant latex, from ecological interests to bioactive chemical resources." *Planta Medica* 85, no. 11/12 (2019): 856-868. https://doi.org/10.1055/a-0923-8215

184 Haruna, Sani, Bala Sidi Aliyu, and Abdulhamid Bala. "Plant gum exudates (Karau) and mucilages, their biological sources, properties, uses and potential applications: A review." *Bayero Journal of Pure and Applied Sciences* 9, no. 2 (2016): 159-165. http://dx.doi.org/10.4314/bajopas.v9i2.30

185 Figure 19: Modified under https://creativecommons.org/licenses/by-sa/4.0 license from: Edvardsson, Johannes, Gunnar Almevik, Linda Lindblad, Hans Linderson, and Karl-Magnus Melin. "How cultural heritage studies based on dendrochronology can be improved through two-way communication." *Forests* 12, no. 8 (2021): 1047. https://doi.org/10.3390/f12081047

186 Plantlet. 2020. "Secretory Tissue: A Laticiferous Discussion." Plantlet. November 25, 2020. https://plantlet.org/secretory-tissue-a-laticiferous-discussion/

187 Møbjerg, Nadia, K. A. Halberg, Aaslak Jørgensen, Daniel Persson, Morten Bjørn, Hans Ramløv, and R. M. Kristensen. «Survival in extreme environments–on the current knowledge of adaptations in tardigrades.» *Acta physiologica* 202, no. 3 (2011): 409-420. https://doi.org/10.1111/j.1748-1716.2011.02252.x

188 Figure 20 reproduced under a Creative Commons Unported 3.0 (CC BY 3.0) Open Access license from Fürstenberg-Hägg, Joel, Mika Zagrobelny, and Søren Bak. "Plant defense against insect herbivores." *International journal of molecular sciences* 14, no. 5 (2013): 10242-10297. https://www.mdpi.com/1422-0067/14/5/10242.

189 "Fierce Ferns Make Insect-Fighting Proteins." 2023. *Nature* 623 (7985): 11–11. https://doi.org/10.1038/d41586-023-03281-2

190 Lewinsohn, Thomas M. "The geographical distribution of plant latex." *Chemoecology* 2 (1991): 64-68. https://doi.org/10.1007/BF01240668

Chapter 8: Evolutionary Epicures

191 Agrawal, Anurag A., and Kotaro Konno. "Latex: a model for understanding mechanisms, ecology, and evolution of plant defense against herbivory." *Annu. Rev. Ecol. Evol. Syst.* 40 (2009): 311-331.DOI: 10.1146/annurev.ecolsys.110308.120307

192 Figure 21: Credit: Rajan, V and Sanjana, T.. Left and middle figures adapted from Agrawal, Anurag A., and Kotaro Konno. "Latex: a model for understanding mechanisms, ecology, and evolution of plant defense against herbivory." *Annu. Rev. Ecol. Evol. Syst.* 40 (2009): 311-331.DOI: 10.1146/annurev.ecolsys.110308.120307

193 Codron, Daryl, Reinhold R. Hofmann, and Marcus Clauss. "Morphological and physiological adaptations for browsing and grazing." *The ecology of browsing and grazing II* (2019): 81-125. https://link.springer.com/chapter/10.1007/978-3-030-25865-8_4

194 Figure 22 modified from: Rajan, Vidya. "An alkaline foregut protects herbivores from latex in forage, but increases their susceptibility to Bt endotoxin." *Life* 13, no. 11 (2023): 2195. https://doi.org/10.3390/life13112195

195 Rajan, Vidya. "An alkaline foregut protects herbivores from latex in forage, but increases their susceptibility to Bt endotoxin." *Life* 13, no. 11 (2023): 2195. https://doi.org/10.3390/life13112195

196 Beasley, DeAnna E., Amanda M. Koltz, Joanna E. Lambert, Noah Fierer, and Rob R. Dunn. "The evolution of stomach acidity and its relevance to the human microbiome." *PloS one* 10, no. 7 (2015): e0134116. https://doi.org/10.1371/journal.pone.0134116

197 "Perissodactyla - Horses, Rhinoceroses, Tapirs | Wildlife Journal Junior." n.d. Nhpbs.org. https://nhpbs.org/wild/perissodactyla.asp.

198 "Artiodactyla - Pigs, Hippos, Giraffes, Camels, Moose, Goats, Bison, Deer | Wildlife Journal Junior." n.d. Nhpbs.org. https://nhpbs.org/wild/artiodactyla.asp.

199 Shipley, Lisa A. "Grazers and browsers: how digestive morphology affects diet selection." *Grazing behavior of*

livestock and wildlife 70 (1999): 20-27. Available from: https://edisciplinas.usp.br/pluginfile.php/7958184/mod_resource/content/1/Grazer%20v.%20browser_Lisa%20Shipley.pdf

200 USDA. 2014. "Silvopasture." https://www.fs.usda.gov/nac/practices/silvopasture.php.

201 Herrel, Anthony, Katleen Huyghe, Bieke Vanhooydonck, Thierry Backeljau, Karin Breugelmans, Irena Grbac, Raoul Van Damme, and Duncan J. Irschick. "Rapid large-scale evolutionary divergence in morphology and performance associated with exploitation of a different dietary resource." *Proceedings of the National Academy of Sciences* 105, no. 12 (2008): 4792-4795. https://doi.org/10.1073/pnas.0711998105

202 Bjorndal, Karen A. "Fermentation in reptiles and amphibians." In *Gastrointestinal Microbiology: Volume 1 Gastrointestinal Ecosystems and Fermentations*, pp. 199-230. Boston, MA: Springer US, 1997. https://doi.org/10.1007/978-1-4615-4111-0_7

203 Lajmanovich, Rafael C., Celina M. Junges, Mariana C. Cabagna-Zenklusen, Andrés M. Attademo, Paola M. Peltzer, Mariana Maglianese, Vanina E. Márquez, and Alejandro J. Beccaria. "Toxicity of Bacillus thuringiensis var. israelensis in aqueous suspension on the South American common frog Leptodactylus latrans (Anura: Leptodactylidae) tadpoles." *Environmental Research* 136 (2015): 205-212. https://doi.org/10.1016/j.envres.2014.10.022

204 Glöckner, Gottfried, and Gilles-Éric Séralini. "Pathology reports on the first cows fed with Bt176 maize (1997–2002)." *Sch. J. Agric. Sci* 6 (2016): 1-8. Available at: https://jeffreydachmd.com/wp-content/uploads/2016/07/Pathology-reports-cows-fed-Bt176-maize-Gl%C3%B6ckner-and-S%C3%A9ralini-2016.pdf

205 Faust, M., B. Smith, D. Rice, F. Owens, M. Hinds, G. Dana, and P. Hunst. "Performance of lactating dairy cows fed silage and grain from a maize hybrid with the cry1F trait versus its nonbiotech counterpart." *Journal of dairy science* 90, no. 12 (2007): 5706-5713. https://doi.org/10.3168/jds.2007-0480

206 Folmer, J. D., R. J. Grant, C. T. Milton, and J. Beck. "Utilization of Bt corn residues by grazing beef steers and

Bt corn silage and grain by growing beef cattle and lactating dairy cows." *Journal of animal science* 80, no. 5 (2002): 1352-1361. https://doi.org/10.2527/2002.8051352x

Chapter 9: Rubber's Alter-Ego

207 Bartlett, D. W. (David W.), and University of Connecticut Libraries. 1851. *London by Day and Night: Or, Men and Things in the Great Metropolis*. Internet Archive. New York: Hurst. https://archive.org/details/londonbydaynight00bart/page/56/mode/2up?q=The+Gutta+Percha+Company.

208 Cited in Goodman, Alvin, Herbert Schilder, and Winthrop Aldrich. "The thermomechanical properties of gutta-percha: II. The history and molecular chemistry of gutta-percha." *Oral surgery, oral medicine, oral pathology* 37, no. 6 (1974): 954-961. https://doi.org/10.1016/0030-4220(74)90448-4

209 "History of the Atlantic Cable & Submarine Telegraphy - the Gutta Percha Company." 2014. Atlantic-Cable.com. 2014. https://atlantic-cable.com/Article/GuttaPercha/index.htm#gsc.tab=0.

210 Zhou, Esri, Li. 2015. "This Map Shows the Full Extent of the Devastation Wrought by U-Boats in World War I." Smithsonian Magazine. May 7, 2015. https://www.smithsonianmag.com/history/map-shows-full-extent-devastation-wrought-uboats-world-war-i-180955191/.

211 Cited in "Sumner Attacked in U.S. Senate." n.d. Www.massmoments.org. https://www.massmoments.org/moment-details/sumner-attacked-in-u-s-senate.html.

212 Figure 23: Public domain. South Carolina Representative Preston Brooks's Attack on Senator Charles Sumner of Massachusetts. History, Art, and Archives. United States House of Representatives.

213 United States Senate (n.d.). *U.S. Senate: The Caning of Senator Charles Sumner*. [online] www.senate.gov. Available at: https://www.senate.gov/artandhistory/history/minute/The_Caning_of_Senator_Charles_Sumner.htm.

214 Figure 23: Public domain. Anonymous lithograph in the format of J. L. Magee's Lithograph of the same title. A factual

error is listed: 'In this print Brooks holds his gutta-percha cane by the knob. According to eyewitnesses, he repeatedly hit Sumner's head with the massive gold knob, instead.' Credit: https://en.wikipedia.org/wiki/Caning_of_Charles_Sumner#/media/File:Southern_Chivalry.jpg

Chapter 10: The Good and the Bad

215 Winchester, S. (2004). *Krakatoa: The day the world exploded.* Penguin UK.

216 Figure 24: Reproduced with permission from "Which Country Produces the Most Natural Rubber?" 2022. Helgilibrary.com. 2022. https://www.helgilibrary.com/charts/which-country-produces-the-most-natural-rubber.

217 "Association of Natural Rubber Producing Countries Forecasts Increased Demand for Natural Rubber – Rubber World – the Technical Service Magazine for the Rubber Industry." 2021. Rubberworld.com. November 19, 2021. https://rubberworld.com/association-of-natural-rubber-producing-countries-forecasts-increased-demand-for-natural-rubber/?doing_wp_cron=1648372904.9381680488586425781250.

218 Ahrends, Antje, and Eleanor Warren-Thomas. 2023. "Tropical Forest Loss from Growing Rubber Trade Is More Substantial than Previously Thought – New Research." The Conversation. November 21, 2023. https://theconversation.com/tropical-forest-loss-from-growing-rubber-trade-is-more-substantial-than-previously-thought-new-research-216407.

219 Jayathilake, H. Manjari, Cheng Zhi Wei, Gerald Tan, Côme de la Porte, and L. Roman Carrasco. "Rubber plantation size and global rubber price are linked to forest loss and degradation in Jambi, Sumatra." *Integrative Conservation* 3, no. 1 (2024): 22-35.

220 Warren-Thomas, Eleanor M., David P. Edwards, Daniel P. Bebber, Phourin Chhang, Alex N. Diment, Tom D. Evans, Frances H. Lambrick et al. "Protecting tropical forests from the rapid expansion of rubber using carbon payments."

Nature communications 9, no. 1 (2018): 911. DOI: 10.1038/s41467-018-03287-9

221 Service, Uniindia News. 2024. "Rubber Farmers Accuse Tyre Manufacturers of Issuing Electoral Bonds to Shield Cartelisation." Http://Www.uniindia.com/Rubber-Farmers-Accuse-Tyre-Manufacturers-of-Issuing-Electoral-Bonds-To-Shield-Cartelisation/India/News/3186533.Html. 2024. http://www.uniindia.com/rubber-farmers-accuse-tyre-manufacturers-of-issuing-electoral-bonds-to-shield-cartelisation/india/news/3186533.html.

222 "A Smallholder's Story - PEFC Rubber." 2024. Pefc.org. 2024. https://rubber.pefc.org/supporting-smallholders/smallholders-story

223 "Rubber | DSIR: Department of Scientific and Industrial Research | Government of India." 2024. Dsir.gov.in. 2024. https://www.dsir.gov.in/rubber.

224 Langenberger, Gerhard, Georg Cadisch, Konrad Martin, Shi Min, and Hermann Waibel. "Rubber intercropping: a viable concept for the 21st century?." *Agroforestry Systems* 91 (2017): 577-596. https://doi.org/10.1007/s10457-016-9961-8

225 "The Future of Global Tires to 2028." n.d. Smithers. https://www.smithers.com/services/market-reports/transportation/the-future-of-global-tires-to-2028.

226 Williams, Jeremy. 2017. "What Can the World Do with 1.5 Billion Waste Tyres?" The Earthbound Report. The Earthbound Report. June 29, 2017. https://earthbound.report/2017/06/29/what-can-the-world-do-with-1-5-billion-waste-tyres/.

227 Kononov, Sergei. n.d. "The World's Largest Tire Graveyard in Kuwait in Flames | Weibold – Tire Recycling & Pyrolysis Consulting." Ecolife.ae. https://weibold.com/the-worlds-largest-tire-graveyard-in-kuwait-in-flames.

228 Wikipedia Contributors. 2024. "Tire Fire." Wikipedia. Wikimedia Foundation. October 31, 2024.

229 Tian, Zhenyu, Haoqi Zhao, Katherine T. Peter, Melissa Gonzalez, Jill Wetzel, Christopher Wu, Ximin Hu et al. "A ubiquitous tire rubber–derived chemical induces acute mortality in coho salmon." *Science* 371, no. 6525 (2021): 185-189. DOI: 10.1126/science.abd6951

230 "EPA Issues Advance Notice of Proposed Rulemaking to Protect Salmon from Chemical Used in Rubber Products | US EPA." 2024. US EPA. November 14, 2024. https://www.epa.gov/newsreleases/epa-issues-advance-notice-proposed-rulemaking-protect-salmon-chemical-used-rubber.

231 Ashworth, James. 2023. "'Plasticosis': A New Disease Caused by Plastic That Is Affecting Seabirds." Www.nhm.ac.uk. March 3, 2023. https://www.nhm.ac.uk/discover/news/2023/march/plasticosis-new-disease-caused-by-plastic-affecting-seabirds.html.

232 "US Playgrounds: Fears Grow over Health Risks from Rubber Particles." 2019. Emily Holden, The Guardian. June 25, 2019. https://www.theguardian.com/us-news/2019/jun/25/lawmakers-concerned-chemicals-rubber-playgrounds-push-safety-rules.

233 Gupta, Mohit, Deepali Prasad, Harshit S. Khara, and David Alcid. "A rubber-degrading organism growing from a human body." *International Journal of Infectious Diseases* 14, no. 1 (2010): e75-e76. https://doi.org/10.1016/j.ijid.2009.03.006

234 Rose, Karsten, and Alexander Steinbuchel. "Biodegradation of natural rubber and related compounds: recent insights into a hardly understood catabolic capability of microorganisms." *Applied and environmental microbiology* 71, no. 6 (2005): 2803-2812. doi:10.1128/AEM.71.6.2803–2812.2005

235 Castañeda Alejo, Sarelia M., Kevin Tejada Meza, María R. Valderrama Valencia, Armando J. Arenazas Rodríguez, and Christian J. Málaga Espinoza. "Tire ground rubber biodegradation by a consortium isolated from an aged tire." *Microorganisms* 10, no. 7 (2022): 1414. https://doi.org/10.3390/microorganisms10071414

Appendix A: The Biosynthesis of Terpenes

236 Boronat, A. and Rodríguez-ConcepciónM. (2014). Terpenoid Biosynthesis in Prokaryotes. *Advances in Biochemical Engineering / Biotechnology*, pp.3–18. doi:https://doi.org/10.1007/10_2014_285

237 Hillier SG, Lathe R. 2019 Terpenes, hormones and life: isoprene rule revisited. J Endocrinol. Aug;242(2):R9-R22. doi: 10.1530/JOE-19-0084. Also, a quick clarification: the terms terpene, isoprene, isoprenoids, and terpenoids are related, but they are not identical. Simply put, isoprenes are unsaturated hydrocarbons with the formula C5H8; terpenes are polymers of isoprenes; isoprenoids are isoprenes with added oxygen groups, and terpenoids are polymers of isoprenoids.

238 Figure 30: Image reproduced by Saurabh Garge based on information in chemistry textbooks.

239 Hoshino, Y., & Gaucher, E. A. (2018). On the origin of isoprenoid biosynthesis. *Molecular biology and evolution*, *35*(9), 2185-2197. https://doi.org/10.1093/molbev/msy120

240 Lombard, J., & Moreira, D. (2011). Origins and early evolution of the mevalonate pathway of isoprenoid biosynthesis in the three domains of life. *Molecular biology and evolution*, *28*(1), 87-99. https://doi.org/10.1093/molbev/msq177

Appendix B: Two Examples of the Duplicate-and-Modify Process

241 Sun, Ming, Yunfei Wang, Caishang Zheng, Yanjun Wei, Jiakai Hou, Peng Zhang, Wei He et al. "Systematic functional interrogation of human pseudogenes using CRISPRi." *Genome biology* 22 (2021): 1-29. https://doi.org/10.1186/s13059-021-02464-2

242 Figure 31: Reproduced with permission from Ross C. Hardison, author. Hardison, R. C. 2012. "Evolution of Hemoglobin and Its Genes." *Cold Spring Harbor Perspectives in Medicine* 2 (12): a011627–27. https://doi.org/10.1101/cshperspect.a011627.

243 Kosfeld, Michael, Markus Heinrichs, Paul J. Zak, Urs Fischbacher, and Ernst Fehr. "Oxytocin increases trust in humans." *Nature* 435, no. 7042 (2005): 673-676. https://doi.org/10.1038/nature03701

244 Young, Larry J., and Loretta M. Flanagan-Cato. "Editorial comment: oxytocin, vasopressin and social behavior."

Hormones and behavior 61, no. 3 (2012): 227. doi: 10.1016/j.yhbeh.2012.02.019

245 Dong, Chen, Grisel Ponciano, Naxin Huo, Yong Gu, Daniel Ilut, and Colleen McMahan. "RNASeq analysis of drought-stressed guayule reveals the role of gene transcription for modulating rubber, resin, and carbohydrate synthesis." *Scientific Reports* 11, no. 1 (2021): 21610. https://doi.org/10.1038/s41598-021-01026-7

Appendix C: The Variety and Value of Plant Secondary Metabolites

246 Bennett, R. N., & Wallsgrove, R. M. (1994). Bennett, Richard N., and Roger M. Wallsgrove. "Secondary metabolites in plant defence mechanisms." *New phytologist* 127, no. 4 (1994): 617-633.https://nph.onlinelibrary.wiley.com/doi/epdf/10.1111/j.1469-8137.1994.tb02968.x

Epilogue

247 Market, Future. 2024. "Natural Rubber Market Forecast: Projected Growth to USD 30,914.3 Million by 2033 | Future Market Insights, Inc." GlobeNewswire News Room. Future Market Insights Global and Consulting Pvt. Ltd. October 28, 2024. https://www.globenewswire.com/news-release/2024/10/28/2970211/0/en/Natural-Rubber-Market-Forecast-Projected-Growth-to-USD-30-914-3-Million-by-2033-Future-Market-Insights-Inc.html.